THE FORGIVENESS WARRIOR

THE FORGIVENESS WARRIOR

* a novel *

Elizabeth Cain

Copyright © 2025
Elizabeth Cain
The Forgiveness Warrior

All rights reserved

No part of this book may be reproduced, or stored in a retrieval system, or transmitted in any form of by any means, electronics, mechanical, photocopying, recording, or otherwise, without express written permission of the author.

ISBN Kindle: 978-1-77419-255-9
ISBN Paperback: 978-1-77419-254-2
ISBN Hardback: 978-1-77419-253-5

Published by 101 Publishing

Also by Elizabeth Cain

they call me Sunny

Once to Every Man Ark for the Brokenhearted

Thirst Almost Paradise

Dancing in the Red Snow

Applause

The Girl from the River

FOR THOSE WHO SEEK FORGIVENESS

AND THOSE WHO ARE WILLING

TO GIVE IT

Nevadan Family Tree

Helen (d.) —— Henry Rose (d.)
│
Jason Rose (d.)　　Julian Rose (d.) —— Serena Skye (d.)
│
Robert Henry Askay Rose (Hank) —— Susan Sun
│
Marta Serena Sun Rose (Sunny) —— Thomas Heart-of-the-Hawk Sentinel
│
Julia Sentinel

African Family Tree

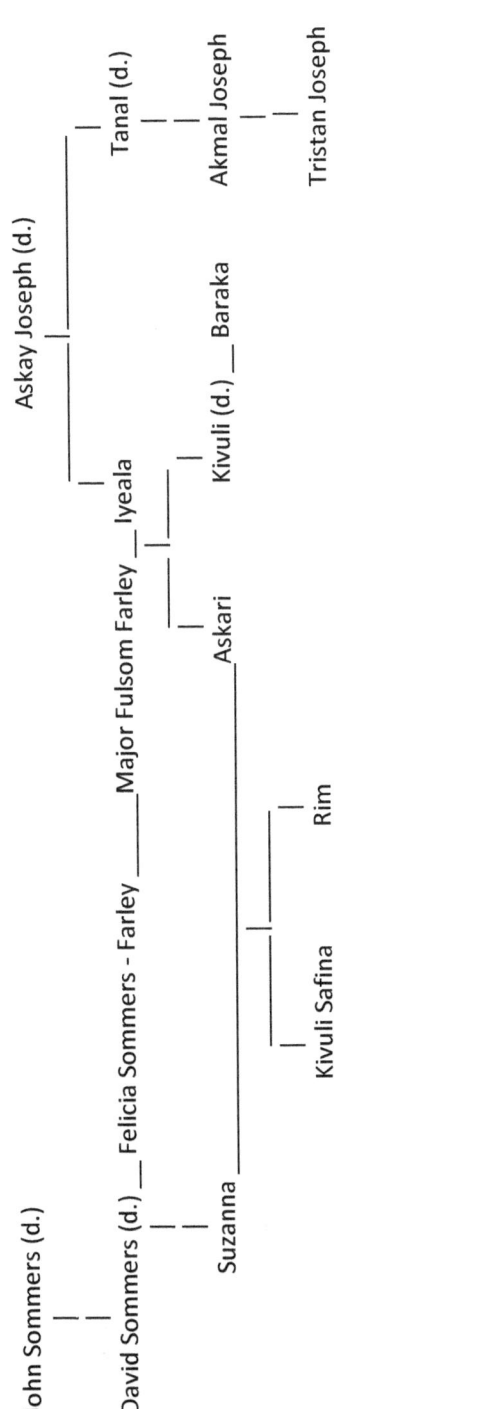

1

maximum security womens prison: Humboldt County, Nevada April, 2013

Liana woke with a start. The damn alarms were going off again. The girl in the narrow bed with her hardly quivered, one bare breast pressed up against Liana's shoulder. The sound of heavy boots thudding down the concrete tiles and the *thwack* of locks being released growled in her head like a rabid dog. "Hey, Tenice, get up!" Liana rasped. "Don't let them catch you here! Ruffle your bedding some."

The just-turned eighteen-year-old rolled away from the older woman and stood up dizzily. She pushed the blankets aside on her own bed just as the burly matron, blacker than the moonless sky in the tiny window of the cell, loomed outside the door.

"Fire in the kitchen! Let's go girls!" the guard shouted.

Tenice covered herself with a tug of her thin hand on the gray sleepwear, but the officer was not to be fooled. As the women staggered into the hallway and turned toward the yard, the black poked Liana in the ribs with a steel baton.

"Up to your old tricks, eh Liana?" she needled.

Smoke filtered into the gym where all the prisoners had been corralled—the building farthest from the cafeteria. Liana was vaguely aware of making the short walk across the volleyball court and the ragged grass field. She was thinking maybe the fire would get out of control and burn the fences down, the mountains beyond the perimeter of the facility seeming a great place to hide, at least until winter.

The women grumbled and pushed against each other, the tension mounting in the cold room, far from the comfort of their dreams, from their wild hopes of doing their time without getting hurt or being blamed for something they didn't do. Rumors spread about who was last in the food service area. A fight broke out over a contraband mirror that now lay shattered on the floor. Shards of glass were swiped up and pocketed. Guards roamed among them but could not stave off little crimes here and there.

Liana lost sight of Tenice, by far her favorite of the month. The girl had killed her boyfriend by shoving him over a cliff in the Ruby Mountains. She said he was going to kill her because she refused to get an abortion, but since he was the one who died, she went to jail, pregnant and justified. The state paired her with Liana, thinking a woman with child would not interest her. *Little did they know.* The girl needed a protector and easily fell into Liana's arms. From as long as she could remember, Liana had always gravitated toward the young ones.

The alarms and sirens had gone off, and the inmates were herded back across the exercise yard, encountering irritating puddles of water left by giant hoses and the fit-looking men coiling them up, some of them laughing at inside jokes about the women in their ghostly gray pajamas. Liana was past ogling those tight physiques and chiseled faces. Girls and women had marked her years in the institution like falling dominoes.

One time in her life she had been crazy about a boy—a twelve-year-old she could command as easily as a kitten—and she had molded him to her will, her sex, until he was seventeen and the kid's mother had put her foot down, talking sweetly to her while devising reasons to keep them apart. Liana was twenty-two then and just beginning to hone her powers, but the mother was a fighter. She offered her riding lessons on some very fine horses that Liana hated, gave her money for clothes, and finally an odd painting of a bronc about to be whipped for bad behavior with the impression of a hand, wielding a treat, reaching through the rails of the round pen. Liana sold it as soon as she could.

She hung around the boy's school, drained his gas tank when he finally got his driver's license, but saw him hitch a ride with another kid before giving her the time of day. She stalked them all the way to his folks' ranch, where he disappeared into the horse pasture. She left cryptic messages on his phone, denying that he was lost to her. She lived on relentless anger and a fiery buzz she called love. But the only thing Liana ever loved again was the little girl she kidnapped…

As she crossed the bleak and unholy space of the prison yard, Liana couldn't remember the little girl's name. She'd only ever called the girl "Baby," even when they were in the shower together and the child sighed against her roaming fingers, a baby no more, even when they walked hand in hand on the beach in California and Baby was almost as tall as she was.

Back in the dingy cell, Liana lay restless and sleepless, trying to recall the girl's name. She pounded her fist against the metal frame of the bunk. An exasperated Tenice said, "What?"

"Tryin' to remember a name," Liana answered testily. The trouble was, eight years after the law had caught up with her and taken Baby away, the girl was a grown woman, round-shouldered and pale beneath an outfit Liana wouldn't be caught dead in, calling herself "Sister Martha."

The nun was perfectly civil to her and didn't let on to anyone that *she* was the reason Liana was there in that prison without the possibility of parole. She fulfilled her ministry with four or five other Sisters, who brought the inmates perfumed soaps and tiny Bibles and rosaries for those who wanted them. Liana figured lightning would strike if she dared touch one of those. Sometimes the nuns would wash the prisoners' hair and listen to their stories. One gal was purely innocent of some crime, and Sister Martha pulled her weight with a fancy lawyer and got the woman released.

Liana thought Baby's eyes hadn't changed much—still unsteady and scared—but she was all right, wasn't she? Safe in the convent with prayers and priests and the Jesus they were supposed to be married to. But it didn't escape Liana that those gals were sexual beings, hiding behind their skirts and their crosses during the day and hankering for someone's bed at night, orgasmic and lonely. She could show Sister Martha a thing or two, but they seldom spoke.

One time, in a group counseling session, one of the nuns asked if any of them wished for forgiveness for their sins and to be made clean as a newborn lamb. The rector from the convent would come and show them the way. Liana laughed out loud, and everyone's head went down, embarrassed for the goodly Sisters just doing their job, but Sister Martha stared at Liana darkly, as if the idea of forgiveness didn't apply to the woman she'd been with for eight, mind-numbing years. Liana stared right back, not conceding a speck of remorse for stealing Baby from her father—the man Liana once loved.

Her heart lurched. Had she forgotten to take her pills in all the excitement earlier? Or maybe Tenice had distracted her with her maddeningly slow foreplay. Suddenly, Liana remembered that day in the yard years ago when she had collapsed with a hideous pain in her heart. The nuns backed away all a-twitter—but not Sister Martha. That Baby-all-grown-up ran towards her, knelt beside her, and began pushing on her chest, up and down, up and down, then clasped her mouth on Liana's own, breathing air into her constricted lungs. From somewhere came her own startled voice: "Sunny?...Sunny?" The nun continued CPR, and an ambulance wailed in the distance.

Yes, that was her name! Sunny. Sunny Rose.

2

the thread begins to unravel: Tanzania, 2004

The first time I realized that life was not going to unfold in a clear-cut and dependable way was the day I started school at the Shanga Center for Disabled Artists in Arusha. I was not disabled, but I was too young to enroll in the elementary level elsewhere, and I wanted to go to school more than anything in the world. That first morning, I walked over through the woods—not scary woods as yet—from the coffee plantation managed by my father, Askari, whom I called Baba. I carried a pale pink backpack and all the dreams of a just-turned five-year-old down the well-worn path in the eucalyptus grove, barely turning once to give my mother a wave, as she stood watching me from behind the freshly-painted white rails of the front porch.

My heart began to pound. Ahead of me in a grassy clearing was the designated building where the woman who lived with the glass-blower's daughter would introduce us to art. There were thirteen of us waiting outside. Except for me, they were children of the Center's residents, some with disabilities genetically inherited or developed from living in environments where their needs were not always met. The teacher appeared suddenly, opened the door, and shepherded us in.

Dust flew as we slammed down carry-alls and art supplies from home and maybe a book or two with titles like *Draw Like a Pro*, full of words some children couldn't read. I couldn't see her face yet. The room was dim, and her back was to us as she opened the blinds and apologized for not cleaning up the desks. She asked someone, who was able, to read aloud the rules she had printed in large, chalky letters on the blackboard. I was too awed to stand up, so I scanned the rules quickly from my seat.

DO NOT SPEAK WITHOUT RAISING YOUR HAND

Too late for that. A boy named Dougie, who never stopped talking, was prattling on about wanting a different desk and being afraid of the quite intimidating spider calmly weaving a web in the corner by the wash stand.

DO NOT TOUCH EACH OTHER'S BODIES OR POSSESSIONS.

The Gabola twins were clasped together in the same splintery chair. Paint brushes and colored markers were already flying across the room from hands that surely didn't own them.

FOUL LANGUAGE WILL NOT BE TOLERATED

The lights flickered off and on as Teacher passed out sheets of art paper and strode to the board to tack up a generously-sized photograph of African animals at a waterhole over the rules and her name, which had been in the top left-hand corner. I had memorized it: Miss Mvua Rain. She turned and silenced us with a look that was a mixture of deep weariness and anxiety. There were dark circles under her eyes and a permanent frown on her face, but I thought she was the most beautiful person I had ever seen. She was slender in a shimmery ivory dress that contrasted with her smooth, brown skin, triple sets of beaded bracelets on her long arms, and her closely-cropped hair that had a thin, bleached line in the shape of the letter M above her left ear.

"Good morning, children," she said, brightly enough. "Today, we are going to sketch, paint, or with colored pens render this picture with our own imaginations. There is no right or wrong way to express yourselves. I'll pass out more materials as needed." She rubbed her eyes as if the unruly lights were enraging her spirit.

I held up my hand.

"Yes? Young lady?" She didn't bother to find my name on the rolls, just nodded.

"If all the paintings are different, how would people feel looking at them?"

She started to answer but was distracted by Chelsea Mbele scribbling on the wall next to the blackboard with flashy streaks, probably from new tubes of watercolors.

"No! No!" Miss Rain cried. "Stop that this instant!"

Chelsea screamed and threw a brush loaded with crimson paint right on Teacher's lovely skirt. She was adding vermillion to another projectile when Miss Rain caught her hands and tied them together at the wrist. The girl thrashed and yelled and let out a stream of words that the rule list said were not allowed. Miss Rain taped her mouth shut with one swipe of the masking tape and held the roll of tape up in the air.

"Anyone else?" she said.

When I got home after school, I didn't tell Mama a thing about what happened, just handed over my waterhole scene, hoping for one word of praise from a woman who doled out those kinds of words frugally, if at all. I did ask her to mark a K with a violet marker in the same place Teacher had emblazoned her letter, but my mother said she didn't have time for such nonsense. Maybe that was why later that night, when I saw her come in the back door holding a bloody knife, I sought to earn her favor by giving her my marble box to hide the thing in. She buried it in the freezer beneath the chicken without a word.

The next day at Shanga School, the art teacher did not show up. One of the disabled kid's mamas came to substitute, and some order prevailed. She was effusive with praise and adored even paintings of rainbows with the colors out of sequence. I watched for Miss Rain to reappear. I had perceived that she held a kind of secret that would be meaningful to my life because of her severe manner, her quickness to withdraw from trouble.

After Mvua Rain had been missing six days, I erased her name from the blackboard. A little drop of red spattered with green remained on the floor where her feet had been. I had not gone out with the other kids for lunch recess, still wrapped up inside myself with the mystery of Teacher's essence erased from the room like amateurs' watercolors stroked over and over with different paints to fix their mistakes until there was nothing viable left.

The glass-blower, Dakimu, stuck his head in the door. "Are you all right, Kivuli?"

"Do you know where she went?"

"I do not, honey," he said and came over and stood by the still-hanging photo of the animals arranged around the pond. "She had some trouble, but it's not your trouble, little one. Come with me. I saw your granpa outside, asking if I'd seen you."

I loved my granpa, famously known as Major Fulsom Farley, a man who had resolved many crises in the world, but my world felt tipped on its axis.

"What will we do if Mvua never returns?" I was only thinking about my own reasons to welcome her back, to please her with my renderings, to move her to smile under her grim countenance, but the glass-blower surprised me.

"You will hear murmurs. Some folks did not like her. She perhaps hurt some, scared others, but I believe in forgiveness. Just look at your Granpa Farley and me. We were enemies. We wounded each other in many ways, terrible ways. But he and I laid our animosity and grievances aside and became friends. Remember that, child…what is possible. What love can do."

We went out into the noonday sun to the chatter of tourists, the tinkling of the wind chimes around the compound, and my granpa reaching out his arms to me. "Everything will be all right, my darling girl," he said.

But one day, a few weeks later, when I scrambled back through the eucalyptus trees after school, there were policemen and dogs and soldiers rummaging about our yard, poking around in the burn pile, pulling out pieces of gray tape, a brown arm bearing a beaded Shanga bracelet, strips of ivory silk stained with ash and blood. *Or was that scarlet paint?* A body was wrenched from the smoldering refuse. I was shoved out of the way, but not before I saw the singed mark of the letter M on the side of Mvua's head.

Not too long after that, Chelsea Mbele's father, who had been a gardener at Shanga and who had disappeared the same week as Mvua, was blamed for her murder, but the authorities were not satisfied. Granpa Farley, still officially attached to the British Air and Ground Patrol—part of the colonization of Tanganyika and beyond the 1961 date when our country was released from British rule and became Tanzania—was able to keep the investigators from our door.

The only key to the horror of Miss Rain's death was her past relationship with Safina, the glass-blower's daughter and my mother's best friend. I found out Mvua and Safina had not only lived together but had loved each other, although in a volatile way. In snippets of conversation, with Safina and my mother, Suzanna, when I pretended I was doing a school project, I heard things like, "You're free." "You never have to suffer again." "Just put her abuse behind you." The two of them were always holding on to each other—a hand on a hand, an arm around a shoulder, a cheek against a cheek.

When I could stand it no longer, I asked my mother one day if she loved Safina too, like Miss Rain had.

She flipped her head around, her blonde hair swinging, the birthmark on her right cheek flaming, and narrowed her eyes. "Not like that! Never like that! Don't ever say that again!"

I felt caught in the space between a brush thick with paint and the paper it's about to touch down on. I barely spoke to my mother for the rest of the year.

3

a breath in time: from Arusha to the Indian Ocean

For weeks after Mvua Rain's body was unearthed from beneath the plantation burn pile, the investigators pursued us for "evidence," as they noted it, certain they could find something incriminating. One time, they dug around in our freezer, and I held my breath. But the knife was not there. *Where was it?* My mother commanded me practically mute when those authorities were around. Another time, she put tape over my mouth and told an officer who wanted to ask me something that I had said a bad word, which was a lie.

Granpa Farley had come to live with us—actually to marry my father's mother, Iyeala—but he'd waited too long. She had died of throat cancer three weeks before he appeared, and it just about killed him. And me, too. He'd been trying to divorce Suzanna's mother, Felicia, for a while, but she was mentally incompetent, and I suppose, he didn't want to shock her too gravely. But too late he did divorce her and settled her in an institution far from any of us, made his way to Arusha, and wandered around the plantation half-drunk with regret.

As the harassment of our family continued, my granpa—his belligerent manner squelched—lay back in the porch swing or in his easy chair in the living room, wherever the detectives accosted him, with a smug smile on his lips like he knew what no one else did. Another time, a female detective got my mother and Safina in the same space and asked offensive questions like, "Were you both having sex with the deceased?" and "Should we subpoena your priest?"

A special team arrived with plans to comb the eucalyptus grove, rake up the fronds and turn over every rock. They got busy with shovels and giant plastic bags. Granpa got up from his favorite chair and picked up the phone. "Say, Dakimu," he said casually, "could you send those leopards over to the plantation? I offed some big rats for them." The pets loped down the path, and the woods emptied as fast as uniformed humans could move. If investigators got too close to the trail between Shanga and the plantation, they became extremely nervous.

That day, Granpa eased himself back down in his chair and said, "There's more than one way to get what you want," and held out his hand for a whiskey Suzanna had poured him. My mother had basically resigned herself to his presence in our house. The edge had gone out of her voice when she spoke to him, but I thought whiskey might not be the best way to forgive someone.

Then, when I was eight and my brother, Rim, was born, my mother moved us all to Dar es Salaam on the coast so we could have a good Catholic education. My father had purchased the coffee plantation and stayed behind, struggling to make a go of it. In Dar, my mother and Safina slept in the same bed. My father did not seem to mind. The "girls", as Baba was fond of calling them, had been inseparable when they were enrolled at the Light of the Word Catholic School at the same age they were enrolling me now. But I did not take to the instruction as they had.

My mother felt obligated to introduce us to her mother, Felicia, who was certifiably crazy. Rim and I had to visit her in a strange hospital where all the doors were bolted shut from the outside, with a white-clad body builder sitting erect in a chair in front of every room. We were searched for sharp objects and had to be very careful of what we said. Of course, Rim was too young to remember that grandmother, but she made a fuss over him and would, with a scowly face, reluctantly hand him back to Suzanna. During the first few visits, she would barely look at me, but finally one day she said, "Why are you so dark-skinned?"

"Mama, I've told you this over and over," my mother replied.

"Well, I want to hear it from the girl," the old lady quipped.

What did I know? I told the truth.

"My father is part Maasai and a little darker than I am."

Felicia's screams brought the guards on the run, and they ordered us out of the room. In the hall on the way to the exit, my mother tried to calm Rim and told us that Safina had been the only black allowed in their house because of her magic, healing ways as a young child, and that we shouldn't think too unkindly of Grandmother's racist fears. "She has her reasons," my mother said cryptically.

"What reasons?" I planted myself under the red exit sign.

Suzanna put her hand on the steel door. "Safina's father…Dakimu was…the one who killed Felicia's first husband—the father I never knew—but we've all, except for her, put that behind us."

I remembered, though Rim could not comprehend it at this point in time, that the day I was christened in the Catholic Church, Major Farley had announced that Iyeala had been his paramour for thirty years and that my father and his sister, Kivuli, after whom I was named and who had died at the hands of one of Fulsom's drunk soldiers, were his true children. Parishioners had raised their glasses to them, and Dakimu had smiled from across the sanctuary, his back to the wall.

Later, Granpa Farley was a fierce defender of Suzanna, all through the rumors and suspicions around the death of Mvua. He told me himself he had hidden things and lied and sent authorities in the wrong directions, which of course, I had witnessed many times. But more than that, he seemed genuinely remorseful for his career of hunting down black renegades, especially Dakimu Reiman, who Felicia cried out time and again was "the ruin of us all!"

I began to pay more attention when the priests talked about remorse and forgiveness. The Church had strict ideas about confession and penitents promising never to misbehave again but not a word about who could do the forgiving besides God, or who, even then, could count on God. Why could only Catholics earn redemption?

One night, when I was about ten or eleven, I found my granpa out on the patio that had a wide view of the Indian Ocean—the tiny boats of the fishermen, the barges waiting to dock, the layers of translucent waves and the dark sea behind them. He was mumbling something like, "She'll never…forgive me…can't forgive."

"Who, Granpa?"

"Your mother."

I waited while he swallowed some amber liquid from a tall glass.

"I gave her the best of everything—horses, books… a lovely, safe place…to live. But I didn't tell her who I was…"

"Can I forgive you, Granpa?"

He set the empty glass on the porch rail. "That is the question, isn't it? Where does true forgiveness come from?"

I didn't answer, but from that moment on, I wanted to know the answer. I wanted to know how people could find this forgiveness in a mixed-up world of betrayals and godlessness. Granpa went on to say that everyone he knew needed forgiveness for some wrong-doing or other, but few he knew had received it.

When Fulsom drank, I didn't always know what to believe, and by the time I had solidified an answer that might work for me, I was fourteen and on my way to America to follow a different lead in my family's convoluted history.

4

a new journey: Africa to Atlanta to Reno, Nevada June, 2013

My father and mother had been arguing for over a year about sending me across the treacherous sea to perhaps a more treacherous foreign land. Baba had good reasons for me to go. She did not. I grew up filling the holes in their stories with what I thought was just and right—heroes and warriors—but what was I? Cut out of white cloth, I could trace my DNA to British colonizers and kings, but about my own black ancestry I knew little.

My Maasai great-grandfather, Askay Joseph, had emigrated to the United States when his daughter, Iyeala, and his son, Tanal, were too small to understand what happened to him. Our family accidentally learned of his employment and ultimate death on a large guest and cattle ranch in Nevada from a young American Indian, Thomas Heart-of-the-Hawk Sentinel, who had come to Shanga to upgrade the Center's plumbing system. Askay's patrons, the Rose family, had given him pages from the old African's dairy so that Thomas might better understand the people he would be helping. He gave them to Iyeala, and she and my father's hearts were lightened by the words in Askay's shaky handwriting, though saddened to learn he had passed away years ago.

Before Iyeala died, she tore out pieces of the journal and handed them around like charms, little poetic messages that best fit the receivers. One she left for Fulsom, which Baba had to give him after she was lying in a grave on the rim of the Ngorongoro Crater. One she left for me.

In the years to come, the idea evolved for me to go to the ranch to represent our family, to show our gratitude and love for the Roses' kindness to Baba's grandfather. There were many things we didn't know. Who were the American ranchers? Why did Askay go with them from Ngorongoro? Why did he never write or send money from his prestigious job? Who were his friends? What jobs did they give him to do? And why did he spend the rest of his life there?

I, with my active imagination, pictured Askay riding magnificent American horses, sleeping in a soft bed and teaching the ranchers how to better raise cattle, preserve soil, and grow crops by valuable tribal methods. Baba heard me one day drawing out these fantasies about the privileged life my great-grandfather must have led and decided I would be the perfect one to travel to Nevada and learn what happened to him.

By the time I entered U.S. airspace in the summer of 2013, Tom Sentinel was married to the daughter of Hank and Susan Rose—Marta Serena Sun, called "Sunny."

I had been in the airbus for six hours, and when I glanced out the window, we were still over the continent of Africa. It was then I got a bit frightened. I understood why my great-grandfather might never have wanted to make that trip home. In his day, the flight must have been much longer with more lay-overs, and who knows how he was treated as a black man who spoke no English. I hoped I had his courage in my DNA.

I was dressed in Western-looking attire, easy to find now in the modernized cities throughout Africa—tight, faded jeans with holes in the knees, a white t-shirt that said *Forgiveness Warrior* in glittering letters. I thought of Mvua with her dull and fire-scarred M. Who could forgive the person who buried her under the combusting slash? *It has to be someone who loved her.* It couldn't just be God or a priest, or even me. At that minute, I didn't want to know who that might be.

The plane veered left, and now when I stared down, I could see the dark, green waves of the Atlantic Ocean, pulsing thirty-thousand feet below. Sunlight leapt like a vast fire from the sea on the western horizon, the setting sun soon to leave us in darkness for the next nine or ten hours. I thought of my father's words as he bent close to give me last minute advice: "Be especially mindful of the Roses' daughter. She had a traumatic experience when she was young." He pulled me against him as if warding off such a disaster from me. I wanted to know more, but my section had been called to board, and my mother was fussing with my hair. "Don't bother the Roses too much," she warned me. "They'll be busy with ranch guests and their animals."

"I'll be good…you'll see," I said, but she was already distracted, pulling my brother out of the path of a bullish passenger with an overloaded cart. " 'Bye, Rim," I called out as I entered the tunnel that led into the plane.

Safina had not come to the airport. She had started a vegetable garden in a roughed-out place in the side yard and needed to transplant seedlings and erect a fence. Lately, it seemed she was planning things to do to give Suzanna more time with my father. I had never been in love and didn't know what I'd do in her situation. She and my mom were both Catholic. It couldn't be right what they were doing—having sex with each other and maybe my father at the same time. I didn't want to believe it, but the signs were all there.

I was not interested in girls, or boys either. I felt the most natural and confident about myself on a horse. Granpa Farley had given me riding lessons on older, retired military mounts when we lived at the plantation, mostly about balance and safety, but could I handle fresh ranch horses? In Nevada there would be more than horses with which to practice my balance and safety skills. Would there be more white people than blacks, more expectations of me than I had ever had to fulfill?

The hours crept by. It was difficult to sleep with noise and light in the cabin. One time, the captain came on to tell us there was a major storm moving east across the Gulf of Mexico, and the plane bounced and dipped like a vehicle crossing the Serengeti. I stopped looking at my watch. Everything was strange and dreamlike. Then, we began a slow descent into Atlanta. No matter how America tested me, I would keep one word in front of me as a shield and a foil—forgiveness.

I breathed easier once we were on the ground, and I only had to wait forty-five minutes for my connection to Reno, Nevada, where the Sentinels would pick me up, and then, who knew how many more hours I'd have to endure in a car to reach my destination? After I found my seat in the new plane, I retrieved a few photos out of my shoulder bag that the Roses had sent my father. One of a middle-aged couple, with a handsome German shepherd between them, was labeled Hank and Susan Rose. They had wonderful smiles. The dog seemed to be smiling too.

There were a couple of shots of cowboys herding huge, white cattle. Their hats were pushed down over their faces so I couldn't see any of their features. Mountains lined the background— jagged, purple shapes that swelled into a deep, blue sky. Another photo was of the Sentinel family, posed on the steps of a wood-railed porch with Tom's hand on the shoulder of a little girl who stood in front of him—Julia. Next to him was his wife, Sunny, not touching her husband or their daughter, her eyes shifted away from the camera as if attracted by something in the distance. They were all wearing riding clothes.

What were they like behind those images? What would they say to me? Askay had passed away twenty-five years ago. *What could they remember that would help me understand him?* I was excited and nervous at the same time. There were so many possibilities in the unformed relationships, the untried conversations. Dakimu had said to me once, "Remember what love can do." So that's what I whispered to myself when I stepped out into the crowded Nevada terminal and saw the Sentinels holding up a sign that read: WELCOME, KIVULI FARLEY!

5

the map of hurtful things

i

Tom was coming toward me with open arms. His smile was just like the one in the photograph. I set my carry-on bags down and waited for the Sentinels to reach me, suddenly overwhelmed by the crowd and the loud speaker announcing flights and the unfamiliar smells. Just behind him was the woman that had avoided the camera, but now I could clearly detect her raven hair, high cheek bones, and haunted, green eyes. She was grasping the hand of a child as if containing an exuberant puppy. The girl called out, "I see her! I see Kivuli! A real African! Askay's great-granddaughter!"

I thought she was not the child in the photograph, she had changed that much. Her dark hair was straight, her cheeks round and glowing, and her body full of dimples and curves in her cut-off jeans and snug t-shirt. She looked nothing like her thin, wan mother, whose hand she tugged.

"Askay's great-granddaughter," the woman repeated, extending her other hand. "I'm Sunny Rose Sentinel, and this is our daughter, Julia."

Her hand was cold, but the grip was firm and friendly. Still, I felt uncomfortable.

"I'm very happy to meet you," I said, trying to look deeper into those troubled eyes. I was glad my father had cautioned me about upsetting her and glad too that I would be staying with her mother and father, Hank and Susan. There might be a way to find out more about what she had suffered without living in the same house.

Tom hugged me and grabbed my laptop case. Julia broke away from her mother and skipped around to my side. "What was it like in the airplane? Was the ocean huge below you? What color was it? I've never seen the ocean," she said all at once.

"Well, actually, you fly for five or six hours, and you look down and you are still over Africa!" I told her.

"Oh, what's there? What kind of people? What kind of animals?" she asked.

"Julia! Don't bother Kivuli now," Mrs. Sentinel insisted. "She must be so tired."

We moved toward the baggage claim area, and conversation seemed impossible anyway. Mrs. Sentinel pulled Julia closer as if to shield her from unnamed terrors. Carts rattled down the tiled floor, travelers rushing about in different directions, and I felt the need of some kind of relief. A black man embraced a young boy in a check-in line, and I thought of my father with his arms around me at the airport in Dar es Salaam.

Thomas slipped his free arm across his wife's shoulders and murmured, "Don't worry, honey. We'll be out of here pretty soon."

Maybe I shouldn't have come. I felt desperate not to be a burden for Mrs. Sentinel. *What shall I call her? Nothing too formal, nothing too familiar.* Then, it came to me in a flash.

"Ma'am," I began as the crowd thinned. She turned to me, and I just spilled it out. "May I call you Sunrose?"

"Oh, I like that! Sunrose—run together like one word," she said.

The beginning of a smile formed on the woman's lips. In Africa, I would have been afraid of someone who, at first, appeared so stern, but I was drawn to this lady with her dark, secretive eyes and protective manner. A small barrier went down.

We walked under the sign "BAGGAGE CLAIM." I felt dizzy as I watched the black platform circling with the piled-up luggage, probably because I had only eaten half a chicken sandwich in the customs line in Atlanta hours ago, and I had no water left. I watched for my suitcases and pointed them out to Thomas. He loaded them on a cart, Julia jumping up and down with excitement, and in a few minutes, we exited through the revolving doors and out into the sunlight, into America.

Tom had the brightest blue truck in the parking lot, a color as rich as the sky. We all climbed in, and he maneuvered through the traffic. The streets reminded me of home, people and vehicles in a frenzied hurry at all hours of the day. I saw black faces, but they didn't look like the African faces I knew. And unlike Dar es Salaam, there were no dirt avenues, no gaping potholes, or yards with no grass. The buildings were clean and the citizens well-dressed. The most amazing thing was that all the stores' lights were blazing, inside and out, in the middle of the day, and potted flowers hung from lampposts and awnings. It was a magical place.

We stopped for a bite to eat at a drive-through vendor, but even though I was hungry, I was too anxious to eat everything. I wanted to be in the part of this country my great-grandfather had called home, to know his friends, to figure out what the words from his diary meant, and to stand on the ground where he was buried. But most of all, I wanted to know if I had a connection to him besides that of our Maasai blood, something I might need from him or he might need from me.

We started up again, and Thomas turned onto the road labeled "I-80 EAST TO ELKO. 289 miles."

"Five more hours, Kivuli. Can you make it?" Tom asked.

"I hope I can stay awake. I don't want to miss anything."

He glanced at me in his rearview mirror. "Do you remember me?"

"You used to work with my father and dig wells next door at Shanga," I said.

He turned his eyes back to the road. "Yes. But before that, I saw you when you were about two years old, outside Manyara. Your family was traveling with your Grandmother Iyeala and stopped for the night in the village where I was running water lines. At first, I didn't know who she was. I started talking about an African, Askay, that had lived with my friends in Nevada. She cried out, hearing his name."

"You had to tell my granma that her father had died in America."

"Sadly."

I tried to imagine that scene—my grandmother hearing from the American stranger that her father had not lived to come back to her, though by that time in her life, she must have suspected the truth.

"Then you gave her some pages from his journal," I reminded him.

"I thought it would comfort Iyeala to see the old man's writings and read his words," Thomas said.

"She was always reading those fragile papers…and near the end, she gave them away. I have one with me now."

He didn't respond right away. Traffic had backed up because of some road construction; we were barely moving.

"I have to admit I never read them," Thomas said finally. "But maybe I will now. Hank has the entire journal, and having you here will certainly rekindle everyone's interest in your great-grandfather."

Julia slapped the back of the seat behind Tom's head. "Can I talk now?"

"Hey!" Tom said. "That is rude, Julia."

"Well, I never get to say anything," she complained.

I expected Sunrose to reprimand her daughter too, but she sat quite still in her seat. *What is going on here?* I thought it was a very long trip for a child and that maybe they should have left her with her grandparents at the ranch. I watched Julia sulk in her corner of the backseat and thought it was a simple enough thing to just let her talk. I asked her how old she was.

"Six and a half," she answered, still perturbed.

"What do you like to do on your grandpa's ranch?"

"Oh, ride the horses!" she said quickly. "Wait 'til you see them. They're all sleek and shiny now after shedding their winter coats. Do you ride?" The little girl barely gave me a chance to respond.

"I definitely ride, but not like a Native American, I'm sure."

"Oh, I can show you!"

"I'm sure you can," I said.

Tom caught my eyes in the rearview mirror again and mouthed "thank you."

We were past the construction zone now and moving normally along the smooth highway. I kept my eyes on Julia. I couldn't help but notice the girl's burnt-sienna complexion and ebony hair, so like an African landscape—light as the plains, dark as the montane woods.

"What tribes do you come from?" I asked.

"Sioux, Iroquois, and Caucasian," Julia said. "Is that right, Momma?"

"It is," Sunrose said.

I was surprised Julia knew the word "Caucasian" but was glad she included her white ancestors in her list of tribes. That was what we would do in Africa, not have one word for a mixed heritage but give credit to each ethnicity.

"Your skin is lighter than mine," Julia observed. She rested her arm against mine. "And your eyes are light brown like clover honey."

The girl had such a direct gaze, I startled a little, but Julia went on. "I like your hair too. Not kinky like in pictures I've seen of Africans. Your curls are soft. Can I touch them?"

"Julia, sweetheart, let Kivuli catch her breath," Thomas chided.

But I didn't mind the girl's attention. The miles were slipping away, the Roses' ranch getting closer and closer.

"My mother used to braid my hair when I first started school, but she tired of that," I told her. "She kept on braiding her horses' manes though."

I closed my eyes. The chestnuts and blacks and bays ridden by my mother galloped behind my eyelids, the crests of their necks adorned with neat knots of braided mane and tiny, white ribbons.

"Horses are her pride and joy. No one can outdo her polished show horses," I said at last.

"Isn't she proud of you?" Julia asked. She lifted a hand slowly and brushed one finger along a wave of my hair.

"I think so. I want her to be."

Sunrose looked around at us. "Sometimes mothers are proud of their children, but things get in the way of them showing it."

I didn't know what to say to that. A small ache began behind my eyes.

"But what tribes are you?" Julia pressed.

I tried to give the short answer. "I'm one-half Maasai and one-half Anglo-Saxon."

"What does that mean?"

"I'm half black and half white," I said. That was not quite true: my father was the one who was half black and half white.

Julia stared at me for a moment. "Oh. I don't know anyone like that."

"Yes, you do, Julia. One of your teachers at school, Mr. Darlington. His mother is a famous black opera singer, and his white father owns several nurseries and does private landscaping. He replanted that area around the pool last year and added some bark walkways between the cabins," her mother said.

She doesn't talk much, but she listens. I liked that. My own mother rarely listened to me. One time I was describing a jump course—no higher than two and a half feet—I had mastered on my lesson horse, and my mother got that blank look in her eyes. So I added an imaginary five-foot brick wall to the exercise, and my mother said, "That's nice, dear." I gave up mentioning the really important things.

"What does *your* father do?" Julia asked.

"He manages two big coffee plantations and owns one of his own. I brought some of his coffee beans for everyone. Do you have something to grind them with, Sunrose?"

"Why, yes," she said.

"Can I try some, Momma?"

"Maybe just a sip," Sunrose said, and Thomas laughed.

"Oh, I have gifts for people who don't drink coffee," I said.

"Tell me! Tell me!" Julia pleaded.

I described the beads and sea-glass and shells in the jewelry and the adventure of the days when my mother and I searched for relics on the beach—days when my mother could tear herself away from the woman who lived with us.

ii

The Nevada miles passed. Towns were far apart and traffic scattered, the lanes mostly filled with trucks as massive as buildings. Once, when we stopped for fuel, I counted twenty of the imposing carriers. Julia asked a hundred questions, jabbering about horses and branding calves, and I drifted from the conversation, my weariness overtaking me.

"And in September, we all go to the fair, and I get to ride this year for the first time!" Julia concluded, after reciting a long list of ranch activities that I barely heard.

I shook myself awake. "What kind of fair? What happens there?"

"Oh, we have animal pens, vegetables, show horses, and Indian Relay races," she answered breathlessly.

Sunrose grabbed her husband's arm, and I heard him say, "It's okay. It's okay."

A measure of disquiet filled the car. Julia stopped talking.

"Do you go to church, Kivuli?" Mrs. Sentinel asked in the awkward silence.

"Sometimes I go with my mother. She's Catholic, but I don't understand any of it. My Granpa Farley is Catholic too, and I love him so much. When I was born, he didn't know I was his *real* granddaughter, but he loved me anyway. My father told me he rocked me and sang to me. Sometimes he cried when he had to give me back to my mother, who is really his step-daughter."

"How could he be your real grandpa then?" Julia asked.

"Julia, that's enough," Thomas said.

"I don't mind, Mr. Sentinel," I said. But I couldn't just blurt out *my mother's stepfather is my father's real father.*

I always had to take a deep breath when I said that. It sounded so peculiar. But none of my relatives was related by blood, and my mother had not known of this unusual connection until she had been married to my father for several years, and he had not known for a while after that. Still, the fact of it often stopped conversations. I looked out the window at the glimmering Nevada desert.

Finally I said, "Well, my mother didn't know that the man who raised her wasn't her real father. And my father didn't know that same man was *his* real father."

"I don't get it," Julia said.

"Lots of people don't," I admitted, looking back at her.

Sunrose broke in to my relief. "Sweetheart, you'll have a whole year to find out about Kivuli's life in Africa. Some things are too personal to pry into."

"Don't I know *that!*" Julia replied.

Several miles out of the quaint town of Winnemucca, Tom reached over and took Sunrose's hand. She kept her eyes straight ahead on the highway and didn't look when a plane landed on a dirt strip to the right of the road or glance left when groups of people rose up into the sky in giant balloons. In about twenty minutes, Sunrose stiffened considerably, and Tom whispered, "Just hold onto me. We're almost past."

"Momma, why won't you ever take me to Winnemucca? That's where the Pioneer Girls camp is…and the junior rodeo!" Julia cried, making Sunrose jump.

I gave Julia my passport to peruse, and soon, she had other questions to ask.

"Why do you have three names?" was the first.

"My middle name is Safina, the name of my mother's best friend. The word means 'ark', like Noah's ark."

"Is she Catholic?

"Yes."

Thomas broke in. "Safina is a beautiful person, an artist, and a teacher. I got to know her when I was working at Shanga."

"What does she look like?" Julia asked.

"She's tall and very thin. Her eyes are darker than Kivuli's, and sometimes she weaves strips of green ribbon into her tight curls. She catches everyone's eye," Thomas said. He turned the rearview mirror so he could see me more directly and I sensed his appeal not to say any more about Safina.

Something darted across the road and zigzagged into the shadows that were beginning to lengthen on the desert floor.

"A wild dog!" I gasped. "You have them too!"

"It was a coyote, kind of a wild dog, I guess." Thomas said. "You'll hear them at night out on the ranch."

"It was so beautiful." We could have been on safari, crossing the endless plains of the Serengeti, but of course, there were no zebras and wildebeests, and this road was paved. A few times after that, I noticed what looked like donkeys and horses galloping in the distance, and there were no fences. I worried about them trying to cross the road.

"Sometimes the ranch dogs try to yip like the coyotes, to talk to them," Julia said.

"Oh, I know what you mean. When you hear hyenas barking in my country, it sounds like a real language."

Sunrose had not relaxed. Maybe she had lost a friend in a car accident on that spot in the highway. Those deaths can stay with you for a long time. But then I saw the sign at another crossroad: State Prison 3 miles.

"Momma, why can't Kivuli stay with *us*?" Julia whined.

"Honey, it's been arranged for her to stay at the main house with Hank and Susan. They knew Askay best, after all. I think Kivuli came to find out more about her great-grandfather," Sunrose explained.

But I want to know about you. Because she seemed the most unknowable. Because she might have secrets like my own mother. Because I remembered words from the scribbles of my great-grandfather: "baby girl in my arms…she Iroquois…not able to save." That baby girl must have been Sunrose—the woman sitting right in front of me!

"But I don't have any friends!" Julia's petulance boiled up again. "You won't let me go to a sleep-over or—"

"Julia!" her father cut in, "sometimes adults have good reasons for their rules. You'll just have to trust your mother and me. Let's try to make Kivuli's first day as pleasant as we can, okay?"

"Okay," she said.

Thomas sighed, but I thought he gripped the steering wheel with a little more force than necessary.

iii

The day was darkening as Thomas turned south off the main highway out of Elko and motioned back west.

"Look, Kivuli," he said.

The sky was radiant. Reds and oranges and golds burst through thin, dark layers of storm clouds edged in purple. The vista stayed and stayed as though it had been painted on the horizon.

"What is this called?" I asked.

"Twilight. Sundown," Thomas said.

"We don't have such a thing where I live," I said. "It's light, and then it's dark, no streaks of color for one to realize day is ending, just sudden darkness."

"Is it scary?" Julia asked.

"Not really."

"I want to see that someday," the child said.

"This is better, I think."

A shaft of the sun's rays pierced the slowly deepening hues. Light and dark played against the distant mountains where the Roses' ranch spread into the foothills, where heavily-traveled horse trails wound into the high country, and animals I had only seen in wildlife books sought their evening shelter. *Perhaps a year won't be long enough*. I watched with amazement as red became crimson, orange became umber, purple became indigo, and gray became black. I would never forget that first sunset on the American desert in the state called Nevada.

The road began to have more rough spots and fewer cars and trucks. Lights from buildings were farther and farther apart; cattle lounged at water troughs or stretched their necks between strands of wire fencing, in search of better grass.

"Those belong to the Roses," Thomas said and indicated a small group of almost completely white beasts.

"Are they free?" I asked.

"Mostly," Tom said. "Some are fenced in so they can be herded to different grazing parcels."

The truck bounced over two steel tracks.

"That's called the Crossroads," Julia said. "A train goes by once a week, and the school bus stops there."

Then the countryside fell into darkness and the road got bumpier. The eyes of small animals blinked at us through the desert night. It was not so different from the outlying tracks across East Africa that I had seen from the backseat of my father's truck. My uncertainty about America dissipated and a new eagerness took its place.

Soon, we were turning again under a black metal sign that displayed foreign words.

"*Rancho del Cielo Azul*," Sunrose read.

"What language is that?"

"It's Spanish. It means Ranch of the Blue Sky," Julia answered. "You'll see why in the morning."

At the end of the driveway was a one-story, wood-framed house with large windows and flowerbeds around a screened-in porch. We had barely pulled up to the front and gotten out of the truck when the main door flew open and the Roses appeared.

"Well, here you are, Kivuli. At last." A woman who looked like an older, sturdier version of Sunrose with brighter eyes and hair pulled back in a ponytail, grabbed my hands. Maybe she was not sure I wanted a hug just yet, but she was smiling. A dog hovered around our feet, wanting attention, but held back when Hank Rose approached us. He was a lean, handsome, almost ageless-looking cowboy. His eyes were not as dark as his wife's. They seemed lit by some inner light. They were just as I had imagined them. Suddenly, I didn't know what to say. These people had actually lived with my great-grandfather, touched him, and heard his voice. They could tell me things no one else could.

iv

Thomas's family waved goodnight and drove up a well-worn track to their own place. I felt a little lost being with strangers again. The Roses took me inside, carrying my suitcases into the living room. There were unfamiliar smells wafting from the kitchen.

I had not seen such a house ever. The walls were covered with paintings. Fresh flowers were arranged in tall, glass vases, and shelves that reached the ceiling were stacked with what must have been hundreds of books. Bronze statues adorned every table. I found nothing that reminded me of Askay. Had he been gone so long, there was nothing left of his life with them?

"You have Askay's eyes," Susan said.

"And his posture somehow," Hank added.

Maybe they were looking for reminders too, of an old African they had loved.

"I've fixed some dinner. I don't know what you may have eaten today," Susan said.

"Well, actually not much," I admitted. "It smells wonderful."

"Whenever you're ready, dear," she replied.

"You can have your choice of rooms," Hank said. "What used to be Sunny's room next to ours, or Askay's on the other side of the house."

"I'd like my great-grandfather's room," I said without hesitation, but still I didn't move, trying to absorb the whole of the lovely, spacious dwelling. I had spent nights in grass huts, the small plantation bedroom I had to share with Rim after Safina moved in, and the crowded apartment in Dar es Salaam. This place would take some getting used to.

Hank gathered both pieces of luggage. "Follow me."

We had not gone far when I stopped to get a better look at a watercolor painting, set in the middle of a row of books with American history titles. It was a landscape: towering gray cliffs with small pines trying to grow out of cracks in the crumbly rock, a field of wildflowers below that, and a hawk sailing across one corner of blue sky.

"I love this," I said. I leaned forward to read the name of the artist. "Helen Rose."

Hank came back and stood beside me. "Helen was my grandmother. This was her favorite place on the ranch," he said, "but sometimes it's hard for me to look at it. She and Henry died there—when their small plane crashed."

"Oh, no." I put my hand on one corner of the watercolor. "Are they the Roses who took Askay from Africa?"

"Yes," Hank said. "It was controversial to some—to ask him to leave Africa, but he was never treated as a hired hand. He was part of us from the very beginning, or so my father told me."

"All those Roses before you, and you too, knew him better than his own children."

"That doesn't seem fair, I guess," he said. "Maybe you'll find something here to redeem us."

"Maybe you are redeemed by the words in his diary, about what you meant to him and how he tried to protect you."

He looked surprised. I explained before he had to ask. "You sent some of those pages from his journal to Africa with Thomas. I started reading them when I was five years old. I understood then just how much he cared for your family."

We went on, down a short hallway and through a door at the end. This room was large too, and one window faced east where I could watch the sun rise. The bed had four posters like my mother's and father's but without billowing mosquito netting. More of Helen's paintings hung on the walls, along with some photos of two good-looking boys, one taller and heavier than the other, both of them forking hay or sitting side-by-side on two matched horses. In one picture, the younger-looking boy held a dog—the other, a rifle.

"Who are these people?" I asked.

"My father, Julian, and his brother, my Uncle Jason. I didn't know anything about Jason when I was growing up. He had been estranged from my family for a long time. When he finally came back to the ranch, my parents were no longer living. Jason just showed up at the front door, on our daughter's second birthday."

"What happened to him?"

"He lived a few more years after that. He was a great help to us on the ranch, knew a lot about cattle from his life in Montana, got Sunny on her first pony, but when we…lost Sunny, he had a breakdown. He died that same year."

"You lost Sunny?" I dared to ask. I felt the weight of the knowledge before I had to bear it.

He straightened one of the frames, and then rested his hand briefly on the photo of his father. "I thought you'd know," he said.

"I don't need to know, Mr. Rose."

"Well, it was a long time ago, but I don't think you can be here very long without hearing about it," he said. He hugged his shoulders, and his eyes would not meet mine. "Let's go eat."

Susan had set out colorful bowls painted with sunflowers and bright blue birds. Into those she dished an assortment of cubes of roasted meat, hominy, two kinds of chiles, onions, and thin slices of cabbage over the top. That's all I recognized. She told me the meat was pork shoulder and the seasonings were garlic, cloves, and cumin. I took a tentative bite. It was so delicious I had no words for it.

"Oh, is it too hot?" Susan asked.

"It's perfect, Mrs. Rose. Just what I need right now."

"Do you have favorites?" she asked, offering me a glass of milk from a wide pitcher.

"I like most everything. Are the vegetables from your garden?" She reached over and squeezed one of my hands. "From your great-grandfather's garden, from the seeds and cuttings he started."

I put my spoon down. *Is this possible?* For sure his hands were in the ground. I squeezed her hand back. We finished the meal, and Susan told me I could be excused to get ready for bed. They'd come in and say goodnight, and she'd bring me a surprise. I wanted to stay, but I couldn't keep my eyes open. I went to my room and unpacked a few things, put them in a mahogany chest of drawers, and sighed, smelling the dark, red wood that had the faint scent of Africa. I slipped into my pajamas and sat on the edge of the bed.

The Roses came in, and Hank said they were there for me, to please not be afraid to speak my mind. That was good to know because I had never been afraid to speak my mind, but I had been expecting to hold back a little here in America, not to shock people with my boldness.

Susan set a plate of cookies on the night stand and said, "Breakfast is at eight, after Hank comes in from chores, but I can always heat it up for you later. Those long plane rides can take a couple of days to get over." She ran her hands through my surely unkempt by now hair and added, "It's so nice to have a teenager in the house again."

They left me then, and I glanced over at Susan's surprise. That was one thing I truly loved—a chocolate chip cookie in the middle of the night! I lay down on the white covers. I wasn't sure my bold streak would extend to asking more about Sunrose, but uppermost in my mind was finding out why my great-grandfather thought he had to save her. It might tell me something ultimate about my African ancestor. I had read enough of the pages from his diary to understand that his life had not always followed a smooth course. There was sadness in his language and hints of suffering. I wanted to know what those sorrows were.

I closed my eyes and imagined Askay resting his head on the feathery pillows for the first time and hearing the unfamiliar language in the voices of his hosts. I took a deep breath. A car went by on the highway, and an animal yipped close by. *Maybe this world is not so different from mine. Wild animals and skittish mothers and fathers and the mysteries about what delights—or grieves—them.* If I could survive anyplace, I could survive here.

6

Rancho del Cielo Azul

I did not exactly leap out of bed in the morning. I ate two more cookies, leaning back against the down pillows. Insistent light streamed through the window. I had no idea what time it was, but I was not going to miss breakfast. I pulled on tight jodhpurs, a tailored white shirt, and my tall black boots, and made my way into the kitchen. Susan turned from the sink where she was squeezing oranges. Her mouth fell open.

"Well, don't you look regal," she said.

"Is that bad?"

"Oh, no, honey." She hesitated. "But come here a minute."

She led me to the front window and drew back the covering. Outside there were men in jeans and plaid shirts, women in leather pants and black leather vests, all of them with huge, silk scarves bunched around their throats. Absolutely no one looked like me.

"Oh."

Mrs. Rose guided me back to the table and set a dish of fluffy eggs, sausage links, and homemade biscuits before me. I lifted my fork tentatively.

"I'll find some things Sunny wore when she came back to us," Susan said. "She was about your size… and age."

"How long was she gone?" I stared at her, while my eggs were getting cold.

"Eight years."

"Oh…I didn't know."

"No one told you?"

"Mr. Rose told me Sunrose had been…lost. In my country that means many things. Sometimes children are snatched by lions. Sometimes they get sold or put up for adoption. Sometimes they run away."

"Well, none of those things happened to Sunny," Mrs. Rose said. Her face tightened, and her hands turned white where she held onto a chair at the kitchen table. She shook her head as if denying a memory, but she didn't tell me any more. She turned to the stove and dished up a spoonful of eggs for herself, then came back to the table.

"You call my daughter Sunrose," she said.

"'Mrs. Sentinel' seemed too formal and 'Sunny' too familiar for a visitor like me," I said. "And she liked it."

"I think I do too," Susan said.

Just then, Mr. Rose came in, stomping his feet, the German shepherd that greeted us last night and whom I recognized from the photo my Baba had shown me, right behind him.

"Off with the boots, mister!" Susan called.

"Okay, okay, but I just have to go right back out." He washed his hands in the kitchen sink while Susan dished up his meal. The dog put his head in my lap.

"How are you doing this morning, Kivuli?" he asked. He did not say a word about my outfit.

Mrs. Rose set the plate down for her husband and ran her hand across the back of his shoulders. I had to look away. I rarely saw my mother touch my father like that. But my mother and Safina—that was a different story. Sometimes they seemed like one person.

Susan ate a few bites, and then she gathered her plate, silverware, and the empty biscuit bowl and began putting dishes and pans into the dishwasher. I saw her shoulders begin to shake, and finally, she left the room. *Did I stir up visions of what happened to her daughter when I asked about the missing eight years?* I could conceive no visions of that time, but it was a blank space I couldn't resist because, even though Sunrose had disappeared up the hill last night into her own secret world, she was the one I wanted most to know.

"Have you thought about school? What grade you'll be in here?" Hank asked, startling me into the present.

"I'm not sure. I've finished ten years of school in Africa. I think I should be in the tenth grade in America. Does that sound right?"

"You can start there. I can get you a tutor if you want. That's how Sunny met Thomas. After we found her, we hired Tom to prepare her for school. She'd had very little education and virtually no friends. I think Thomas fell in love with her then, but, you know, they were both so young," Hank said, "and Sunny was…withdrawn."

I let that comment stand for a moment. Whatever had happened to Sunny, it was still on Mr. Rose's mind too.

"My father met my mother when he was sixteen and she was thirteen," I said. "My mother had me when she was fifteen."

Hank stared at her. "That's around your age!"

"I can't imagine it. But my mother was on her own then. Her mother was…not available."

"You mean 'not around?'"

"I mean in her bedroom…or raving."

Hank shook his head. "Goodness. That must have been so hard on Suzanna."

"Well, she had Safina, my father, and her horses. They pretty much saved her, I guess."

"You must miss her already," Hank said. "Do you want to call her? When I spoke to your mother last week, she seemed reluctant to let you fly all this way and stay with people you don't know."

I thought back to that time when the police, with their dogs, ran all over the plantation looking for evidence in a *murder*, questioning anyone who came near my family, and scaring me with their guns and suspicious eyes. Now Suzanna was worried about me?

"Could I talk to her right now?"

"Sure. Have you finished your breakfast?"

"I can't eat any more."

Hank picked up the house phone and dialed the long-distance operator. "Yes, the time in Dar es Salaam? Eight p.m? Can you place a call for this young lady? She'll give you the number."

Moments later, Suzanna said, "Jambo? Hello? Kivuli, is that you?"

In spite of my dark feelings, I was glad my mother had answered.

"Yes, Mama, I'm here… at the ranch. Tell Baba I slept in Askay's bed last night…it felt like I was in Africa."

"Oh, sweetheart, how wonderful! Your father is out with Fulsom. He'll be sorry he missed you."

"I haven't been close to any horses yet, but the desert is so beautiful. The sun takes forever to go down, and a German shepherd has taken a liking to me!" I said in a rush.

"Maybe you should keep a journal like your great-grandfather did. Then America could be real for your children someday," Suzanna said.

There was a distracting noise on the line, and I was afraid I'd been cut off.

"Mama, is everyone okay? Baba and Granpa? Rim? Safina? Mlinzi?"

"Honey, you've only been gone one day! Everyone is fine, just missing you so much. Give everyone a hug from Tanzania," her mother said. "And stay out of trouble."

"I'll try, Mama…I love you…"

We were disconnected, and still imagining the sound of my mother's voice, I handed the receiver back to Hank.

"Who is Mlinzi?" he asked.

"The horse I'm the closest to, at this time in my life. His name means 'guardian.' He used to be a military horse, so he knows what he's doing."

"A military horse? How did you have access to a horse like that?" He pulled on his scuffed-up boots and retied his bandana.

"My granpa is a major in the British Air and Ground Patrol. Well, I think he's more than a major now, but everyone calls him *Major* Farley, almost like Major is his first name."

He smiled. "I don't think we have any horses to match his, but we'll find you something that fits. I'm going back out. Come to the barn when you're ready."

"When I'm dressed for the part, you mean?"

"You look fine to me," he said and slipped out the front door.

Susan came back in the room, bearing jeans and long-sleeved t-shirts and carrying a pair of old Western boots, more scuffed than Hank's. She had put on fresh make-up, and I noticed again how striking she was. Her skin was unblemished, and her almond-shaped eyes were clear and honest, though she might have been crying earlier. She must have heard the end of my conversation with Hank because she said right away, "I know all about you and your horses."

"You do?"

"I don't think your father ever wrote an email to us that didn't mention you and those horses."

I tried on the boots, wondering what else Baba had said about me.

"I know when you finished your first jump course, albeit only six inches high!"

Soft wrinkles formed at the corners of Susan's eyes when she smiled.

"And I know about the time your granpa made you get back on after your horse veered away from an oxer and you ended up on the ground!"

This was more than my own mother knew.

Susan put one hand over Kivuli's.

"And.... I know about the art teacher," she said.

All at once, I felt certain I was in the right place and understood why my father had wanted me to come to Nevada. And why my great-grandfather Askay's words to his forsaken children made so much sense: "Oh Africa, send your daughters so American daughters see another vision of themselves and feel tie to land where love began."

7

horses

The horses were going to be my touchstone. I walked up toward the barn, my heart racing at the sight of animals grazing in surrounding fields, tied to hitching posts, and being led to various places for their morning jobs—colors and shapes I only knew from photographs: cremelo, pinto, red roan, white with brown flecks all over, dished faces, blue eyes, muscled chests and forelimbs, and some with striped manes that only stood up four inches from their crested necks.

No one spoke to me, but I didn't care. The horses would, in their own intuitive way. They did not keep secrets. They would let me right in. But before I had touched one of those beauties, I came to the tack room door. There was a painting hanging on it, signed by Helen Rose. The canvas was battered, maybe water-damaged, the frame scratched, the colors muted, but I could clearly make out a wild, dark horse poised to buck or charge at the fence where several men stood with equally dark looks. They had spurs on their boots and whips in their hands, ready to punish the animal that perhaps had not given in to their demands. I recoiled. It was so unexpected.

Hank appeared beside me. "Noticed another one of my grandmother's paintings, I see."

"Yes. But I don't know what it means. I'll have to study it more. I just hope the horse will be all right."

"Why do you say that?" Hank asked. "Maybe it was a bad horse."

My granpa had taught me that bad horses usually meant bad owners or trainers. The painting raised a lot of questions. "It could have reasons to be bad. Maybe it should get a second chance."

"Look closer."

I moved until my eyes were within inches of the picture. Then, I saw an arm reaching through two rails of the corral and a hand holding something out for the scared animal.

"What's in the hand?"

"Does it matter?" Hank said. "What could it be?"

"A sugar cube? A grass stem? It could be…" I had to go out on a limb here, "forgiveness."

Hank nodded thoughtfully. He paid no attention to the ranch hands milling around, waiting to get their saddles and bridles.

Then he said, "That's sort of a human idea, no? What do you think the horse wants?"

I didn't have to think too long to answer that. "I think he wants to start over."

"My grandmother would have been crazy about you," Hank said. "And my mother too."

He looked at me with more intensity than he had earlier, as if he recognized my value beyond my relationship to my great-grandfather.

"Why is the painting damaged?" I asked.

Hank ran one hand over the dented frame, and a chip of wood fell onto the scuffed floor.

"Let's just say it's had a life of its own," he said, stepping aside so the wranglers could get to work.

"Will you tell me about it?"

"Maybe. It's complicated."

"I don't mind," I said. What could be more complicated than living with my mother and Safina during the week, with my father on his plantation four hundred miles away on weekends, sometimes with the three of them and Mvua's ghost in Arusha, and going to Catholic school in Dar when I barely believed in God?

"Anyway, I have to leave you with Tom and Julia for a while. I need to check out a particularly dangerous trail with Sunny this morning before our summer guests start arriving."

"What trail is that?"

"Oh, the loop around the Cliffs. A creek crosses the bottom of the ascent, and it can overflow in the spring. We built a bridge there, but that gets busted up sometimes, and it's a boggy mess. We might be gone all day, depending on conditions," Hank explained. "I think Julia can keep you entertained."

"I'm sure she can, but I don't need to be entertained. I want to work." *Does he think a fourteen-year-old just sits around playing video games all day?*

I didn't want to babysit a six-year-old either, particularly one as unevenly-tempered as Julia. Then I thought of the arm through the rail for the fractious horse that Helen Rose had imagined. The lesson in the painting was for more than the equine.

Julia and her father came in from a side door, and Hank went out of the barn with two horses to meet Sunny, calling to Tom to find me a good mount. I glanced longingly after him. I felt split right down the middle. I was not in Julia's sphere, nor was I in Sunny's or Tom's, privy to their conversations or trail rides. I could get fit with a horse easily enough, but what about with the humans on the ranch of the blue sky?

Julia went off down a row of barn stalls, and Thomas beckoned me into the tack room.

"About Safina," he began, as if continuing the conversation from yesterday, "when I left Africa the last time, she told me about her relationship with your mother, in case I had any lingering hopes that she and I could get together."

"Oh, that's good, I guess."

"And then, sometime later, your father started corresponding with Hank, asking more about Askay and making plans to come here. I asked him to give my love to Safina, and Askari wrote back that all of you were living in Dar es Salaam together. By then, I had realized what that meant."

"Do you think that's weird?"

He peered around the door to see where Julia was. "Frankly, Kivuli, I do. It does not suit my Catholic beliefs."

I stared at him. "My mother and Safina are both Catholic. Their priest, Father Amani, loves them. I grew up thinking it was all right."

He closed the door. "I just thought you should know it's a sensitive subject in this family because of what happened to Sunny."

"I don't know what happened to Sunny," I said. *But I'm going to find out.* "I have issues with Suzanna and Safina, but it doesn't have anything to do with them being gay. Of course, I'll be discreet around Sunrose and Julia."

"Thank you, Kivuli. I hope you don't take my caution as criticism. I'm very glad you came instead of Askari. I think you will add a touch of grace for the horses, and for us."

Julia had haltered the pony Tom had given her for her sixth birthday and led him to a hitching post inside the barn. She'd tied him with a quick release knot and was bent cleaning his feet. *Who was I to judge this child?* The pony had excellent conformation and a totally white face that had two serene blue eyes. His body was almost all white too with a couple of brown patches, one right over his head.

"I've never seen a horse like this," I remarked.

"It's a Medicine Hat pony. He's a real Indian horse, blessed by the gods," Julia said.

"Whose gods?" I couldn't resist asking.

"The gods who take care of everybody, even if they don't go to church," she said.

I thought that was the most interesting definition of God I'd ever heard, especially from a child I assumed was Catholic.

"But don't tell my mother," Julia added.

"Oh, don't worry. I know how to keep things from mothers," I said. *I guess that puts us on the same level.*

Tom had grabbed a couple of halters and was going along a row of stalls. I caught up with him. He moved with a lighter step than Hank's and spoke in a less serious tone. He looked fitter than I remembered, as though his time with horses had given him muscles that designing water systems could not. Though he was much younger than Hank, his wavy hair was already graying. His smile was steady in a clean-cut face that bore no wrinkles. He stopped by a stall where a brown gelding, maybe more of a dark chestnut, stood enjoying his oats. He reminded me of my mother's horse, Jester.

"What's this one like?" I asked, admiring the horse's pretty head.

"He's a good one," Thomas said. "His name is Lazo."

"Spanish?"

"Yes. It means 'rope'."

I took Lazo's halter and a grooming bucket and went in his stall. He turned his back to me. My Granpa Farley's horses never did that, and I knew why.

"Oh, he does that," Tom said. "Just go catch him up."

But I didn't want to do it that way. I moved to the horse's left side and said his name. Nothing happened. Then I slapped the halter lightly against my thigh. Lazo swung his head around. I took a few steps back and waited. The gelding turned and came to me.

"A thoughtful horsewoman," Thomas said.

"I just try to do what my granpa would. I might make mistakes. I guess the horse will show me if I do," she said.

Lazo put his head down for the halter.

"You should talk to Sunny. She followed her dad around after she came back from California. She knows a lot about communicating with horses. Hank had learned, apparently with some teenage resistance, to try his mom's way. I remember as a kid, not much older than Sunny at the time, how Hank worked a horse in the round pen. I was full of questions, and Sunny answered every one of them. Of course, those days, I was following *her* around!"

I let that "back from California" go unchallenged and tried to lead the horse out to the grooming post. He didn't want to leave his morning grain and planted his feet. I kept pressure on the rope but didn't pull on it. My Granpa Farley had horses like this at the military base in Dar, and I had learned long ago what to do. When Lazo moved the slightest bit forward, I released the lead as quickly as I could. Soon, the horse came with me willingly.

"I don't suppose you just figured that one out," Thomas said.

"No. I arrived here with *some* feel. My granpa knows a lot about horses, although he can be impatient with the whip. I was kind of a sponge for his horse sense when I was growing up."

The ranch hands moved about turning horses out, separating some for special attention, and conversing amiably but didn't include me. *Do they think I don't speak English? Do they think I am untrained and not worth their time?* For a moment I forgot my purpose. I wasn't here to impress anyone but to adhere myself to Askay's little known life among the Americans and give it resonance and shape for my father and my family back in Africa.

Thomas brought our tack over, and I had to admit I didn't know anything about the cowboy saddle. He showed me patiently while Julia cinched her own, talking to the pony as if he were her best friend. And maybe he was. A flood of sympathy rose in me for this girl who lived in the shadow of her mother's trauma. Maybe Julia needed to forgive her mother. Maybe she needed an older sister to share some of the burden.

"I've got to gather up some horses for the shoer," Tom said. "Will you girls be okay? Just stay around where I can see you."

"All right, daddy. We'll practice the trail stuff in the arena."

"Fine. Grandma Susan will have lunch for you at noon," Thomas reminded us and went on with his ranch duties.

I was left with the six-year-old after all.

We led the horses to the outdoor arena and lined them up by the mounting block, Julia first. As she swung into the saddle, she said, "What is one big question that pops into your head right this minute?"

What happened to Sunny in California? But I didn't ask that. I said, "If you could pick one place to show me on this ranch, what would it be?"

"Oh, that's easy. Heaven's Door."

I felt a little chill, but I didn't know why. I got on Lazo and rode up next to Julia who had started down the rail toward the first obstacle. "What is Heaven's Door?"

"Oh, that's where my great-grandfather Julian and great-grandmother Serena were struck by lightning. When the wranglers or the guests go by there, everyone leaves a scarf or a piece of bridle or something to honor them, but I've never been allowed to do that."

While I was getting over my shock, I tried to think of something reasonable to say. But the words got stuck in my throat.

"I'm sure even *you'll* see Heaven's Door long before I do," Julia added.

She side-passed her pony up to a standing gate, opened it neatly, and went through, latching it behind her. I rode around that challenge and watched her back through a narrow L-shaped pattern. The pony's feet did not touch any part of the ground poles. I skipped that one too.

"So what's *your* question?" I asked her as we approached a fake-looking river made out of a blue tarp.

She flipped her reins from side to side to encourage her horse to step lively upon the plastic sheet. "What was my mother doing when she was six years old?"

"I don't know, Julia. Why don't you ask her?"

"She says she doesn't remember." The girl glanced back at me with such wisdom in her eyes.

"Just ask me in twenty years or so if I remember riding a trail course with an African from Tanzania. Some things you don't forget."

She kicked the Medicine Hat pony into a canter and headed for a fat log to jump. She didn't hear me say, "There are some things a mother has good reasons to forget."

I splashed through the plastic creek and met Julia coming back across a rickety bridge. We paused face to face. She talked on.

"I asked Momma if she had a horse growing up. She said, 'No.' That's all. Just no. I asked her to tell me what she was doing when she was eight, or ten. Nothing."

Julia turned her hands up to the sky as if that expressed how that "nothing" made her feel.

"One time, I said 'What *do* you remember before that picture Grandpa Hank has of you when you were twelve sitting on a pretty grey horse?' She said 'I remember a grey horse in a green field that I wasn't allowed to touch, and I remember a shiny chestnut and a woman reaching down to lift me up behind her. We galloped out into the ocean. The horse was not afraid. He took big, strong strides in the surf, and salt water and foam burst all around us. I screamed, and the woman told me to hold on tight.' I told momma I thought she was dreaming because there was no ocean around here, and she said, 'Yes,

I think I was dreamin', and she stopped talking completely."

"My mother does that too," I said.

"She does?"

"Lots of times."

"But was she ever just a little girl?" Julia asked in a pensive voice.

"She had a strange childhood, full of disappointments and joys," I told her.

"But my momma's is like a big hole," the girl said.

"Sometimes there are big holes in life, Julia. You just have to fill them up with your own dreams," I said. "Hey, are you hungry yet?"

"Yeah, but I want to show you something first."

We tied the horses to an arena rail and climbed up in the grandstand that bordered one side. From the top bench I could see miles of desert stretched out like some inland sea with jagged peaks along the horizon perched like rogue waves in a storm.

"That all belongs to my grandpa," Julia said.

In the distance two riders were coming toward the ranch from the edge of a wide mesa. Little puffs of dust rose up behind them as they moved at a steady lope. In a few moments, I recognized Hank and Sunrose, gliding easily through the summer air, the sky above them the most remarkable shade of blue. To Sunny's left, being careful to stay out of the way, was the German shepherd, whose name I did not know.

8

Dog

Liana got to thinking about that German shepherd she let the little girl call "Dog." It was easier than explaining that his name was Paraíso, the second—the first being the Paraíso she had stolen from the child's father—Hank Rose. She and the girl certainly were not in Paradise, running from the cops, the truant officers, and park rangers who asked too many questions. No place was safe. But Dog kept the girl more or less on an even keel. Now there were blank spots on the map of Liana's mind—names of towns, numbers of highways, and features of campgrounds.

Liana resented those blanks because they were the markers of a life that once had purpose. She glanced over at Tenice who had her eyes in a thick book. They'd gotten pretty close recently—having sex in that narrow bed, playing cards during lockdowns, and seeing who could lap the most miles in the yard when they were allowed outside. Maybe if she talked about what had happened, the memories would become clearer.

"Did I ever tell you about my dog-breeding days?" Liana began.

Tenice turned the book down on her chest. "What? You bred dogs?"

"German shepherds. Yeah. Quite fancy ones—very high pedigrees. I stole the first one but didn't steal the papers so they couldn't be registered. Everyone wanted those puppies anyway. Quality always sells."

"Wasn't that illegal?"

Liana raised her arms and waved them around at the cell walls. "So?"

"Never mind. Go on." Tenice settled back in her bunk.

"I traveled the country. I had a nice van so I didn't have to spend on motels. Had a little cook stove, a water tank, a porta-potty—"

"Get to the dogs," Tenice interrupted.

"They were somethin'. The first one had a thin strip of merle-colored coat right along the back of his head. Prob'ly would have labeled him inferior for show, but everybody went crazy over that merle. Half the litters would have it, half not, or some other combination. People paid for that mark.

"Then, that shepherd got hit by a truck. The asshole didn't even stop to see what he'd done. It just about killed me. I'd had him about six years by then. I really loved that dog. I went back over my route to find one of his offspring with that merle stripe, not expecting to get one. But I did. I had to pay twice what the gal had paid me for the breeding. But he was worth it and just a year old. Plenty of time to train him and build back my business.

"Then I got myself some help—a companion, someone who could walk the dog, feed 'im and groom 'im…and keep me company. Took a couple of years to educate the kid—"

"Wait a minute. What kid?"

"Never mind all that. I took care of us."

Liana had not meant to get that close to the crux of her life. But there it was—the darling daughter of Hank Rose, living in that van with her and Dog for eight years and no one the wiser.

"What was the kid's name?"

"That don't matter either."

Tenice slapped her hand down on the mattress. "Don't just lead me on with your dog story and then leave out the details!"

"I had sex with the kid, okay?"

"Christ, Liana! What possessed you?" Tenice sat up on the edge of the bed.

"Well, I'm suffering for it, aren't I?" she said. "But here's the good part. About a dozen years ago—before your time—the Catholic Convent of Winnemucca sent a troupe of Sisters to redeem us, and there was that girl—all grown up, married to Jesus, and full of forgiveness."

"You molested a *girl*? She forgave you?"

"Not in so many words. But she saved my life once when I had a heart attack in the yard. Put her pretty mouth right down on mine and gave me air until the ambulance arrived."

"Not that you deserved it," Tenice said.

"No, I reckon not, but then, she's out there, and I'm in here."

They sat without speaking while the night shift delivered their suppers and ran the metal detector over their bedding and their bodies. Liana stirred her spoon around in the mashed potatoes.

"I'd sure like to know what happened to that Dog with the bit of merle."

9

True Passion

By the time Julia and I put our horses away and got back to the house, Sunny and Mr. Rose were already there. Susan had made olive and cheese sandwiches and reheated last night's posole. Thomas was still shuffling stock for the farrier so Sunrose packed up a couple of sandwiches, a carton of soup, and a dozen ginger-molasses cookies, which she said were the shoer's favorite, and went back to the barn.

When I tried to sit down in my chair at the table, the shepherd's paw was resting there. He looked at me with sad and mysterious eyes. He had chosen me, for some reason, to test. I was outside his routine, his carefully managed set of humans. I might do something interesting and different. I found myself not wanting to disappoint him so instead of commanding him to remove the paw, I stared at it with an image in my head of the paw on the floor. In a few seconds, he took his paw down. I made a big fuss over him.

I had only eaten one bite of my sandwich when the dog was back at my side with a ball in his mouth. Hank called out, "No, Pass, not while we're eating!" The shepherd didn't move but waited for me. I had noticed earlier that he had a bed at one end of a frayed sofa and another one closer to the front door, where he could keep his eyes on whoever was coming or going. I stared at the bed by the door, and pretty soon, he trotted off and curled up there with the ball in his mouth.

No one paid any attention, but I thought there was a lot of responsibility with this game and said a little prayer of thanks to Temple Grandin for her insight about animals and mental pictures.

Soon the ball was rolling around under my feet. When I reached down to pick it up, Hank finally said something.

"Kivuli, you're teaching my dog bad habits."

"I'm sorry, Mr. Rose. But what if he is teaching me? Don't I have to pay attention?"

"To a point," he said. "To be honest, I'm the only person he ever brings his ball to. Maybe I like it that way."

"Yes, sir."

I was relieved when Sunrose came back in and she and Hank began discussing what they would need to repair the bridge and other sections on the cliff trail. They had a good relationship, I could see, respecting each other's ideas, agreeing on which horses were likely to spook this early in the season on a new bridge, and listening even when they didn't agree. Sunny thought they should design some go-arounds on potentially difficult sections for horses and riders. Hank countered that he wouldn't have a horse that couldn't safely do that loop, that she and the boys should just get the horses fit for any circumstance. She said the dangers were one thing, the unknowns were another.

"Don't I know that," he said, putting an arm around her shoulders.

She looked over at me. "We could ride to the Cliffs tomorrow, Kivuli, if you're up for it."

"Momma, I want to go," Julia pleaded.

"Honey, you have Catechism tomorrow. Gramma Susan is taking you."

"That stuff is boring and it doesn't make any sense," Julia whined.

"Sometimes childhood doesn't make any sense. You have to learn to give things a chance," Sunrose replied without raising her voice.

"Is that what *you* did?"

Sunny's beautiful face paled, but she looked unflinchingly at Julia and at me and answered. "Ultimately I did, Julia. That's exactly what I did."

Her eyes were as sad and mysterious as the dog's and much harder to read. It seemed as if when she spoke, there was another being next to her—guiding, correcting, approving every word, telling her, "Don't be distant, but don't say too much." Maybe someone like God.

Hank pushed his chair back from the table, signaled to the dog, and went to the front door. The shepherd tipped his head back to me, seeming to say, "Where's the ball?" I had hidden it in my lap, and I struggled to get the soft, blue shape out of my head. Instead, I imagined him leaping out the door after Mr. Rose, and he disappeared in a flash. I put the ball in his bed.

Susan packaged some leftovers for the Sentinels for dinner, and Sunrose and Julia went home.

"Now, my darling African, let's go out to Askay's garden," she said.

We knelt in the dirt side by side, and she showed me how to thin the baby carrots, but soon my vision was blurred by tears. "Mrs. Rose, I think I should go home."

"Oh no, sweetheart. Come here." She enclosed me in her arms, but I couldn't stop crying.

"Your family has enough trouble without me. I'm afraid I'm making things worse."

She took the edge of her gardening smock and wiped my face. "I will tell you something. Hank doesn't realize it yet, but you are just what this family needs. Will you feel better if I tell you about the dog?"

"Oh, yes!"

We got up and sat on a bench in the shade. The Nevada sun could match the sun on the equator in the middle of the day. Susan adjusted the awning for more relief and began:

"When we recovered Sunny, she was twelve years old. There was a beautiful German shepherd with her, a male she called Dog. We brought him home with her, of course, but Hank hadn't paid much attention to him, having to deal with all the detectives and the psychologists and the traumatized child herself. One day, we were bathing and grooming Dog, and Hank cried out for me to look at a mark on his chest. It was a strip of merle-colored hair. It had been hidden in his dirty and matted coat, and then Hank knew this Dog was a descendant of the first German shepherd he'd had as a boy!

"That first shepherd was a female named Paraíso, but she was killed, along with one of her pups. They both had the merle marking. Then another of that litter was stolen, also with that mark. I don't know what happened to the others, but by then Hank was in college and on to another life. The shepherd who came back with Sunny was aging, and after Sunny went off to the Convent, Hank bred Dog to a lovely female shepherd that belonged to one of our daughter's high school friends and kept one of those puppies with a merle stripe on his shoulder. That is the one you see now, the one Hank is so protective of. Does this help you understand things a little bit?"

"Yes. But couldn't there be other shepherd pedigrees with a merle marking? What is the dog's name? I thought Mr. Rose called him Pass."

"Pass, for short. The dog's name is True Passion," Susan said, putting one hand over mine. "There's a connecting factor identifying these dogs that can't be denied."

I couldn't ask Susan more right then. It didn't seem proper. I wanted to know who stole the first puppy. I wanted to know where Sunny had been and for how long before she turned twelve. *How could she possibly have had that merle-striped shepherd?*

It was just the three of us that night at supper. Hank came in at dark with Pass. The dog grabbed the ball out of his bed and got it to Hank's hand before he could sit down. True Passion ignored me completely, and I tried to believe he would someday warm up to me.

"I'm sorry I was sharp with you, Kivuli," Hank began. "It was just hard seeing you spark something in Pass, when Sunny, in many ways, abandoned Dog after he'd been her only friend, and then she never has been especially fond of Pass. I felt you were slipping into the place I so badly wanted Sunny to fill…"

"It's all right, Mr. Rose. But can Pass and I at least be friends?"

"Friends would be okay. Just no tricks."

"Yes, sir."

"And Kivuli, you might as well call me Hank. No one calls me Mr. Rose."

"Yes, sir."

I collapsed in Askay's bed early that evening but I couldn't sleep. I couldn't stop thinking about what Julia had asked—"Was your mother ever just a little girl?" That was another story. What drew me inexorably to Sunrose was the fact that the "hole" into which no one could see was filled with *something*, maybe something Sunrose would never tell. *There are things in my own childhood I may never tell.* But I dearly wanted to and fell asleep with the first words on my lips: "When I was five years old, the police found a body…"

10

the cliffs

Sunrose and I rode out at dawn. It was fifteen miles to the Cliffs and back, which was quite a trek for me. While my mother and Safina were experienced trail riders, I had been schooled primarily in arenas on level ground. The desert rose and fell, the footing tricky, and the features of the landscape blunted by a dense fog. Sometimes I could only see a faint outline of Sunny in front of me. She said the mist would lift, but until then, it was like riding blind.

I tried to ask questions about the workings of the ranch—what were the activities for the guests, the cattle business, the wranglers' duties. Who were those men and women and why did they treat me so aloofly?

She said, "Don't talk, just ride. We'll take a break at the top."

She rode with verve. I followed with trepidation. I felt like I'd be swallowed up at any instant. We wound through forests of cactus and down small ravines. We were supposed to be conditioning horses for cautious and inept dudes, but I was the one clinging to the saddle on a not particularly steady horse. The Palomino gelding was balky and perturbed. He'd been taken away from a warm stall, where he'd had his head in a bucket of oats, into this madcap morning ride in chilly air. Sunny encouraged me, but I was not enjoying the jaunt. I put my head down and soldiered on.

We'd been trotting for forty minutes when I called out, "Sunrose! I need to walk. I'm getting a stitch in my side!"

First that silly, but smart, shepherd had tested me and now this formidable, ex-nun, who'd had an unmentionable childhood. I hadn't known about her religious vocation…or maybe I had. I vaguely remembered Thomas helping my father with Shanga's plumbing and his courting of Safina, telling her his girlfriend in Nevada had run off to a convent, and would she like to go out. Not much chance for that, but Tom didn't know she was gay, and Safina let him pine after her unaware.

I took a deep breath. The cramp was gone. We walked on past mile marker six.

The sun finally broke through the shroud of fog, and we got our bearings. The desert sparkled with dew on every thorn and patch of bunch grass. Bees were already busy at the pink blossoms of prickly pear cactus. Other flora that I couldn't identify yet spread in yellow and white tendrils across the sand.

"A ripe canvas for Helen," I said.

"The poet in the girl speaks," Sunny said respectfully. "Look up."

There in front of us rose a granite massif that seemed impenetrable, shooting up for a thousand feet out of the gentler, undulating plain. Access to the ascending trail was on the other side of a three-foot deep creek, roaring with spring run-off. The bridge was splintered in a hundred pieces. Sunrose said building material would be delivered to the site that day by truck and a new bridge installed.

"Are you game for it?" Sunny cried over the turbulence.

"This horse is not letting you go without him!"

We plunged in! It was not as risky as I had feared, and we emerged wet from the knees down onto a narrow path that began to climb up into an outpost of limber pines and ponderosa and kingcup bright with orange buds. But I couldn't wallow in all that beauty because the trail had serious gaps that had to be straddled or jumped with steely nerves and a secure hand on the reins.

The horses were not fazed. They'd been here before, and our early speed had taken the edge off their spark. I wondered how the "boys" would make a go-around any safer. We climbed a few switchbacks and stopped on a wide spot for the horses to breathe.

"It's not as steep going down the back side," Sunny promised.

"Oh, that's good," I said, thinking anything less steep might still be challenging.

In twenty minutes, we entered a clearing at the summit, dismounted, and tied to a permanent iron hitching rail long enough for ten horses. There was a footpath to the edge of the cliff where a security fence had been placed for guests to comfortably view the country below. Sunrose and I leaned against it and observed the sunlight filling all the dark places in the land, turning arroyos crimson and revealing yucca plants still holding onto their creamy blooms. There was a slight breeze and hawks soared above us.

Sunny looked at me. "For that brave ride, you deserve to ask one of your questions."

I asked, even though I knew the answer, how long she'd been missing from Susan and Hank's life.

She stared at me like, damn—that's your first question?

"Eight years," she said, keeping her eyes on the shadowy landscape.

I gasped, hearing the darkness in Sunny's voice.

"I'm over it," she said.

I didn't think so, and I worried I might have ruined my chances to learn more.

But she nodded. "Go ahead. Ask another."

"Is there one place in all that time that you cherished? That you'd go back to in a heartbeat?"

"You know how to get to the heart of the matter, don't you?"

"I like to know what's important to the people I live with, even if it's only for a short time."

"Well, here it is: a stretch of beach at Santa Barbara, California, an incoming tide with four-foot waves of Pacific Ocean, riding behind a stranger on the back of a chestnut horse…"

"Julia told me you said something like that once."

"I guess I did. I haven't told her much…about that time."

"Why that place of all the places in your life?" I pressed.

"It's the first place I remember being alive."

We stood on the precipice and waited for the echo of those words to fade. Then, Sunrose said, "Now, tell me about you."

We unpacked the snacks Susan had made for us and moved back under the shade of a ponderosa. Mountain jays swooped down for cracker crumbs; the horses picked at the sparse grass at the edge of their tethers. This would be the first person I said these words to, maybe the only one.

"My mother killed someone. It might partly have been an accident, but she didn't go for help or tell anyone where she stashed the body."

"Christ, have mercy," Sunny cried, making the sign of the cross over her heart.

"My mama is Catholic, but I don't know if she ever confessed it… or if she's even sorry. She'd say she's over it, like you did, but *I'm* not over it."

Sunrose fingered the crucifix at her neck. Thunderclouds lurched over the edge of the Cliffs, and the horses lifted their heads nervously.

"What would make it right for you?"

"I want someone who loved the dead woman to forgive my mother."

"Oh my, Kivuli, such a grand passion. I will pray for you…and your mother. What is her name?"

"Suzanna."

We were solemn going down, and careful, more danger now than the misstep of a hoof or the swipe of a low-hanging branch—the danger of our circumstances, as yet unspoken, the danger of truth.

11

the heart of the matter

As soon as I got the chance, I unpacked my computer and googled that place in California where Sunrose had ridden into the surf—Santa Barbara. It was over seven hundred miles from Rancho del Cielo Azul. I traced my finger along what seemed like the main route. Here is where the hole in Sunny's childhood had been filled. *What did she remember? Who would she tell? Eight years. Why was she gone so long?*

Susan called me for lunch, and after that, I had tack to clean up at the barn. I did not wait to be asked. When the first paying guests arrived, I went to work. When the wranglers arrived in the morning, they would find the stalled horses fed and their water buckets filled. Sometimes I could get a few groomed before I'd hear a gruff "we'll take over now." Then I'd straighten and sweep the tack room, sometimes the bathroom, though I hated that job.

Hank or Thomas had already taken groups to the Cliffs. Did Hank tell them the story of his grandparents who flew into a wind shear at the top of the peak and were slammed to their deaths? Did he tell them about the African they took off the rim of the Ngorongoro Crater to work for them in America? *Did either of them ever say that black girl who helped you on your horse is his great-granddaughter?* I was the only sign of Askay anywhere on the ranch.

Then one morning, one of the wranglers said, "Hey, Kivuli, could you settle that Paint a bit in the round pen? I need to use him today, but he may be too much to handle right now for any of these clients. Work him as hard as you want so he'll be happy walking."

"Yes, sir."

I learned the horses' names. I retrieved them for the shoer, even out of the mud from one of the far pastures. I cleaned hooves at the hitching rail and gave kids a boost into the saddle. Each horse I took to the round pen got more than an energy drubbing. They got everything my granpa had taught me—giving pressure and releasing, using my inside leg into the outside rein for straightness, not accepting the movement of one hoof for mounting and dismounting. When a client messed up, I repeated patiently the ways to convince the horse to think it was *his* idea to do what the rider wanted.

One older, spoiled gelding, Tuff-as-Nails, had a bad habit of crowding the horse in front of him on a single-file trail. That was the easiest quirk to fix of all, and the guest didn't have to keep yanking on the horse's mouth. Sometime in the middle of July, Thomas asked me if I knew why Tuffy didn't run up on horses any more. I just smiled. When Tom said, "Good job," my self-esteem soared.

On a rare day without clients, Hank caught me standing in front of Helen's watercolor with a half-oiled bridle in my hand.

"Hey, Kivuli, taking a break?" he asked.

"I was hoping you'd tell me why it was damaged. You said you might."

Hank sighed. "You don't give up, do you?"

"I like to find out the whole story about things."

He brushed one of the chipped corners of the frame with a reluctant hand. "A very damaged woman stole it and sold it and it went all over the place and through a lot of different hands. We didn't reframe it because it represented the very worst that could happen and reminded us all to take care."

"What woman?" I asked.

Hank leaned against the wall of the tack room. He seemed to be deciding how to answer, but finally he said, "The woman who took

Sunny. Years later."

My hand went to my mouth. *Sunny was kidnapped?* All at once, something flashed in my mind: words I had read from the pages of Askay's diary, pages I had found in my father's plantation invoices, some in my mother's dresser, some in Safina's books, like book-marks. I had saved them all and brought them with me, hoping someone in the Rose family could make sense of them, but these words were perfectly clear now—"mad woman writes…I open letter by mistake… it say hank I will stab you when you least expect…if woman comes I will take stab for hank…he never have to know." I pressed my hand to my heart.

"Don't let it bother you too much," Hank said. "We've had a lot of time to…adjust."

I didn't think anyone had adjusted very well, but I couldn't tell Hank my own great-grandfather had known something dreadful was going to happen and didn't warn him. I stared at the painting, appalled that the mad woman's hands had been on it and had been on Hank's and Susan's little girl. But I touched it anyway, tracing the arm in the painting with my fingers.

"I wonder what it would be like to hold out that arm for someone."

"Well, my father told me Helen had painted her own arm there," Hank said.

I felt caught between two worlds—the barn with its summer scents of contented horses in their softly-bedded stalls and the cold reality of the child Sunny being taken from her family.

"Did the kidnapper hurt Sunny?"

Hank turned away from me, and the painting, and looked out the side window where he could see a corner of the Sentinel's house up on the hill.

"She hurt Sunny beyond repair."

"In my country…I've heard of kidnap victims being killed when ransom isn't paid or when the victim becomes too much trouble."

"Well, I guess we can be grateful the woman didn't *kill* Sunny, but she sure as hell killed Sunny's spirit, her dreams, her idea of herself. She left very little of her childhood, her innocence—just a slim view of what life could be."

I shivered and took my hand off of the watercolor. *A slit for the eyes.* That was what my mother had left the teacher, Mvua. I would dig that article out of my handbag and force myself to read it again. I would look at my mother's own crime.

Hank straightened the bent frame against the door as best he could. He didn't seem angry with me, but I wouldn't blame him if he were. The painting stood for so many things—pain, fear, damage, and loss.

"What was her name?" I asked, pushing my luck.

"Who? The woman who took Sunny?" Hank gave me a cold look.

"You don't have to tell me."

"You're right. I don't, but you're probably going to hear it anyway. It's Liana," Hank said and grimaced afterward as though it made him sick. "She told some reporter back then her last name was 'Rose.' Figure that one!"

"I'm sorry, Mr. Rose—Hank. It's just that Sunny almost told me, that day we rode the Cliff loop."

"The key word being 'almost'," he said. "I don't think you'll ever hear that name or anything else from her."

I had tried for years to get the image of Mvua wrapped up in gray tape except for a slash for her eyes, and her mouth too, out of my head, but here it was again. Dangerous women, behaving dangerously, all of them needing forgiveness, except for Sunrose. She was the most innocent one. Hank still stood there as if he might not mind saying more.

"Could Sunny have ever gotten away… from the woman?" I didn't want to say the name.

"I don't think so. We asked ourselves that over the years, but we never asked Sunny. She must have been so scared. She was trapped, with just a vague memory of where she really belonged. We dreaded making her relive all that again." He shook his head as if not wanting to imagine it himself. "But hey, Kivuli, I just came back from fencing off a section of bog in the north pasture, and I had to give Pass a bath. I tied him in the sun, but could you brush him out and bring him to the house?"

"I'd love to!"

He took the bridle from my hand and got me a bucket of clean horse grooming tools from the tack room. We walked out together. An older wrangler passed us going to the barn and said to no one in particular, "You can't know what a pleasure it is to grab a freshly soaped bridle every morning…" My heart did a little dance.

Hank squeezed my shoulder. "That's Ty," he said. "In case you'd like to know, he was close to Askay."

Then, I whipped around to catch a good look at the tall, bowlegged cowboy slipping through the barn door. I thought the day couldn't get any better. Hank left me with Pass, and I began combing out his coat and talking to the dog like we'd been friends forever. As I stroked down his left side, the teeth in the comb broke open a line of merle-colored hair on his shoulder. It was hard to keep from crying.

When I got back to the house with Pass, Susan had left me a note on the kitchen table: "Take a rest, darling. You work too hard. I'm in the garden, but when I'm finished, I'm going to bring you some of Sunny's tenth grade text books to see what might interest you at school this fall. Hank has gone out to worm horses."

"Okay, Pass, I guess you can come with me." He wagged his tail. "I see you've forgiven me."

We went down the hall to my room, and I sat at the newly-varnished desk where Askay must have written much of his journal, where he wrote the words that *he* would take the stab that was Liana. True Passion curled up at my feet. I opened my laptop. My hands were shaking. I didn't want to hurt anyone, but Sunrose's kidnapper might still be alive. In the google box I typed two words: Liana Rose. There were fifty-three of them. But there was only one in the state of Nevada. Newspapers across the country detailed her crime—the abduction of the Roses' daughter from the Nevada State Fair. *The fair!* Photos showed a run-down trailer in Elko and an old "Missing Child" poster at a rest stop on Highway 101 in California. There was a quote from a teacher, an Allen Bowen, who said "I knew something wasn't right when that woman enrolled the little girl here at Solvang Elementary." In one report was a statement about Liana's capture in Santa Barbara, California, and subsequent trial and imprisonment at the Nevada State Womens Prison in 1996.

Then, I found a more recent article that said the prisoner, Liana Rose, had been moved to a new facility twenty miles east of Winnemucca. I typed the name of that institution, but the prison website indicated that no information about inmates was available. There was a list of rules for visitors, but I didn't want to read them. Did I think I was actually going to go there?

The Roses were trying to forget this woman. I should forget her too. But if I was so fierce to find forgiveness for my mother, I should want that for Liana too, as crazy as it seemed. I felt quite sure Helen Rose would never have held her hand out to *this* criminal. *I'm the one who has to do it! I have to reach through the rails and offer something good.* The only way I would be able to figure out what to offer would be to stand before Liana and see what kind of remorse she might harbor and what kind of salvation was possible. I could never expect Sunrose to do it. I was on my own.

12

omissions

Someone was knocking on my door. Pass jumped up and greeted Susan, who had an armload of books. I closed my laptop and grabbed a couple of texts off the top. She spread them out on the desk and moved a chair up next to mine. The dog stretched out on a Navajo rug by the bed. I glanced at the thickest volume.

Susan read the title: "*Earth Science*. What do you know about that?"

"I know the earth is four point five billion years old."

"Good for you. I never remember facts like that," Susan said.

"I love school. My problem is there are always more questions than answers. Or omissions."

"Oh, yes, I know about *omissions*," Susan declared. "Sunny was always arguing with her teachers. I remember once when her class was reading about all of those famous explorers who discovered the New World, and she stood right up and said, 'All those ships carried *slaves!* Those captains sold millions of people in chains!'"

"Here's another omission," I said. "At one time, half of the populations of most African countries were slaves. Africans captured slaves for the Portuguese to export, for sure, but did you know they sold slaves to the English, Dutch, French, and German colonizers and to tribal rulers for bondage in our own country?"

"I didn't know that," Susan admitted.

I didn't think that was taught in any school in the world. No country wanted to own the truth about slavery or how to soften its ramifications. We leaned into each other and were silent for a moment.

"I so want Julia to have a well-rounded sense of history," Susan said. "But we have certainly omitted things about her family's *personal* history."

"I sometimes think I know too much about *my* family," I told her. "I know facts but not reasons. I know about crimes but not about forgiveness. Is that a good thing, forgiveness? What does it mean in the long run? Some things can't be taken back."

I was thinking about my mother's crime of killing Mvua, not Liana's crime of kidnapping Sunny, but Susan said, in a facetious tone, "I'd be open to any insight about forgiveness."

"I haven't figured out everything about that, but I like to hear stories of real people forgiving or being forgiven," I said.

Susan leafed through a couple of books. Her face took on that strained look as it had at the breakfast table that first morning. She read a couple of other titles: "*Math for the Twentieth Century, Advanced Biology.*" Finally, she looked up at me. "Do you know what happened to our daughter, our Sunny?"

"Hank told me someone kept Sunny from you for eight years. My father told to be especially considerate of Sunny because she had suffered trauma as a child. I don't think anyone wants me to know more," she answered.

"Well, I'm going to tell you more—one of those stories you like about forgiveness," Susan said. She got up then, went to the window, and drew the curtains back farther, as if she'd rather look at the light than into my eyes. "Our daughter, years after she was recovered, saved the life of her abductor."

"What?" I could hardly believe what I was hearing. "How?"

"When Sunny was in the convent, the Diocese had a prison outreach program. The sisters ministered to the inmates in the Nevada lock-up for women. She discovered that her abductor was incarcerated there. Our daughter had always thought the woman was in prison in

California since that's where Sunny was rescued. But no. The kidnapper had been right here in Nevada. Anyway, one day Sunny performed CPR as the woman was having a heart attack."

"Oh, Mrs. Rose, what a brave thing for Sunny to do! It seems like forgiveness to me. But I don't understand Catholics at all."

"I couldn't have done it," Susan admitted. "I don't know if that means my daughter forgave her. I didn't want to know then, and I don't want to know now. I could hardly bear that the woman was still breathing! But, among other equally inexplicable passions, those Catholics are big on forgiveness."

I thought about my mother with the bloody knife in her hand, Mvua gasping for air, and asked a possibly unanswerable question. "Do you think each case is different? That bad acts can be judged by unique parameters?"

"I can't imagine what those might be. But Kivuli, I didn't mean to burden you with events over and done with—our unhappy saga," Susan said. "I guess when the subject of forgiveness comes up, things are not quite over."

"You are so right," I agreed.

"I'll let you get back to whatever you were doing. I need to think about supper anyway." She touched the frames of the photos of Julian and Jason Rose. "So much those boys suffered and so much they never knew about suffering," she whispered, "but about forgiveness, they could write a book."

I mumbled something about helping her with dinner, and she said I could pick some squash and tomatoes from the garden about four. She gave me a quick hug. When she reached the door, she turned and said, "Not being able to forgive has affected my whole life."

I stretched out on top of the comforter and closed my eyes. A sudden strong wind rattled the window sills, and an unnatural darkness enveloped the room. I could hear wranglers calling back and forth about catching horses and nailing down boards that had come loose on the barn. When thunder boomed in some far canyon, Pass jumped up on the bed and curled up next to me.

13

Henry Dancing Horse

In the second week of July, Hank and the boys led a big group on a full-day ride, but they left Lazo. He paced around in an outside corral, whinnying after his friends. It was a good time to get him attached to *me*. I took him out to the round pen that had a rail fence like the one in Helen's painting. It didn't take long for the horse to teach me what to do. I started on the ground. When I moved toward his haunches, he sped up. When I stepped toward his shoulders, he slowed or turned the other direction, depending on how much pressure I put on him. When I stopped asking for anything, he halted, and then if I backed away, he walked right over to me.

"You already knew that, you silly thing! You were just testing me."

I had found an English saddle under a stack of western saddles in the tack room, but I got on his bare back with just the halter on his head and tried to direct him with my legs and with my hands out to the side of his neck. I asked him to do the things he was already doing with me on the ground, things he understood. It worked fairly well. Tracking to the right around the arena and turning in that direction was easier for him than traveling to the left, so I gave him extra praise when the left-hand way shaped up.

I mostly walked. He had a big trot, and I wasn't sure I could stay on. I made it a few times around the ring each way, swinging the lead rope over his head so I could influence his head, then closing my legs around him, being careful not to drive him forward, and he came to a nice stop. I threw the lead rope to the ground but stayed on his back, talking to him and petting him wherever my hands could reach.

"If you weren't so young and a bit dark-skinned, I'd say I was watching Serena Rose all over again."

I glanced around, but the sun was in my eyes. The voice came from between the rails, a man's voice. Lazo nickered. The horse knew him.

"Hop down, in case I startle him. I'm coming in," the man said.

I slid off the horse as I heard the creak of the gate, the measured footsteps, but Lazo blocked my view momentarily. Finally, the man was standing in front of me. I looked up into a rugged, brown face framed by long, black hair streaked with gray. A beaded headband contained his locks. He held out a hand.

"Henry Dancing Horse," he said.

"Kivuli Farley," I said.

"What kind of a name is that?"

"Maasai and British," I said, looking him straight in the eyes.

"Well, I'll be damned. You are that little African everybody's talking about. They didn't say you were a *horsewoman*," he said respectfully.

"I've proven myself to them a bit," I said.

"Serena will be smiling in her grave."

"Hank's mother Serena?"

"The one and only."

We moved to a spot of shade by the rail, and I picked up a brush I had left there. I groomed Lazo's sweat-streaked coat with long, even strokes, interested in the old man but a little unsure of myself.

"Is there a family graveyard someplace around here?" I asked.

"What an odd question. Are all Africans so direct?"

"It's not so odd, Mr. Dancing Horse. My great-grandfather might be buried there," I told him.

"Your great-grandfather? I believe I might have heard something about that. You are Askay's great-granddaughter."

"I am."

Dancing Horse peered over Lazo's back to the distant hills.

"I'll take you to the place he's buried, after you canter this horse from his bare back with your arms out in the air."

"I think I'd prefer a saddle for that."

"You want to ride like an Indian, don't you?"

"What makes you think that?"

"Something about your approach to the horse and the way you already ride him," he said.

I was beginning to like this wild-looking man. He spoke to me like an equal.

"What does Serena have to do with me?" I asked him.

"Everything. She came here to the ranch when she was twenty-something, all fired up for a job with the horses and fell in love with the boss before she'd gotten off her third horse! Whose trouble she had pretty much fixed, by the way. She was talented, but it never went to her head. Kind of like I imagine you becoming."

"Was she as good as Helen? I mean knowing what horses need?"

"You've seen the painting, have you?"

"Yes. I think about it a lot."

The Indian reached into the nearby bucket for a comb and smoothed Lazo's auburn mane.

"I didn't know Helen," Dancing Horse said, "but the painting has saved a few lives. Those who seriously agreed to *look*. Let's put your horse away. We can talk some more in the shade of the barn. It's damned hot out here."

"Who are you, anyway?" I asked.

The man took Lazo's lead and opened the arena gate. The horse waited to see if Dancing Horse wanted him to go first or follow behind. The gate was only wide enough for one of them. He seemed to be directing the horse with his mind.

"Maybe I should take lessons from you, but I still need to know who you are. How do I know you're real? The sunlight can play tricks on a person."

He laughed. "Let's just say I'm Hank's token Indian, and maybe a little more."

"I don't think so! He's married to an Iroquois woman!"

"You've done your homework," he said.

"Some of it," I said. "But there are things I don't know."

"Like?"

I could be vague and never learn anything, or I could shock him and drive him away.

"Like where is that kidnapper, Liana?"

"Why in hell do you want to know that?" he asked, raising his voice.

We turned Lazo out in the lushest pasture and wandered back to a couple of chairs by the side of the barn, where folks could sit and watch the horses do their turn-out antics. Dancing Horse retrieved two bottles of cold water from an ice chest he had brought.

"So," he said.

"I can't explain it yet. I just want to ask her something."

"Yeah, well, they'll never let a child in *that* visiting room," he said. "Especially one as crazy as you."

"I'm not crazy, Mr. Dancing Horse—just curious," I said.

"And how do you think you're going to do this, Miss Not-So-Crazy?"

"Tell me where she is, and I'll tell you."

"The Womens Prison outside of Winnemucca, but I think you knew that," he said.

I frowned, suddenly recalling Sunrose stiffening the day I arrived when we passed that town on the way to the ranch. "You can't always trust the Internet, and that stuff happened a lot of years ago."

He sipped his water thoughtfully and gazed out at the heat mirages forming on the desert.

"So how are you going to accomplish this feat?" he asked.

"I'll say I'm a relative wanting to see how she's doing with her heart condition and all."

"You know about that, huh?"

"Susan told me," I said.

Dancing Horse squinted at me as if now he couldn't believe *I* was real.

"You some kind of private detective or something?"

"I just want to *talk* to her."

"But why are you digging into things that don't concern you?" he asked.

"Just forget it," I said, feeling I had started something I couldn't finish.

"Oh, no. Anyone who handles a horse like you do can damned well handle a *conversation*."

I tried to think if I had known anyone like this outspoken Indian in my entire life. He waited for me to speak as if we were playing a game and it was my turn to move. I didn't flinch.

"I hate what that woman did to Sunrose, and I don't know all of it. I hate something my own mother did. But that's not why I'm here, in America. It's just that I knew a few things about Sunny and the Roses and about Askay's life when I arrived, but when I met the actual people, I wanted to understand how all the pieces fit."

"Are you sure you're, what? Fifteen? Sixteen?"

"Fourteen. But I've always liked things to make sense. I can see myself in that prison. I'm less afraid of talking to that kidnapper than my own mother," I said, but I felt my bravado slipping away.

"Well, you just might get away with it, except your Maasai might show," he said. "Or your age."

"I'm pretty good with make-up. My mother has a birthmark that she knows how to cover quite nicely. And I could add a few years to my face."

Dancing Horse shook his head, his gray locks falling around his craggy face. "You have it all figured out, don't you? Except for your own safety."

"What could she do, in prison?" I stared out at the far hills where the Cliffs baked in the summer sun. Out there, Helen and Henry Rose were tossed to the ground in their flimsy airplane. Nothing seemed safe.

"Did you know Liana?" I had come this far, I might as well see how far I could go.

The aging Indian held the bottle of water to his lips but didn't drink this time. It seemed that he was going to ignore me. Then he answered in a voice of dark resignation.

"Yeah. I buried the dogs she killed and gentled the horses she ruined and picked up the pieces of the twelve-year-old she shattered," he said.

"You mean Sunny?"

"Hah! I guess you don't know everything, 'cuz I mean Hank. She started hurtin' on that boy when they were both just kids."

I had no idea what he was talking about. The only thing I knew for sure was that Askay had intercepted the note the "mad woman" meant for Hank, the "stab" she had promised to deliver, when they were both *adults*.

"I do know a very rueful thing about Liana that no one else knows," I admitted.

"Aren't you mysterious."

"I don't know if I can ever tell it. Please don't mention it to anyone," I added quickly.

"Oh, no, I wouldn't ruin your plans. I might back you up, if we get to where we trust each other."

We sat in silence for a while. I felt as ancient as the Indian but very new in my knowledge of the world and the trouble people found themselves in. I felt uninhibited with Henry Dancing Horse, even when he seemed to be reprimanding me. He didn't talk down to me. He didn't hide things. He tried to see my point of view. He answered questions as though he could see into the future.

"Are all Indians like you?" I asked.

"I doubt it," he said. "I had the benefit of Serena, fine horses, and Askay."

After that, whenever I needed help with a horse, I sought out Dancing Horse, who worked part-time on the ranch. I had a hard time explaining to the horse the concept of "follow me" or "you go first," doing gates or loading in the trailer. But the Native American would take the lead rope, approach the problem with a clear intent, and Lazo would do exactly what the man asked.

"I don't get it," I said to him once. "What do you have in your bag of tricks that I don't?"

"Oh, about fifty years, I'd say."

"There's something else, Mr. Dancing Horse, and I think I need to know what it is."

He looked at me intently for a moment. The lines in his face softened, and his eyes gentled.

"How do *you* find out things about a horse?" he asked.

"Watch. Wait."

"Hmm. That could work."

14

altars for forgetting

On the afternoon of a thunderstorm, I hiked up the rise where the Sentinel home stood overlooking the main barn and a wide stretch of valley grasslands beyond that. I had not been in the Sentinel's home, and I didn't know what to expect. The dangerous weather had kept everyone off the horses and given me this chance to be close to Sunrose and Julia.

"Mom! Kiki's here!" Julia shouted when I came through the front door. She had given me that nickname at the beginning, but I didn't mind. Something of her own choosing was a small star in her cap.

Sunrose had made us meatloaf sandwiches and mint tea, which I loved.

"I thought you girls would like to sit by the back window where you can see the lightning strikes in the hills," Sunny said.

As we walked through the house, I tried to ignore the clutter and signs of neglect, but I couldn't avoid the dozens of Catholic symbols perched on every shelf and dresser, the candles arranged in small shrines, statues of saints and holy figures, and rosaries draped wherever there was an empty spot. On the walls were pictures of Jesus and Mary, some artwork of Julia's, and photos of horses. Not one of Helen Rose's paintings.

The three of us ate in the changing light as dark clouds threw shadows on the table. We hugged each other when thunder broke over the land. I told stories about the leopards I had grown up with and how they hid in the rooms of the plantation house when a storm approached. As awkward as it might have been, I loved being there, in the Nevada house with a mother and daughter struggling to have a smooth relationship like the one I wanted with my own mother. Still, I wondered about things, so when Julia leaped up to answer the phone, I asked Sunny why she didn't have any of Helen's watercolors displayed.

"They remind me of something…unpleasant. I've asked Tom to remove the one on the tack room door, but he says some of the wranglers who've been here for a while use it as a talking-point with people who are new to horses."

"Yeah, I get that." Sunny didn't have to know what else I got about that particular one. "Some of the paintings have a lot of hope though."

"That depends on your definition of hope," Sunrose said.

"I guess I'm too young to have a firm definition of hope, but I'm planning to go home with one," I told her. "I haven't always been a beacon of hope in my mother's opinion."

"I think you would be a lovely daughter to have."

"My mother might stumble over that adjective."

"But why?"

"She's had a complex life. I don't know all of it, but I don't hold it against her. I feel cut off from her though, sometimes."

Sunrose pulled the crust off of her sandwich and looked to see if Julia was still out of the room. "I wonder if Julia will hold my life against me."

Before I could say anything, the girl was back. "Grandpa says Pass is missing!"

"Oh, he hates these storms," Sunny said. "He'll turn up. We can't very well go out looking for him."

I shuddered to think the dog had followed me and was now cowering all alone someplace. I should try to find him, but after hearing the story about Julian and Serena Rose being struck by lightning, I was not eager to be out in the storm.

"Grandpa just says to keep an eye out in case he shows up here," Julia said, grabbing a sandwich and crashing down on the long sofa next to me. "Momma, you need to put more catsup on my meatloaf."

"I know. I've been quite forgetful lately," Sunrose said.

"It's okay," Julia said.

Thunder resounded through the house. A few trinkets rattled on the shelves, and then a sheet of rain hit the bay window. We all stopped eating for a moment and stared out at the outlaw storm. "This is something for this part of the country," Sunrose said. "Higher up I'd expect it, but the desert usually stays dry all summer. Things change, I guess. Things can frighten one, but here in my house is everything I trust."

Her Catholic treasures teetered as thunder shook the timbers and the power surged off and on. We seemed to be on the edge of another world.

"I was in a storm like this once," Sunny said, "crossing the High Sierras. It was the day before Christmas, and all the mountain towns along the way were filled with colored lights and decorated pine trees. I thought we were going to Heaven. I couldn't wait to see God and the angels."

"Did you get any presents?" Julia asked.

"I…don't remember. It was a long time ago," Sunrose answered faintly, the next clap of thunder drowning out any more words.

Julia set her plate on the table and clutched one of my hands. She seemed to know this was one of her mother's memories from the hole in her childhood. The wind blew some loose boards against the front door, but Sunny jumped up and cried, "Someone's knocking! I forgot about Bible Study! I didn't think anybody would come today."

"Come on, Kiki, we can go play with my dolls," Julia said.

We carried our dishes into the kitchen and then went into Julia's bedroom. The bed and several dressers were lined with dolls of all kinds—ones with Indian necklaces and fringed vests; others with cowboy outfits, spurs and chaps; and still others with white lace dresses like wedding clothes. Julia made up a story about them and told me their names as the narrative unfolded. Almost all the dolls had a part in the drama, except one that Julia kept pushing aside, covering it with part of her bedspread.

I thought the doll had once looked better. It had a Native American face and should have been dressed as a fancy dancer with ribbons and bells, but the doll's clothes had been stripped and replaced with a plain, brown dress that was misshapen and stiff.

"Who is this, Julia?" I asked, drawing back the covers.

"Oh, that's the little Indian girl who was kidnapped. I don't know her name. I don't know what she was called then. I don't play with her," Julia admitted.

"But why not?"

Julia patted the doll in a careless way. "What if it was my momma?"

I didn't have an answer. The unexplained place in Sunny's childhood had found its way into Julia's. Maybe Sunrose was going to use the doll to tell Julia what had happened to her when she herself was six or nine or twelve. Maybe the doll would come alive on a beach in California or with its hand on a leash walking the German shepherd called Dog.

"Let's go back and watch the lightning," Julia said.

On my way to the main house later, True Passion fell in behind me, wet and shivering. He stuck by me all the way to the ranch house kitchen. Susan and I gathered warm towels from the dryer and rubbed him down. I felt so grateful that he was all right.

15

Heaven's Door

The morning after the contentious storm, I counted twenty horses at the hitching rail. Only nine guests had arrived the night before. Something was up. All the wranglers were saddling their horses, and there was Sunrose with Julia, and Susan was leading her mare out of the barn. Dancing Horse sat on a tall pinto, surveying the scene. When he saw me, he rode over.

"You're riding with me," he said. "We're going to Heaven's Door."

Everyone's going to Heaven's Door? And then, I knew. In a lightning storm just like yesterday, Julian and Serena Rose had been killed. We would be riding by the ravine to honor them. I hurried to tack up Lazo and waited with Henry at the back of the pack. Hank and Susan led out with Tyrone, and the Sentinel's fell in the middle somewhere. Pass loped along at the front. We moved quietly across the watered grasslands and onto the desert floor, guarded by ghostly Joshua trees that I had just learned grew farther north in Nevada than ever before, and pink hedgehog cactus glowing in the shadowy early light. Some riders had fancy tack on their horses—silver bits and tooled saddles.

There was very little conversation. The story of Hank's folks was passed around through the clients so by the time we reached the deep gorge that marked the entrance to Heaven's Door, no one was surprised to see a post driven into the ground with remnants of other visits to this place. Hank, and then two or three others at a time, dismounted and climbed down to the post and left a memento with many other headbands, scarves, crops, and saddle tags, now mostly in pieces. There were no crosses. After Dancing Horse climbed back up and remounted, he said, "Twenty-nine years ago today."

There was so much I wanted to know. *What happened to their horses? Why did they die? Did lightning always kill you? What were the last words they said to each other?* Some of those things could be known, others not. Sunlight washed over the scene, slowly filling in the cut in the land where the Roses had tried to escape the strike.

"Thanks, everyone. Let's go on up," Hank said.

We started on our way again, winding single-file into the country called Heaven's Door. Wildflowers laced the woods with the colors and patterns of a Maasai wedding dress, and raptors flew so close I could feel the wind from their wings. The trail narrowed, and there were steep drop-offs on one side and loose-shale cliffs on the other. The horses moved steadily on.

We stopped for lunch, and I made a place next to Dancing Horse in the shade of a wide-trunked cedar. Hank pointed out the columbine, paintbrush, larkspur and other mountain flowers that graced the hillsides and the creek that rippled down from a spring higher up; the land had been his father's dream, he said. I wondered if Julia would understand the passing on of dreams from generation to generation, or if she would always be burdened by what she didn't know about her mother.

"Where are their graves?" I whispered to Dancing Horse.

"In the family cemetery…near Askay's."

"I guess I'll never see it…'til I can ride like you."

"You're getting there," he said, and smiled for the first time that day.

I looked out across the bunch grass meadows where the ponderosas and aspens met the sky and then closer to the orange and yellow columbine and cobalt larkspur lining the stream. A golden eagle perched on a short dead snag, but the horses made him nervous, and after a while, he flew away. The place felt holy. It felt like a heaven should.

Hank had begun to tighten the horses' girths and load the saddlebags. "Let's head out, folks," he called. "Thunder storms building up!" I cinched Lazo, offered him the bridle, and stepped into my stirrup. Dancing Horse waited until the clients passed by and then swung into the saddle. We followed, hustling the stragglers, as we felt the electricity in the air. Once we got down onto the desert floor, Hank split us up. Thomas took his family and half the clients on a short cut, and the rest of us stayed with Hank. It was fitting that we celebrated the life and death of Julian and Serena with the threat of lightning not far behind.

I kept my eye on Pass, knowing how scared he might be. Promise of no tricks or not, I sent out a strong image of the shepherd right up beside Lazo, and in a few minutes, there he was, matching my horse stride for stride. When we reached the barn and all the horses were stalled and guests safe in their cabins, Hank threw his arms around me and hugged me tightly. He didn't have to say a word.

When I called home that night, my mother did not like me putting myself in such danger. "Where did you go anyway?" she asked.

"We went through heaven's door and back."

16

the black priest

Susan wanted me to go with her one day to the small town north of the ranch where Julia and I would attend school in the fall. It would be one less day for me on a horse and one less day to be on the computer, but I couldn't say no. I had finally read the rules for visitors to the Womens Prison, and I couldn't think of anything else. You had to be eighteen or with an adult to visit anyone incarcerated there. It would be easy to change the "4" in "14" to an "8" on my ID, and I certainly knew how to use cosmetics to lighten and age my face. You only had twenty minutes with the worst offenders, and some of them were not allowed visitors. The hours were Monday through Friday from eight to four. Gifts could not be wrapped. You couldn't touch prisoners or make any sudden moves.

Susan slowed down at the Crossroads and checked to see if I had my seat belt on. I felt guilty for thinking about the criminal Liana, who had hurt the Roses—and Sunny most of all—but the imagining of the kidnapper would not let me go. It was as though Liana herself were dragging me into the story.

"You and Dancing Horse have found some common ground, I guess," Susan said.

"For sure. We have the horses—and he doesn't shy away from my quirks."

Susan thrust her arm out to protect me when she swerved around a pothole, but she didn't know the real danger I was in, wanting to confront her daughter's abductor. I ran the window down and stared out at the foreign country going by. Cactus flowers bloomed out of the brown earth, and green shoots of desert vines spread out from pools of summer rain. I could feel the aura of the Serengeti, my Nevada questions boiling in my mind.

"Why do you think Sunrose left the convent?" I figured that might be a neutral question.

"I've not wanted to ask," Susan said. "Why do you care about that?"

"It's kind of mixed up with some questions I have about God," I told her.

"Well, you'll like my little surprise then," she said.

In a few miles, I noticed a sign that read "Welcome to Ochala Junction: Population 830." We went by a general store and the post office. I counted three bars and as many churches. What I suspected were one-hundred-year-old houses were clustered around a central park with a fountain and swings. The lawns were neat, and dogs were behind fences, mostly. After four or five blocks, Susan pulled up to a church with a tall bell tower that reached into a tide-pool blue sky. A robed gentleman stood on a stone sidewalk watering a mass of colorful bedding plants.

"A priest?" I said. "A black priest?"

"Not just a black priest. An *African* priest," Susan said.

"Really? Way out here?" I was amazed.

"He came just before we found Sunny. He's the one who sponsored her at St. Mary's Convent. I thought you'd like to spend some time with him."

"I don't know. I'm not Catholic," I said, but then I reconsidered. Perhaps this was just the man to have in my corner if I made a mistake I couldn't take back.

Susan stopped at the curb. The priest came over to the passenger door just as I opened it.

"And whom do we have here?" he asked.

Susan leaned over and said, "Father Zenwa, this is our guest, Kivuli Farley. I'm off for some shopping. Can I leave her with you?"

"A girl who'd choose me over a new outfit? Definitely leave her!"

I walked with him toward the parish house as Susan drove away. He stopped and pulled a few weeds from a bed of marigolds.

"An African priest?" I said.

"And you?"

"An African teenager."

"Ah, I have heard. The great-granddaughter of an African I did not have the pleasure of knowing."

"Yes."

"May I ask why you have traveled so far?" Father Zenwa asked.

I took in his chiseled, unwrinkled brown face and short, thick frame. His eyes had a sparkle, youthful and somewhat mischievous, although he must have been at least middle-aged. How much should I say?

"My father wanted to find out what his grandfather's life had been like in America and to thank the Rose family for loving him. But I've imagined learning Askay's secrets," I said.

"Hmm. Perhaps a priest is the last person with whom to discuss such things," he said, "although I was not privy to his secrets."

"I might like to reveal my own."

"In that case, you have come to the right place," he said, looking me straight in the eye.

He led me into his study. The walls were lined with books, and, it seemed, the floor and a few chairs too. There was hardly a place to sit down. The priest lifted several volumes from two chairs and stacked them on other piles.

"Excuse the mess. I'm reorganizing."

"Oh, that's okay. I love books. This is like a dream room," I admitted. "But now that I'm here, I'm a little shy to talk to you, an important Catholic from my own country."

"I'm certain your heart's agenda is as important as mine," he said.

"Heart's agenda. I like that."

I sat in one empty chair and he in another. A slight breeze came in through a screened window. I was not uncomfortable, but I feared what I might say.

"You are from Tanzania?"

"Yes. I live in Dar es Salaam now, and I was born there, but in between, I lived in Arusha."

The priest reached down and lifted an over-sized book from a pile on the floor. It was titled *What to See in Tanzania – People and Places*.

"I was just reading it, in case I ever get to that country," Zenwa said. "I'm from South Africa, but I feel like an American now."

"Like Askay," I said.

"Yes." He was close enough to touch my cheek. "You are fair. You have a mixed heritage?"

"From Askay to my grandmother, Iyeala, to my father, Askari, my Maasai blood is deep. My mother's family is all from England, but there's a twist—my father's father is a British major."

"The Maasai blood is stirred," the priest said.

The breeze whisked some papers off the priest's desk. He got up to collect them and then offered me a glass of orange juice. I sipped the drink and thought right away it wasn't freshly squeezed like Susan's.

"So, did Susan leave you with me for a particular reason besides that we might reminisce about Africa?" Father Zenwa asked.

"Maybe she wants me to be a Catholic?"

"I don't think so. She follows the Iroquois way, the way that existed before there were Catholic missionaries rounding them up and refusing to let them speak their own language."

A priest who does not like omissions. I turned the pages of the big book, my heart comforted by the reminders of home. "Oh! There's Shanga! The center for handicapped artists in Arusha! We lived in the coffee plantation next door. I brought sacks of coffee beans from the farm. Would you like one?"

"I would dearly love coffee from Africa!" Zenwa exclaimed.

I closed the book and looked for a way to explain my deeper qualms.

"My great-grandfather was Catholic. He came here to help the Roses. I know about many of the things he did. He raised a garden, cooked for them, took care of Hank when he was in trouble growing up, and wanted to save Hank from a vicious act that he knew was coming. But I don't know how he fit in with these Americans, why he cared about them so much he never went back to Africa to his own children," I said and swallowed the last of the juice as if swallowing the rest of what I might reveal.

The priest remained silent, so I went on.

"What I dearly want to do is finish something Askay couldn't."

"And what is that? If you can tell me," Father Zenwa said.

I was certain he wouldn't repeat it, but he was not Dancing Horse. This man might have judgments, *requirements,* to consider. And I couldn't say anything about Liana without telling him about my mother's crime. I was afraid of what he might say about that.

"How long will you be in America, my child?" he asked, as if to give me space to think.

"A year."

"Well, we have plenty of time then."

"No. It doesn't seem like enough time," I said. And then, I made my choice. "To find out what forgiveness can do."

He perked up a bit at that. "Who needs forgiving?"

"Liana."

The name rang like an alarm in the room.

"Oh, my. How do you know about Liana?"

"My father warned me to be careful what I said around the Roses because their daughter, Sunny, had been traumatized when she was a child. I was to be careful around her too, in case she still suffered because of it."

"Did he tell you that name?"

"No. But I've heard more of the story from Mr. Rose himself, and Thomas, and Dancing Horse, even Susan." I looked away at last, down at my own hands. "Then, I found out where Liana is, on the Internet."

The priest made the sign of the cross, but didn't speak.

"I only wanted to know about Liana and what she did because I found something my great-grandfather wrote, something that might have stopped Liana before she could hurt Hank. It's too late for that, but it's not too late for Liana to be sorry, for the Roses, *anyone*, to forgive her. I don't think the crime should be excused or forgotten, but forgiveness, that's a different thing, and I need to know if it's real, if it's possible."

"Anything is possible...with God."

He reached for a Bible and began scanning the pages, but I stopped him. "I want there to be forgiveness that has nothing to do with God."

The priest turned his eyes up toward the ceiling, or maybe heaven, as if he couldn't believe I'd say such a thing. Then he looked at me again.

"Where do you think the idea of forgiveness comes from?"

"From Jesus on the cross—to Christians, at least," I said. "But where was Jesus when Liana stole Sunny right out from under her parents' eyes?"

He didn't answer right away as if he was seriously considering my question.

"Maybe he was there when Sunny saved Liana's life," he said.

"I know about that. But I don't know if that's the same as Sunny forgiving her. I'm not saying Sunny should have anything to do with Liana, but maybe *I* should."

"Why on earth?"

"Who else in this world can tell me about forgiveness? Maybe someone like Liana, someone at the bottom, is someone I could ask."

"I don't think that's a job for a little girl from Africa. It would be better for you to befriend Sunny herself."

"I could, if I knew more about what happened to her. She has this huge blank place in her person. No one's said anything about Sunny's years with the kidnapper."

"That's because no one knows. She was twelve years old when she finally screamed for help."

I moved to the edge of my chair and gripped it with both hands.

"She was screaming?"

"Liana had locked her in a car in a heat wave."

"Oh no! That's not—"

"Forgivable?" the priest finished for me.

"Maybe not." I had never thought of things as completely unforgiveable. "But what would Liana have to do for penance anyway? She can't just call Sunny up and say, 'Hi, how are you?' How can she earn forgiveness if there's no one to give it?"

The priest took my hands from the chair and clasped them in his. His answers meant so much more to me than just what he might say about the kidnapper. I remembered the look on my mother's face when the detectives started snooping around the smoldering slash pile. A look that was suddenly open and raw, not the blankness that I was used to, as though a secret had been verged upon. I had not known what it meant or how to get inside that place where my real mother lived.

"We get our answers in the least expected ways," he said.

"I'm thinking of getting my answers from the worst person possible," I whispered, letting go of his hands.

"Who is that, my dear?"

"Liana herself," I said.

Father Zenwa got up and poured himself another glass of orange juice. He opened a drawer in his desk and got out a small bottle of clear liquid. Then he shook his head and put it back.

"I don't think you should do such a risky thing," he said. "Promise me you'll consider not going to the prison. It will only defeat you and make things worse for the family who has taken you in."

There was a knock on the door.

"I'm back," Susan said from the other side.

"Come in, Mrs. Rose," the priest said.

"I've just about finished, but I thought I should see how you're doing."

"I've been given many things to think about," Father said.

"Isn't it supposed to work the other way?" Susan asked.

"Not in this case, apparently. Shall we meet again, Kivuli?"

"I hope so, Father."

The priest reached into one of his stacks of books and handed me one entitled *Healing in the High Desert*. "You might find some answers in there, dear child. Don't stop looking," he said.

I started out the door with Susan but turned and looked back at Father Zenwa. "You didn't ask me why I wasn't a Catholic."

"I thought right away you were a person who did not like easy answers and probably had not studied the catechism too closely. As you can see from the titles of my books, I also do not find all the answers in my own Church."

I thought the Catholic answers were not necessarily so easy.

17

graveyard news

I had said too much to the priest but still not everything that had sent me down this path to the possibilities of forgiveness. Though he had never known Askay, he could surely have had an opinion about Askay's mistake, since it led to the misery of his parishioners. I stared at the dark screen of my laptop, as silent with its answers as Father Zenwa.

The Roses were outside with two families who had just arrived from Florida, being treated to Susan's best barbequed ribs. One of the women was afraid of dogs, so they left True Passion with me. He was stretched out on my bed, the closest one to the old Dog who had seen everything that Sunny had suffered.

My fingers tensed on the keyboard. If I allowed my best instincts to take over, I would type my great-grandfather's name into the google box instead of Liana's. So that's what I did.

ASKAY JOSEPH, a subsistence farmer from Tanzania, East Africa, wins Best Bloom of Show at the Nevada State Fair for his black rose, Remembrance, the first black rose in the world. Mr. Joseph is the gardener, cook, and companion for the ranching Rose family of Ochala Junction. He has two children still living in Africa—a daughter, Iyeala, and a son, Tanal. The patent on his rose is pending. Elko Tribune October 1952.

My great-grandfather rose from the page! His *Remembrance* was now over sixty years old. He had spoken the names of his children. He had been a "companion." Who was alive to whom he had been a companion besides Hank and Susan? There was a wrangler. What was his name? Ty?

I should use the time to arrange Askay's diary notes into some kind of order—chronological or by tides of thought. Maybe there were more clues about why he had once written "she Iroquois…could not save her" when he died three years before Sunny was kidnapped. He couldn't have had any idea what Liana's stab was going to be.

As I reached in my bag for a handful of notes, my cell phone rang. I answered instinctively, "Jambo."

"Jambo? Really?"

"Oh, Dancing Horse! It's an African greeting."

"I figured that. Hey…I've been thinking I should release you to go up to the Roses' cemetery any time. I've no right to make you pass a test."

"I live for your tests, Henry."

"Yeah, right. Just so you know, tomorrow is Tyrone's day off, and I told Hank I'd help guide the Floridians to the Cliffs. I made the date with Ty for you."

"I'm not sure," I said, feeling nervous right down to my roots. "I'm not sure he's accepted me yet."

"It was Tyrone's idea. He was a little shy to ask you and gave the task to me."

"It will be an honor, Henry. You tell him that. I just don't know if I'm ready to meet those souls from the past."

"Well, I think it will be good for you, give you some perspective. And keep in mind that Ty knew every single person that's buried there. So be on your horse at nine, okay?"

"Okay. And Henry? I owe you."

"Silly girl. Get some sleep."

Hank came and got Pass at 10:30. I sat up in the bed.

"I hear you might go up to the graveyard tomorrow with Ty."

"Yeah, I'm going. Anything I should know?"

"You should know all those folks were loved…and forgiven, when necessary. Ty has my permission to tell you about Miranda, who is buried on the opposite side of the ranch. If you are a 'forgiveness warrior' as your arrival t-shirt stated, you should know everything. Goodnight now."

"Goodnight, Mr. Rose…Hank."

When I got to the barn in the morning, Tyrone was the only one there. He'd fed the horses and had Lazo and his black mare hooked to tie rings outside their stalls.

"The Cliff-riders go out at eleven so I thought we'd just as well get out of their way," Ty said.

"Fine with me."

It didn't take long to tack up. We rode down the driveway and then turned east through a wide gate and let the horses walk on a long rein. Ty told me Hank didn't use this pasture much. It was about twenty acres and he liked to keep it as green as possible close to the ranch so it would look nice for visitors and clients.

"We'll go out the far side onto open range," he said. "From there, the cemetery is about five miles, where the Ruby Mountains dip into the desert."

"I don't see the trail marked at all."

"No. We discourage folks from riding this way."

In a few minutes, Ty opened and closed the gate from the back of the mare, and we eased into a trot. The terrain climbed steadily through silver-tipped sage and hillocks of bright yellow dandelion. I was glad I had a lot of rides behind me because this wrangler liked to *move*. After about three miles, we entered a deep canyon and tempered our pace. A stream tumbled beside us, edged by junipers and tall grasses, and imposing red bluffs rose up on either side of the faint path. Hawks screeched at us— intruders with our prancy equines. The air suddenly felt more like mountains than desert with the scent of cedar and pine.

As the ravine widened, I saw a small cabin, a rail corral with a shelter, and a stair-step waterfall where the creek coursed over the red and charcoal stones. Ty said this was the honeymoon cabin of three generations of Roses, and Tom and Sunny Sentinel, and that the graves were farther up. We untacked and turned the horses loose in the pen and climbed to the fenced plot. The gate was coming off its hinges, likely where deer or elk had broken through. I noticed only one cross among the headstones. *Could Askay have been the only Catholic?*

"We'll take them as they come," Ty said.

On the first gravestone were these words: HELEN AND HENRY ROSE—*We are flying still. We didn't leave you. We are on a different path.* I thought anyone who had seen Helen's painting with her arm through the round pen rails was on the path of forgiveness, one way or another. The next marker read: JASON ROSE—*Home at last, forgiven, and at peace.* I put my hand over the word *forgiven* and Ty said, "He turned his back on his brother the day Julian married Serena. No one ever knew why, but Hank and Susan forgave him when he returned to the ranch many years later."

The next site had this engraving: *We took our blessings from all who would give them and thank God we are on the last trail together*—SERENA AND JULIAN ROSE. "I guess here's where I could tell you about Miranda," Ty began. "She was Julian's first wife, and she became severely mentally ill. She…burned up two of his horses in a horse trailer, escaped the institution where she was committed after their divorce, and pursued him—to shorten the story some—right out onto the ranch with a gun. I can relate this part because I was there. A bunch of us wranglers spread out on the desert with Julian and Serena and ended up by a mesa called Towering Peak. The first one to see Miranda was Serena. I came up behind her in time to see Serena throw a rope around the crazed lady and cinch it tight. Serena was amazing. She talked to Miranda in a soothing voice, and every time the woman did what Serena asked, like throw the gun down or agree to accept help, she released the rope a bit more. She made promises to Miranda and urged Julian to approach her from where he had taken cover from the threat of gunfire. The two of them got Miranda out to the highway where the sheriff was waiting.

"They pleaded with law enforcement not to incarcerate Miranda, and Serena visited her regularly in an institution in Elko. That's the first place Helen's bronc painting went. That and Serena's 'arm through the rail' you might say, changed Miranda's life. She never got out of the mental ward but became a model patient who helped others along the way herself. After she died, Julian and Serena buried her at Towering Peak."

My throat had tightened to the breaking point by then, when Ty rested one hand on the grave marker and told me the Roses were buried out here in the same grave because their bodies were fused by the lightning. He said after Askay saw them that day, he barely spoke for months and died within the year.

Off to one side was a more recent burial with a plain, gray stone. *Here lies Carla in loyalty and love for Serena.* "They were…partners…before Julian hired Serena, but Carla never let go, was always hanging around and begging Serena to come back to her. Hank's way of forgiving her for the trouble she caused in his mother's life was to promise Carla, as she lay dying of cancer, that he would bury her here in the family graveyard."

Finally, we stood at the white cross by a weathered mahogany plaque with these words carved into the hardwood: "ASKAY JOSEPH—

surrogate father, ultimate friend. May he rest in the arms of Nevada and Africa in God's eternal love. Kyrie eleison. Christe eleison."

I fell to my knees. I could hardly breathe. My great-grandfather would never know I came to find him, to understand his place in the hearts of these Americans, to be a bridge between the Ngorongoro Crater and the valley of the ranch of the blue sky. Ty put his hand on my back. "Let's go now, Kivuli. This has been too much for you."

I picked up remembrances from the ground on the way out—a heart-shaped stone, a piece of glass, a stiffened strap from someone's bridle—and laid each one on a grave so when I left the cemetery, something from me would remain.

18

cross your fingers, but do not tell a lie

When we rode back onto the ranch proper, it was eerily quiet. The Cliff-riders were not expected back yet, but we got worried when we found Julia by herself in the pool. She told us her dad had gone out with the water truck to check the cattle tanks because of the heat. Her mother had sent her to find Gramma Susan because Father Z would be there in a few minutes.

"Gramma wasn't anyplace around so I jumped in the pool to cool off," she explained.

"Susan has book club today," I reminded her.

"I forgot."

"Let's go to the house and make some lemonade. I don't think Ty will mind putting the horses up."

"Not at all," he said, giving me a look of relief that nothing bad had happened.

I dismounted and handed him Lazo's reins. Julia floated over to the edge of the pool and climbed slowly up the tile steps. We walked back down the lane, Julia kicking little rocks in her path with her sandaled feet.

"I wish my momma wasn't crying," she said. "Do you think the priest will fix her?"

"That's his job, sweetheart." I pictured Serena lassoing Miranda to save her from her mental aberrations, her lack of self-esteem, and her tendency for self-destruction. The priest would never think of something as radical as that.

"I wish I could have gone riding with you and Ty," Julia said.

We crossed the lawn and stepped up on the porch. I reached into the mudroom closet for a thick towel. "Here. Let's dry you off a little before we drip on Gramma Susan's floor."

"I wish you were my sister," Julia said.

"My, you have a lot of wishes today," I said. "Any more roaming around in that head of yours?"

"I wish my mother didn't need that priest. He just makes her cry harder."

"Sometimes you have to cry before things get better, you know."

"No, I don't know. My momma sometimes doesn't talk to me for *days* after she sees Father Z!"

"I told you my mother acts the same way. I think mothers have a lot of problems to figure out," I said, making sure she was completely dry and not shivering.

Susan had left a large bowl of lemons in plain sight. I cut them and let Julia press them onto the juicer. We added fourth-cups of sugar and tasted it until it was just right.

"But does your mother say her rosary ten times a day?" Julia continued.

"Sometimes."

"Does she say 'Only God understands me'?"

"I've never heard that." *Had I?*

"Well, I think Momma should want her *family* to understand her."

"Yes, you are probably right," I said.

We sat on the couch gulping the cold juice. What answers would I have wanted when I was six? The truth, or something to make me feel better.

"Where'd you guys go anyway?" Julia asked, sliding closer to me.

"To the cemetery up by the cabin."

"Did you see Julian and Serena's grave?"

"Yes. There's a beautiful stone marking the spot that says they felt blessed by all their friends."

"Did you know my momma was born three weeks after they died?"

"I didn't know that. Serena might have helped Sunrose through her tears better than the priest."

A car pulled up outside. I got up and went to the door. Father Zenwa stood there with one hand on his shiny crucifix. I hoped he couldn't hear through walls.

"Come in, Father," I said.

"Oh, hello, Kivuli. I'm looking for Hank."

"He took guests out to the Cliffs. I'm not sure when they'll be back. Could I give him a message?"

"No. It's a private matter."

Julia put her hands on her hips. "Why is everything around here a big secret?"

The priest put his hand on her head and explained that he had taken a vow to keep secrets when he was ordained, she wouldn't want him to go back on his word, would she? He looked so uncomfortable I asked him to sit down and sent Julia to the kitchen for a glass of lemonade.

"I'll gladly have the drink, Kivuli, but then I'll excuse myself. I can call the Roses later. I can see you have your hands full," he said.

Julia returned with his lemonade and continued to pout about being excluded from Zenwa's talk with her mother. Of course, *I* wanted to know why Sunrose had called the priest. There wasn't enough lemonade to quench my thirst for Sunny's secrets. Even her lies would be welcome—some words to connect us, just as I longed for meaningful words to connect me to my own mother.

Horses scrambled up the driveway, their hooves clattering, the clients whooping and hollering like they'd just completed the trek of the century. Sunrose could be feeling that joy, that lightness, if she'd gone with them. The excuse of having to stay home with Julia was a weak one. Their daughter could have gone with Thomas on his errands. Sunny could have taken a chance on life. She could have walked away from the statues and the rosaries and taken a chance on the grace of the desert world.

The priest gave me a warning look as though he knew what I was thinking.

"She is still Sunny Rose," I said, when Julia went to get more lemonade.

"She has not been Sunny Rose for a very long time. You should forget this plan of yours."

"You sound like my father."

"Why is that?" Julia said, holding the pitcher of ice cold juice like a shield.

"He always warns me not to get involved in people's troubles."

"If I was in trouble, I'd want you, Kiki." Julia said, her lower lip trembling.

"At this age your troubles are very small, my dear," Father Z admonished.

"That's what you think," she said in her best petulant tone.

Susan heard her as she came in the back door with an armload of groceries. "Julia! Apologize to Father this instant!"

"I'm sorry," she said in a tiny, uncontrite voice, "but Gramma, Momma has been crying all day, and Father won't tell me what's wrong. She's *my* momma." Julia's tears were very close to the edge now.

For the first time, I felt some anger at Askay. Why couldn't he have acted more responsibly? More sharply? Why couldn't he have shown the note about the stab to Hank…or Susan? Or maybe Tyrone—someone who knew Liana and had seen her in action? Even if Askay wasn't sure who made the threat, all those people would have suspected it was Liana.

The truth was that Askay caused the hole in Sunny's childhood. I could not keep silent about this. So right in front of Julia and Susan and the priest and Thomas, who had just stepped through the front door, I said, "Everyone is laying blame on this or that, on Sunny's strength or weakness, on who can best listen to her or heal her, wanting her to find solace at the feet of God, when it was an unconscionable human failing that led to the damned eight years!"

I'm sure everyone thought I meant the unredeemable kidnapper, but I meant my great-grandfather—Askay Joseph—the man I came thousands of miles to honor with my presence and my love, who needed as much forgiveness himself as I could muster.

"Father, would you like to stay for dinner?" Susan asked with shocked politeness.

I excused myself. I just wanted to be alone, and maybe the Roses wanted to hear what Father Zenwa had to say about Sunny. Hank had just looked in from the mud room where he was removing his boots and said Sunny was waiting for Tom and Julia up on the hill.

I sat at the computer for a while trying to think of uncomplicated subjects. Finally, I wrote an email to my father describing the ride to the graveyard, telling him how I left tributes on the headstones, and relating what I had learned about the people buried there. I ended with: "You didn't tell me everything about Sunny Rose Sentinel!" In five minutes, there was a response: "You should leave that alone, Daughter. Enjoyed your notes about Askay and the other family buried on the ranch, but I hope you are not dwelling on all those old stories. You should be light-hearted at this age. You should concern yourself with those who are living and trying to forget the past, as we all are. Your loving father."

What is he doing up in the middle of the night? My father. A good man. A man who had forgiven many things in the past but surely had not forgotten them. A man who seemed to be telling me to leave the subject of the kidnapped Sunny Sentinel alone. I dreaded to think what he would say if he knew I had the actual kidnapper's location on my laptop.

I heard muffled voices in the living room. My hands rested on the letters of Liana's name. It was still a foolish idea to go see the woman, and I should not follow through with it. But what if the kidnapper could say something, anything, to relieve Sunrose of her current turmoil? And my own. I didn't move for a few minutes. Then I typed "Santa Barbara, California."

Susan opened the door. "Dinner's ready," she said. She looked exhausted as she placed a vase of fresh flowers on my dresser. "Father Z said you'd had a tense conversation about our daughter's dark times that led to your outburst."

"I apologize for that, Mrs. Rose, but the priest is not the only one who keeps secrets. I'm wrestling with one of my own. I'll have to tell someone sooner or later, but I'm resisting the priest." I moved the blooms to my desk where I could smell their scent while I worked.

"The roses are Askay's, of course," Susan said.

"Do you still have 'Remembrance'?"

"The black rose. It blooms when it wants to. I'm hoping to have a few for the fair at just the right stage in the budding."

"How could he have given such a rose to the world…and failed… in other ways," I said. I touched the burgundies and yellows I could not name.

"He gave everything he knew how to give. We don't fault him for a thing," Susan replied.

"Not yet," I whispered to myself.

"Come on, dear. Father is waiting to ask the blessing."

We went to the dining room and sat at the table. Father Zenwa began in the usual fashion, addressing God's goodness and thanking him for small favors. But I had to swallow hard when he said, "And forgive us our trespasses as we forgive those who trespass against us."

I glanced over at Susan who gave me a pensive smile. Hank passed the brandied carrots.

"This is very sumptuous fare, Susan," the priest commented. "But I won't stay too long. I'd like to drop by the Sentinels before I go back to town."

"We'd appreciate that, Father," Hank said.

I could only think of one thing—the photograph that had been on my computer screen when Susan had interrupted my search—a lovely town on the coast of California, with flowers, open air markets, intriguing restaurants, and miles and miles of sandy, white beaches. Someplace along there, Sunny had ridden into the surf on the back of a chestnut horse and come alive.

"There is nothing like a good meal to put everyone on a balanced path," Zenwa stated.

And then, I was reminded of Safina's father, Dakimu, searching for the right path after his unholy acts, hearing a story from his priest, so I spoke up. "One time, there was a man Father Amani in Africa knew who was on a familiar path across a wide swath of the savannah, traveling on foot back to his village from a neighboring settlement. Suddenly in the distance a haboob rose up and coursed his way. He was afraid but noticed a deep gulley close by and huddled down in it until the dust storm passed. When he stood up, there was no ditch in the land. Father Amani always says if we are on God's path, there will be a sight or a sound that has no other explanation."

"Well, my dear," Father Zenwa said, "wouldn't that answer some of your own questions?"

"I'm still looking for the ditch," I replied.

"What happened to Dakimu?" Hank asked.

"That night a wild leopard appeared at Dakimu's door. Dak had already made amends to many of his enemies, but he continued on that path."

"No other explanation, indeed," Zenwa said. "It will be a lovely story to take with me on the road home."

We finished our meal in relative silence.

Soon the priest was gone, and the Roses told me to get some sleep, they'd take care of the dishes. Pass lay crashed under Hank's chair. "A little too long a trip for you, Dog?" he murmured. I got up, thinking how interesting it was that Hank called True Passion *Dog* now and then but never in front of Sunny.

"Hey, I thought one of your guests was afraid of dogs," I said.

"Well, she didn't get off her horse the whole ride! I hope she didn't pee on one of my nicest guest saddles," Hank noted.

I could not help but smile all the way to bed and all the way to sleep.

19

the tent camp, August

Ty passed me in the aisle way between the indoor arena and the outdoor arena. He had three bridles in each hand. Behind him marched six new guests of various sizes and ages, obviously overwhelmed. They had come from one arena for a read-through of client rules and expectations and were going with Tyrone to the other, where six beginner horses were tied for basic horsemanship, not that they'd ever get as far as bridling a horse, but Ty could make it look fabulously simple.

He leaned into me. "I hear you're going with us to the tent camp."

"I am?"

"Hank probably hasn't had time to tell you. This is the largest group of guests he's had to wrangle up there. It's all hands on deck. You have two days to get ready," he finished and grinned.

I counted eighteen folks in various stages of ranch dress carrying suitcases and studying the numbers on the guest cabins. A couple of kids raced by me yelling, "I'll beat you to the barn!"

"Hey!" They barely slowed down but turned to see who had interrupted their flight. "Have you been to Rules yet? Number one for *children* is "no running and no screaming."

"Who are you?" one of them asked.

"I live here. I'm the rule enforcer."

They took off. *Oh, for Serena's lasso!* The ride to the tent camp would take the stuffing out of those two. It was twenty miles east/southeast from the ranch, the trailhead between the summer grazing pastures in the Ruby Mountain foothills and Heaven's Door. I was afraid we'd run out of summer before I was allowed to go. I avoided my laptop and counted the hours.

Hank sent Pass on ahead with the cook crew so he could ride part way in a wagon. Julia moped around, but she knew her grandpa never took children under ten on the overnights, and her mother had enrolled her in a Pioneer Girls' religion badge program. *Heaven help the instructor.* Sunrose and Susan were baking every day, and it gladdened my heart to hear their genuine laughter radiating from the kitchen. They would stay at the ranch to care for the horses left there and manage the cattle buyers that showed up every year about this time.

I was not missing my Tanzanian home in the least and already thinking a year would not be long enough to figure out how to *be* Askay and do the right thing. The day we rode out to the tent camp, I took my biggest risk ever. I went in the kitchen and grabbed Sunrose's hand and led her down the hall to, *I need to say Askay's room here,* and opened my computer. "I only mean this in the best way," I said, and clicked on the file of all the photos I had found of the beaches at Santa Barbara, some with horses, many with four-foot waves rolling toward the white sand. Sunrose scrolled through them one by one, and then she turned and gripped my shoulders and said, "Thank you."

Hank and Thomas guided the first nine riders with two wranglers on either side with pack animals. After a five-minute wait, Dancing Horse headed the next nine, again with wranglers and pack horses on each side. Tyrone and I rode drag, keeping our eyes open and everybody shaped up. The sun turned the eastern sky a shade of red I had never seen. Hank's nine disappeared over a slight rise in the land and a couple of our pack horses got excited.

"This won't last long," Ty said. "By the time we catch up, we'll all have to go single file, and we'll be climbing."

Our nine were matched with the quietest horses on purpose so their eagerness to be with their buddies would help us maintain a good pace. No one fell off. There were two water troughs in the first twelve miles, but it was too early for the animals to have built up much thirst. Many of them didn't drink until the second stop, and most of the clients dismounted to stretch their legs. Tyrone sent our outriders on with the pack horses as soon we'd be in a long line. That left three of us to keep our nine guests on track. I loved being treated like a working wrangler.

By late morning, we began a series of switchbacks that wound another seven miles, then merged into another steep trail the last five miles to an eighty-five-hundred-foot summit and the overnight camp. The line of horses and riders could easily have been a mile long by then, everyone craving deep breaths and a drink. About half way up, we each got a chance to pause at a wide creek crossing.

"I guess Julia is about ready to "speak in tongues," don't you think?" Ty said.

I looked around at the dark green pines towering into a cloud-studded blue sky, the rushing snow-melt brook where the horses ahead of me dipped their muzzles into the icy water, and places where magenta and lapis wildflowers swayed on the bank's edge.

"This is church enough for me," I said.

"You know it. This very scene is like a stained glass window," Ty replied.

I had reached the crossing myself by then as the queue of horses and riders inched forward. Lazo dropped his head into the rippling stream. I took a drink from my canteen and then moved on so Ty could water his horse. It had been suggested that we eat an energy bar about then so I savored the oats and chocolate chips in lieu of a real lunch. After that, the trail rose sharply, and everyone began to feel the effects of the sun and the altitude. For a while the only sounds were the heavy breathing of the animals, the creak of leather on leather, Steller's jays and ravens calling to each other and the gurgle of springs bursting from wet grottos. Once a band of black-tailed deer started to breach the trail, then braked and wheeled away into the woods.

At last, in the late afternoon, Hank veered off the trail into a small clearing. Permanent tents dotted the high meadow and spring water ran down a steep slope on one side. There were hitching rails, covered tack boxes, and a central cook fire with fixed grates. Log benches surrounded the fire and a few tables stood between the tents and the benches. The ground had been raked of twigs, and two outhouses had been set up back in the trees.

I dismounted at a railing marked "STAFF" and watched the wranglers untack the guests' horses and hand riders their personal gear from the panniers on the pack string. I heard Hank tell everyone to take it easy the rest of that day because of the altitude, especially those people who had come from sea level. Everything seemed to move in slow motion—the horses munching their oats from burlap bags, and the fire Thomas finally coaxed into being sending soft curls of smoke toward the cobalt sky. It seemed to me that I had stepped into a dream.

In a little while, Ty and Dancing Horse turned the horses out to graze with a trusted bell mare, and Hank filled Dutch ovens with stew and cornbread batter, resting the pot directly on the fire. I sat down next to him but didn't say anything at first; now and then, he got up to stir the lamb and vegetables.

"My Granma Iyeala used to say, 'When you're stirring a pot, it's a good time to think'," I said.

"Wise woman. Askay's daughter, after all."

"Are you thinking about your daughter?"

"No, actually, I'm thinking about my mother and Carla," he said, surprising me. "They used to come up here. I think before *and* after my mom and dad got married. I thought Carla was just my mom's riding instructor most of my life. But one day, after Julian and Serena had been buried at the cabin, the woman called me."

How does Hank know I know who Carla is?

"She insisted on going to my mom's grave, and I knew it was what Serena would want, so I took Carla there. She left a locket on the gravestone, but I went back and got it and buried it in a corner of the indoor arena where Carla had given my mom dresságe lessons."

He ladled a spoonful of the broth into a paper bowl, blew on it, and then tasted it carefully. "Yep, needs some salt," he said. He looked at me. "Tyrone said you might be asking questions about her, so you'd just as well hear the story."

"I think the way Serena was in the world has a lot to teach everyone. So I'm listening," I said. "Did your mom ever talk about Carla?"

"Not to me. But I found a poem Serena had written to the woman. It seemed like coded language. I haven't read it in years. Anyway, when I learned Carla was in a nursing home with a terminal illness, I went to see her. She didn't talk much. She was in a lot of pain, I guess. I sat with her for hours. At one point, she said, 'I never loved anyone but Serena in my whole life. I never got to tell her.' Right then, before I could change my mind, I asked her if she wanted to be buried in the canyon. She said, 'You would do that for me?' I said I'd do it for my mother. Carla died a week later."

I supposed that was one of the "old stories" my father didn't want me to get involved in, but now there was a poem, words that could speak to me about love I wasn't sure I understood.

"Can I see the poem?"

"You can probably make better sense of it than I can. Your father told me how you excelled in creative writing, especially poetry," he said. "I'll look for it. But there's something else you should read. Your great-grandfather's journal. The pages Thomas took to Africa were only a part of the whole."

"I've been putting it off. I don't know why." *Yes, I do.*

"It's a history that must be written slowly on your heart, like Serena's has been on mine," Hank said. "Then it will be a part of your history, your reason for coming, yes?"

He got up to get the salt, and I stirred the stew, letting my mind drift to history that was not mine.

That night, a meteor shower rained down over the campers' heads. I watched until my neck hurt, knowing I would never see those stars or falling pieces of those stars in Africa below the equator. When I looked down again, I tried to imagine Serena and Carla there alone by a warm fire, the woods around them darkening, their horses nibbling sweet feed. Maybe their hands touched, or maybe not, but the thought of them sharing this place filled me with tranquility.

True Passion nosed around the camp seeking treats and trying out different guest's sleeping bags, but he stuck the closest to Hank and to me. When half the night was gone, he found me and didn't move 'til dawn.

Hank was already up when first light broke over the mountains. He was stirring a rich-looking pancake batter. I added milk when he needed it and asked him about the wild animals that lived in the area of the camp.

"Black bears, elk, pumas. Occasionally you'll see boar and turkeys back down below six thousand feet. Mexican wolves sometimes make it this far north. They're endangered in the Southwest. Hunters and civilization have driven them out."

"We have a lot of endangered animals, almost all the big cats," I said.

"Well, those pumas, or cougars as they're also called, aren't endangered around here. You might see one before you have to go home. It's an attractive cat, for sure."

"I'm partial to leopards, of course, having been raised with two of them right in my house most of the time. Do people ever tame the cougars?"

"I don't think you'd call it "tame" exactly, but I've known folks to keep them," Hank said. "Here. Turn these pancakes."

Guests lined up for their breakfast. I greeted everyone warmly. A slender, very tanned woman with short, blonde hair and jeans tucked into her cowboy boots wanted only one pancake and one piece of bacon. I suggested she'd need more to eat for the demands of the day's schedule.

"Oh, I know, but if I can't get into my jeans, I can't do the schedule either," she said.

I laughed. "That's just what my mother would say!"

The woman seemed to take a longer look at me then. A couple of people went around her.

"Aren't you a bit young to be working for this outfit?" she asked.

"I'm a guest too," I admitted. "I'm staying with the Roses for a year. My home is in Africa. In Tanzania."

"Oh my, how interesting. I'm Faith Collins. I teach art at the public school in Ochala Junction."

"I think that's where I'll be going! I'm Kivuli Farley. Do you want a fresh pancake? That one must be cold by now," I offered.

"Oh, give me one more. I'll break all my rules for the joy of discovering a girl from Africa at the top of a mountain in Nevada!"

Faith Collins moved along toward the table with maple and wild cherry syrups, and I thought the day couldn't bring anything better than that American schoolteacher. After everyone was served, I loaded my plate with three pancakes and four strips of bacon and grabbed a seat next to Hank on one of the log benches.

"That's what I like," he said. "A girl who eats. When Sunny was your age, she hardly ate anything, always reading her books or her Bible."

"Oh, Mr. Rose! A teacher I might have is here! Do you know her? Faith Collins?"

"I don't know her personally, but I've seen her paintings and collages. I think Susan has her eye on one in a gallery in Winnemucca."

Pass had been curled at their feet, but suddenly he jumped up. The bell mare had gone out of sight, and Thomas was trudging over the hill after her. The shepherd whined, knowing he was not allowed that particular job. I thought it would be wonderful to be so sure of what you were meant to do.

The guests fixed their lunches from homemade bread, meats, cheeses, Susan's sugar cookies, and ranch apples laid out on another table. I filled sacks for myself, Hank, and Tyrone while Thomas and Dancing Horse saddled the mounts for the eleven guests who'd signed up for the day's ride. In thirty minutes, Ty led out of camp with Hank somewhere in the middle and Henry and I at the back. Pass stayed happily with us and didn't dart off the trail after prey, which might have startled the horses.

The trail curved over the summit of the mountain and down the other side for a few miles into a granite bowl where there was a remote camp on a pristine lake, one shoreline rimmed with fir, spruce, and ancient, twisted mahogany. I had to leap off Lazo and hug the first gnarled branch of old wood I saw. Hank told everyone there weren't many places, at least in the west, where mahogany trees had grown, and these were damaged and half-dead after living through centuries of fires, frost, and wind gales. They were protected, and no one was allowed one small stick. Later, Hank put a four-inch nub of the hard, ochre-colored wood in my hand.

"I think we can make an exception for you," he said.

We ate in the shadow of an immense black cloud emerging from the horizon. Hank seemed nervous, but the storm moved south, and he allowed the guests another hour to fish or hike. I wandered around the lake. The wind had died completely, and I knelt down on a mossy berm and bent over the still water. My reflection did not waver. It seemed to seal my connection with the land, to America, my face staring back at me from the clear pool.

Hank signaled to everyone after a while, and horses and riders climbed back over the summit of the mountain and into the tent camp. The guests who had stayed in camp were mixing spaghetti sauce in one of the Dutch ovens and buttering bread with garlic spread. Men from the trail ride group cleaned the trout they had caught and laid slices carefully in the ice chest to be fried for breakfast.

The clouds swarmed back in over us later, and we all huddled around the fire. But before we could organize our own camp songs, wolves began to howl from nearby cliffs, the sound echoing down the canyon below them. I imagined them calling for their mates struggling up from Arizona and Mexico. Or maybe just announcing themselves to the humans in their midst.

A few drops of rain sizzled on the fire. Hank and Thomas went out and gathered the horses, tying them securely to hitching posts and hi-lines in the trees closer to camp. When the storm covered as much of the sky as we could see, the wolves stopped singing. The night was cold then, and the fire dwindled in the wet air. I crawled into my sleeping bag and listened to the rain pelting the tent and the horses moving restlessly at their posts.

The morning dawned bright and cloudless. The early light cast prisms on the sodden leaves that plastered the surrounding rocks, where possibly the wolves had serenaded us. We ate flour-coated trout and scrambled eggs, then saddled the horses, while Hank and Tyrone smothered the fire with water and dirt and loaded the pack horses. Thomas took the lead out of camp to set a safe pace for trekking downhill. Wranglers gathered the pack animals at the back with Pass who would be picked up about half way back by a four-wheeler. I waited there holding Henry's pinto while he straightened the campsite. The last thing I saw was Dancing Horse leaving bits of fish and crusty bread on the flattest rocks on the edge of the trail. I would have given anything to hide in the forest to see what might appear.

We zig-zagged down the side of the mountain and broke out onto the open desert. The horses seemed flighty, and I saw Faith Collins' blue roan veer sideways and stare hard at the low hills to the north. Lazo stiffened under me. Suddenly, a herd of wild horses filled the horizon. They moved toward us, tossing their heads and darting carelessly around the sage and cactus. Hank ordered us to form a tight group, and he and Thomas with several of the boys rode out to meet them, their ropes whirling. Some of the guests dismounted while they could and helped each other keep a tight hold of the reins. I leaped off and grabbed Pass's collar.

Pintos and bays, buckskins and greys raced by. I had never seen anything like it. Tears ran down my cheeks. We could be on the Serengeti with migrating herds of zebra and wildebeest surging across the dry plains. The dust rose around us, the wild animals scrambling to avoid the knot of horsemen huddled like safari rigs on the desert. I could not catch my breath. In a few minutes, most of the stampeding herd had gone by, but we were all shaken.

Hank galloped up. "Everybody okay?"

One gal got her foot stomped on, and an older man had his shoulder wrenched. Hank promised immediate medical care when we reached the ranch, and already we could see the pre-arranged vehicle rushing toward us. The shoulder injury and Pass got a ride back. The sight of the barn in the distance brought a huge cheer from the riders. But I strained my eyes to see the last of the stragglers fade into the mirage of trees at the edge of the mountains.

The rest of the month, Hank kept the guest rides to the west of the highway. I knew he was wary of the wild horse bunch and hoped they wouldn't cross the paved road. The land was not as dramatic to the west, but I loved the massive rock formations and surprising lush oases around refreshing springs. It was windier than in the mountains of the tent camp or Heaven's Door, and I thought it would be a much scarier place to be lost in. One day, a monstrous rattlesnake coiled threateningly on a flat rock ten feet off the trail. Hank turned everyone down a steep, shale slope to avoid the creature.

"I don't want to kill it," he said.

A balky horse lost his footing, and a client tumbled to the ground. The uncooperative white gelding raced off toward the ranch. It seemed this territory had its dangers too. Hank cut the ride short, since someone would have to hike back, but we stopped for lunch by one of the cool springs and tied the horses to scraggly jack pines. Then he told everyone the story about his mother saving his dad after he was struck by a rattlesnake not far from where we were.

"My mom had only been working on the ranch for two days, but she was already in love with the boss. She held him all the way to the ER after the boys got him to the truck, and the next day he kissed her in thanks. It was a new beginning for both of them," he said.

Only Hank, Ty, and I knew his mom had been in love with a woman before that. It was a lovely secret to share. The guests nodded and smiled as if conjuring up their own visions of Julian and Serena being drawn together by the snake, though most of them didn't know their names. When Hank signaled for everyone to mount up, I offered my dependable Lazo to the client, who was an inexperienced gentleman, and I began the long walk across the sparse and haunting desert.

20

prisoners

As summer merged into fall, I had to face another big transition, one more challenging than learning to ride in a Western saddle in jeans. I would be going to public school for the first time. I would have male teachers, change classes every hour, and adjust to clothes rules. At The Light of the World Catholic School in Dar es Salaam, where I had been enrolled since the second grade, the instructors were nuns, boys were separated from girls, and clothes decisions were governed by uniforms. We prayed three times a day, and at least two of our subjects were based on religion—like *The Lives of the Saints* or *New Testament Ethics*.

Here, in Nevada, in America, I was going to find out who I really was. I was going to speak my mind and stand up for underdogs. I was going to check out books from the library that were not on the shelves of Catholic Education 101. I was going to ask questions for which I'd received a ruler on the wrist by a strict Sister or two.

But first, I needed to go shopping. I only had the one acceptable outfit that I had arrived in. I couldn't very well show up at school with "Forgiveness Warrior" emblazoned on my chest, although later in the year, it might be all right. I stood in Susan's room one day in front of her full length mirror and studied the image. I had a dancer's figure like my mother. My hair hung in soft waves down to my shoulders. I could almost pull it back and tie it away from my face, but I thought that made my eyes look too large. I had my mother's refined features and my father's long arms and strong hands, stronger now from my summer with the horses.

"I think someone is contemplating a new wardrobe," Susan said, coming in with an armload of clean clothes from the dryer.

"What do you think? Tights and tunics? Jeans and t-shirts? Or khakis and jackets?"

"Honey, I think Sunny wants to get some outfits for Julia. We'll go to Elko Saturday. I'll be your personal fashion coordinator!"

"In that case, I'm glad you're not my mother! *She* always looks fabulous, but I always look like an eight-year-old!"

"Kivuli, you are going to be a star, no matter what you are wearing. You're pretty and smart and generous. You are going to make friends like Sunny never could, and I'll be proud of you."

When we finally made it to Elko that next Saturday, after a thirty-minute hold up, once for the train and then behind the chip-sealing truck, Sunrose was so nervous she hung onto Julia like the girl might be snatched away any minute. *Oh God, that's it! These crowds on every corner and people rushing in and out of revolving doors must be like a nightmare to her.* I told Julia to take my hand so she wouldn't have to hang on her momma so much.

Things were easier for a while. In Lacy's we bought jeans with holes in the knees and crystals on the back pockets, brightly-colored tanks, white t-shirts with sayings printed on them like "Just Ride" and "Girl Power." At Fabulous Footwear we chose Mary Jane shoes since sandals were not allowed at school. Then, we had to find winter boots, down jackets, and turtlenecks at a sportswear store. I kept a hold of Julia, and Sunny and her mother walked behind us arm in arm. Susan tried to keep the conversation light, but I felt more tension than facing a flighty horse in the round pen.

We stopped for lunch at a Chinese restaurant. It was very dark inside, and I had trouble reading the menu. An exquisite Asian girl came to our table and poured hot tea into china cups from a beautifully painted teapot and set a plate of vegetable egg rolls before us. We had just begun to relax and had taken a few bites of the appetizer when a black lady approached our table in an inconsiderate manner.

"Sister Martha? Is that you?" the woman asked, pushing at Sunny's shoulder.

Sunrose put her fork down. "Do I know you?"

"Sure. Number one-o-two. Remember? You got me out of that prison after I was indicted by mistake. You got me back to my kids. They grown and gone now, but they good, because of you. You still go there? To the prison?"

"Why, no, I'm married now. This is my daughter, Julia," Sunrose said. She put her arm on Julia's.

"You married? I thought you married to Jesus, sister," Number 102 said.

"Things change," Sunny said. "But I'm glad I helped you. I'll never regret helping my inmates."

The woman kept staring at Sunrose and Julia and made no move to leave. She had very dark skin and her hair had been straightened. It hung around what would have been an attractive face except when she opened her mouth to laugh, I saw at least four missing teeth.

"What about that Number 4? Ooo-wee, she was somethin'. But you saved her life, bad as she was. Ever know what happened to her?"

"No." Sunrose clasped her crucifix.

"Me either. I hope she dead," the falsely accused woman said. "No room in the world for her kin'."

I squirmed in my seat. Sunrose had no idea I knew who the black woman was talking about, but I felt like shaking this ex-inmate for dragging Liana into the room. I settled on confronting the woman.

"What kind of person is that?" I asked.

"The kind you don't want to know," the rude woman said, rolling her eyes.

Other customers were watching us now because the black woman had raised her voice, and Sunny had turned white as a sheet.

"Please excuse us," Susan said. "We're having a shopping day with our girls. We're a little busy."

"Busy eatin' lunch? No time for a friend of Sister Martha's? A *black* friend?"

I could not keep quiet. I stood up to block the presence of this ingratiating woman and found that I was almost as tall as Mrs. One-o-Two.

"They have plenty of time for me," I said, "and I'm black."

"No way, girl. You white in my book," 102 said.

Susan responded then. "This young lady is a Maasai from Tanzania. That's black in my book."

"Well 'scuse me," the woman said. "Didn' mean no offense. Didn' know Maasai was so white. Didn' know a nun could divorce Jesus. Good luck with that, Sister Martha."

Sunny's eyes followed her as Number 102 walked out. I sat back down, but the food had lost its appeal.

"You helped that lady?" Julia said. "Why was she so mean?"

"I don't think I understand a single human being in this world," Sunrose said.

"You understand Daddy," Julia said.

"Yes…I understand Thomas."

I started eating again, thinking that would get things back to normal, but soon the appetizers were gone.

"Why did you go to that jail with those nuns anyway?" Julia asked.

Sunrose glanced at her mother and then took a sip of her tea.

"I wanted to be of service to people who were suffering," she said.

"But those were bad people," Julia said. "I don't think you can fix bad people."

"I have to believe you can, Julia," Sunrose said.

I wanted to believe her more than anything. It was the theory of my life, that there must be redemption, somehow, even for the bad people.

The smiling waitress brought bowls of fried rice, chow mein, and sweet and sour chicken. We ate in silence, the mood spoiled by the ex-prisoner. Sunny kept her eyes on her plate. Julia pushed soy sauce and fried noodles toward her, but her mother's attention was lost.

"I will never be able to be me," Sunny said finally.

I despised that black woman, the first American I didn't like, but Number 102 had given me a view into Sunrose's emotions—her profound reaction to the mention of prisoner Number 4. I was more determined than ever to meet Number 4 myself, but there were so many barriers to it—my loyalty to the Roses, obligations to Dancing Horse, Tyrone, and the horses, commitments to school and the promise I made my father to not cause Sunny any more distress.

Out on the rangeland between Ochala Junction and the Ruby Mountains, the wild horses were being driven into a catch pen eighty meters by eighty meters by eighty meters, a triangular shape whose points could be opened for a convenient chute and closed behind the fleeing herd. A few days earlier, the band had crossed a downed fence on a prestigious ranch and wreaked havoc, adding six more equines to clutch, one a one-hundred-thousand dollar stud of the highest caliber. He was found mauled to death by the renegade stallion and half-eaten by wolves.

Nevada State law prevented any of the horses from being mishandled or killed so Hank Rose pacified the ranchers by offering to help capture and house the animals until they could be sorted out and brands or pedigrees provided to establish proper ownership. It was a tedious and unrewarding job, for volunteers or owners trying to extract their stock that had been missing, sometimes for years. One wrangler's arm was shattered by a flying hind hoof as he attempted to get a rope on a gelding—a well-broke horse who had only been running with the wild ones for two months.

Winter in the high desert could be harsh, temperatures dropping below zero and water sources few and far between. But the horses moved to the Rancho del Cielo Azul would have the best chance—blankets and shelters for the old and injured and the best hay available. Preparations had already begun there.

When we turned under the ranch sign, I wondered what was going on. A semi piled with lumber was parked in the yard, and wranglers were spread out in the near pastures digging post holes and pounding extra siding on the barn. Existing shelters were being refurbished with wider roofs and hay racks. Hank's truck was not in the driveway. Susan went in the house to call him. Sunrose and Julia and I accosted one of the boys who was pushing a wheelbarrow full of wet cement toward a line of holes with big timbers laid out nearby.

Sunrose asked first what they were all doing. It was the only thing she had said all the way home. "Did my father buy some new horses?"

"Oh…no. We're getting the place secured better for the wild horses," he said.

Julia looked at me. "The wild horses you saw on the tent camp ride?"

"Must be. I guess we should be excited, but I want to know what's in store for them. It could not be good," I said.

"My dad will do the right thing," Sunny promised, and she and

Julia turned up the hill to their place.

I went back to see if Susan had found out anything more. She was still on the phone. I heard her say, "But, darling, will this be safe for our horses? Or our clients? We have guests booked until Thanksgiving. Okay." She hung up and grabbed my hand. "Dancing Horse has already caught the wild stallion and has him in a separate holding pen!"

My heart raced. Henry Dancing Horse seemed like God to me in that moment. But the horses would be fenced in. Wasn't there more to life than rich hay and a manmade shelter? If they had a chance, wouldn't they break out and run for the hills? I was thrilled to see them up close, maybe take part in their gentling, but I dreaded to see the look in their eyes.

21

wearing your heart on your sleeve

The first day of school, Susan offered to drive Julia and me to the Crossroads, the farthest point the bus would come, but as we turned onto the highway, a stream of trucks with stock trailers pulled onto the ranch road. Some of the vehicles had rifles mounted against their back windows, and I cried, "Stop! Stop!" I had trusted Hank when he promised there would be no guns involved in the rescue. He'd told me ranchers were coming with trailers to go out to the catch pen and bring the horses back to his ultra-reinforced pastures for some vet care and distribution to legitimate owners, but I was suddenly afraid for them.

Hank grabbed me as I ran back to the closest rig. "I can't go to school thinking someone's going to hurt those horses!"

"Honey, no one's going to hurt them. Some of these people are here to pick up their own horses after the vet gets a good look at them."

"But what about the others? The truly wild ones?"

"We'll geld the colts and separate the mares from any foals that are at least six months old. The youngsters might go to prison programs that use respected training methods. I will not allow any of them to be abused, believe me."

I climbed back into the Roses' truck, but I wasn't convinced of the outcome for the poor animals. My heart pounded at the unfairness of it. They would be so scared: trailers and barricades and food they weren't used to. Before we reached the Crossroads, Susan told us she was going to personally assist the vet and please not to worry. Then, as the yellow bus lumbered up, she got out and hugged each of us. I thought she hugged me especially tight.

Soon, my day got better. On the third stop after the bus began its loop through the vast ranchland, a Native American boy, maybe a little older than I, came down the aisle and sat next to me. I moved over to make room for his backpack, extra bag full of books, laptop, and drum.

"Are you going to need all that on the first day?" I asked.

"I like to be prepared," he said.

"Apparently. I'm Kivuli."

"Kivuli? What is that? Not Sioux."

"No. It's African. Actually, my name means 'shadow' in Swahili."

"I have a feeling it doesn't suit you," he said.

"You could be right," I replied, liking him immediately.

The bus jerked to another stop, and some very loud boys clambered on. They ignored me, and the Indian boy, at first. I went on. "I was named after my aunt who, I've been told, was on the shy side."

He grinned at me. "I'm thinking you were named after her for some other reason."

I looked out the window at the yellow fields flashing by and the odd-colored cattle bunched here and there and tried to banish the image of my gun-shot Aunt Kivuli from my head.

"Anyway, I'm Trace Martin. I'm a junior," he continued. He shifted the drum so it wasn't wedged between us.

"I'm in tenth," I said, returning his gaze, "but I might skip. The school wasn't sure what my level was after nine years in Catholic school in Dar es Salaam."

Trace's eyes widened.

"Dar es Salaam. . .Tanzania?"

"There's another one?"

"No, but I thought you were an African-*American*," he said.

"Just an African-*African*," I said. "Are you an Indian?"

"An *American* Indian, a Lakota Sioux," he answered. "Man, I'm sure glad we got that all straight." He tapped a rhythm on his decorated drum.

"Thanks for sitting with me," I said.

Someone three rows behind us called, "Hey, gay boy, you got a *girl*friend already?"

"Hey, white boy, mind your own business!" Trace shouted back.

It was noisy on the bus now, almost filled to capacity. I tried to find other faces that might be friendly, but no one said "hi."

"*Are* you gay?" I finally asked. "I mean, I don't care. It's just that I've never known any gay men, only gay women."

"Well, I'm not gay, but you're in luck. I can introduce you to two very classy gay men—my dads," he said. "But they're just like regular people, you know. They don't have green hair or sit around kissing all day."

"That's good, because the gay women I know are very weird. And one of them is my mother."

"Oh, Tanzanian Kivuli, I like you already!"

I studied him then. He had a great smile. His eyes were slightly almond-shaped and the pupils as dark as a moonless night sky, with little flecks of white like stars hidden deep. His skin was a shade darker than mine, clean and smooth. It was hard to describe his haircut, some kind of cross between what I imagined was traditional Native style and the locks of those brash boys still tossing rude comments behind us. He had a wrestler's body, lean and hard. He was wearing new jeans and a couple of layers of shirts with gaping holes through which I could see the smooth, brown skin of his chest.

The bus rumbled on, stopping a few more times, and the seats filled up. I noticed that there were kids from various ethnic groups. To me, diversity was what made life interesting and valuable, so it bothered me that I didn't see anyone sitting with a person of a different race. Maybe when I got to know Trace better, I could ask him about it.

The bus finally stopped at a single building with a couple of different wings. A large sign on the front of the building read: "OCHALA JUNCTION PUBLIC K – 12" in black letters. I hesitated to go in, but Trace took my arm.

"Come on," he said. "You'll be fine. I'll bet there's no one here as confident as you."

We stepped off the bus, but I did not feel confident.

"Meet you here after school?"

"Okay."

Trace ambled off, his drum banging against his right knee. A bell rang—once, and then twice. I couldn't find my locker. Everyone rushed past me without a glance. A couple of books fell out of my arms, and I felt like a wild horse being forced into a trailer.

A teacher came out into the hall. "You're not allowed in the hallway after that last bell," she said.

"I'm new, and I don't know where my locker is," I said.

"Oh, the first day is hard for everyone. You'll get used to everything."

The woman went back into her classroom and sent a student out to help me. The girl seemed peeved she had been given the job. "I don't *have* a locker yet!" she complained.

The girl found my locker and left me there in the middle of my question about directions to Honors English. A small boy who reminded me of my brother Rim rushed by and kicked one of my books that had fallen out of my arms again. He didn't look back. Ten minutes after the bell, I walked into my first class and took a seat at the back of the room. Then, I put my head down on my desk.

"Didn't get enough sleep last night?" the teacher, a Mr. Seavey according to the chalk board, asked. He came down the aisle toward me.

"Let's see...you are—"

"Kivuli Safina Farley," I said, "and if I don't get some respect around here, I'm going back to Africa, and you all will miss the brilliance of my company."

The class erupted with laughter and a few cheers. Mr. Seavey did not seem to think such a reaction was in order, but he didn't give me a tardy slip. "I'll remember that, Miss Farley," he said.

I barely heard what he said after that. I started thinking about the wild horses and what might be happening at the ranch. I wrote a few notes as Mr. Seavey talked about the assignment for the next day. He wanted us to bring a piece of literature—poem, essay, or letter—that had meant something in one's family, something one heard as a child or something written by a family member that was revealing or provoking—no nursery rhymes.

"But that's poetry," someone argued.

"I'm looking for writing that is deeper, more symbolic of family struggle or courage," the teacher said.

He had my attention now.

Faith Collins met me at the door of Art 101. The pretty teacher had let her hair grow longer, and it framed her face in golden waves. She looked younger than I remembered; her clothes were flamboyant and rustled when she moved around the room. She had hung works of art in different mediums on all the walls, and I noticed her name on a couple of them.

Miss Collins stood behind a table where she had set several objects—bowls of fruit, vases of flowers, and statues—and gave instructions.

"Each of you choose one of these items and draw it, then place your work in a file in your notebook, face down, where you can't see it. You're going to do this every day first thing and not look at your work until Friday. Okay, you may begin."

One of the project pieces was a blue, glass horse posed in a *levade*, which might seem to many observers to be a rearing horse, but I knew the difference. Granpa Farley had taught me that in a true *levade*, the horse's body remains at a forty-five degree angle to the ground and the hind legs are bent at the hocks. It would be fun to recreate this lovely, balanced horse on paper. No one chose the blue figure, so I took it to my desk and began.

"That one is the most challenging," Faith said, as she stopped by my desk. "Good for you for selecting it. Don't try to copy it perfectly the first time. Add details as you go through the week. Turn it around for different views. Do you know what the horse is doing?"

"Yes, Miss Collins. A beautiful blue *levade*."

"I should have known you would know!"

I struggled through Spanish, and then it was time for lunch. The cafeteria ladies were friendly and introduced me to girls they knew. I ate with strangers and listened to their stories about life on the reservation, their broken families, their fair projects, and their animals. A few mentioned their boyfriends and their after-school jobs. I didn't see Trace Martin any place, and I felt lonely.

The first day of school was not always easy in Africa either. There were so many rules, new ones every year. Some classes were segregated by race or gender, mostly, we were told, to control bullying. My mother had rocks thrown at her at that very school when she was in the second grade! The nuns organized students' schedules, activities, and our thoughts, it seemed. No one was allowed to be rude, like that boy who kicked my book down the hall, but also there would be no opportunities to make friends with such a boy. Dangerous relationships were avoided and hidden, not that anyone in *my* family bothered with that. I wondered if here, in America, dangerous relationships might be encouraged and admired. I didn't have to look far for such a relationship for myself, no farther than a Nevada jail cell.

Another bell rang, and the crowd in the cafeteria began to clear out. My Pre-Algebra was taught by an amazingly small man named Mr. Littlefield, which everyone thought was hilarious until he scribbled his actual name on the board: Eric Largeman. We didn't know what to believe, but we stopped laughing. "Okay. Now that we have that out of the way," he said, "let's solve some problems." I found I enjoyed the simple equations; they were neat and satisfying. I was the first one to solve them, at least among those I could see from my seat. I noted the homework assignment just as the bell rang.

I was thankful my next class was clear across the football field in a portable building. I took deep breaths of the high desert air and pretended I was on Mlinzi, trekking across the savannah. The World History teacher, Garrett T. Glen, was dressed in a suit and tie and seemed very young. He had beautiful blue eyes that challenged me immediately. He announced we would begin by studying the democracies and ideologies of politically free, civilized countries. He said these words as if they were proper nouns, and I actually wrote them like that in my notebook with capital letters. When I studied the list the teacher handed out, I couldn't find my country on it. I raised my hand.

"Mr. Glen, why isn't Tanzania on this list?"

"Tanzania? An African country," he began. "I believe they have a socialist government. That doesn't qualify as liberated, I'm afraid."

I stood up. This was just too much.

"Is England a civilized country?" I asked.

"Of course."

"And Germany?"

"Yes, of course."

"Did the British help free the German people, including Jews and homosexuals, from Hitler's tyranny?"

"You could say that."

"Did you know that Tanzanians fought alongside the British in that war?"

Mr. Glen cleared his throat. "I did know that. Just where are you going with this?"

I felt a little desperate to get my point across so I softened my tone, a trick my father had taught me to disarm people.

"But did you know the British forced these Tanzanian soldiers into concentration camps after the war? They separated men from their families and wouldn't let them read or speak their own languages. Does that sound civilized to you?"

"I don't know where you got your information, young lady, but—"

"From a reputable source, sir. From a British major who studied carefully the history of what his country did in Africa because he didn't want to believe those kinds of things could happen. Then the Americans helped Tanzania break free from British control in the sixties. The new, native officials decided socialism could best heal the people from colonialism, and if you had just put Tanzania on your list, I wouldn't have had to say all this."

There were eruptions of "You go, girl!" and "Right on!" This approval from two different classes more than made up for my earlier disappointment in the bullies. Garrett Glen sat down, and when there was quiet again, he looked directly at me and said, "I certainly hope you're going to be on my debate team. And by the way, who is this British major to you?"

"My grandfather."

The biology teacher was a Native American woman called Thea Standing Eagle Bell. She held several degrees in genetics and evolutionary theory, according to the framed certificates on the wall behind her desk. I loved science and couldn't wait to read some of the volumes in the bookcase that stretched around three sides of the room, though science was not as easy for me as some of my other subjects.

My father had studied the sciences after he was hired to manage the coffee plantation in Arusha. He always encouraged me to look more deeply into life's beginnings and the theories that explained the evolution of plants and animals, how natural selection and mutation worked, and how the human genome could tell us so much. But I could only go so far in these pursuits. Sooner or later I would get lost in the complexities.

Mrs. Bell called me up to her desk after class. "I'm so happy you're with us this year, Kivuli. I want to learn what brought you here and make sure you are fitting in to your satisfaction," she said. "I have a pen pal, oh I know that's old fashioned, but we enjoy writing, emailing now, so much. She's a Xhosa woman in South Africa named Lindiwe Tukani. Now isn't that just a lovely name?"

The weight of all the confusion of that day fell from my heart, and I went out to meet Trace with a lighter step. He was walking with Julia toward the bus, and he reached out and took some of her books. A boy raced by and shouted, "Man, you either like 'em black or you like 'em young! At least they're *girls*."

Trace calmly replied, "Aren't I the lucky one."

I caught up with them. "Doesn't that kind of stuff make you mad?" I asked Trace.

"Actually, it's a game for me. What those guys don't realize is by the end of the year, we're going to be friends. When you think about the world, it's all we have—our friendships," he said.

"Then there's heaven," Julia interjected.

"She's working on a religion badge for Pioneer Girls," I explained.

"I never would have guessed," he said. "How'd you do today?"

We found a seat as far from the rough crowd as we could.

"It didn't start out too well, but I like my teachers. One of them is so good-looking, but I had to put him in his place."

"Oh, boy. So who is my competition?"

"Garrett T. Glen."

"Well, with a name like that, I'm not too worried. I'm his star debater anyway. I can keep an eye on him."

I handed him my class schedule so he could see where I crossed out "Equestrian Drill" and wrote in "Debate Team."

He raised his hands in mock surrender and then added the word star on my schedule after Debate Team. I told him if we were both going to be stars, I needed to know more about him. His eyes seemed to get darker for a moment, and he put the drum against his heart. He started telling me about his real parents, how they surrounded him with books and art, gave him music lessons, encouraged him to have friends in different tribes as well as white friends, let him go to whatever church he liked or no church, and above all *dream*, dream big.

"It was a good life," Trace said. "But then my father lost his job, and he and my mom went out drinking with the last of their grocery money. They weren't used to drinking. They fell asleep in the truck where it ran out of gas on a train track. They never woke up."

I grabbed the hand that was not holding the drum. The kids in the nearest seats chanted something about "young love, sweet love." But I was lost in the story.

"Don't mind them," Trace said. "And don't let go."

The bus turned off the highway and stopped a few times at ranch gates and dirt lanes leading off into the sage-covered hills before Trace spoke again.

"The authorities sent me to some relatives up in Canada, but I kept running away. I was ten. I hitchhiked and got rides clear to the border, but of course, I was corralled there like a wild horse."

I sat up stiffly in my seat.

"What?"

"I'll tell you later. Go on."

"My cousins, or whoever they were, had enough of me pretty quickly. And I was sort of unadoptable. When Tim and Stuart offered to give me a chance, I said, 'Oh, you bet, I'll take them.' They had just gotten married and wanted to adopt an infant. Well, you can imagine the trouble they had with that. Neither one could give up his job, so a school-age kid was best anyway. They were so wonderful. They let me cry and break things, and I bolted a couple of times. They'd find me a few miles from home under a jack pine or in some fast food parking lot. They'd take my hand and say, 'As long as we're here, we might as well eat. Do you like Whoppers?'"

"What terrific guys," I said, "but I'm sorry about your mom and dad, shocked really. They sound like great parents too, and they must have been so young. It isn't fair."

"Yeah. I still can't go by that trestle. Do you have some place like that in your life?"

I pictured the trash pile where the corpse of Mvua had lain smoldering, but I couldn't tell him that.

When the bus reached Trace's stop, he said, "This is the best first day of school ever."

"Mine too," I said.

22

a question of vision

Susan was waiting at the Crossroads. Julia and I started talking at the same time. "I met the nicest kids and the meanest kids in the school," I said, crashing in the backseat.

"I think she has a boyfriend already," Julia added.

"Hey, believe me, I'm not looking for a boyfriend, just a friend. Oh, Mrs. Rose, what happened to the wild horses?"

"You'll see," she said.

When we drove onto the ranch, I couldn't believe my eyes. There were at least thirty horses circling around in one of the turn-out pastures. All the trucks and trailers were gone, and a few wranglers hung on the perimeter of the herd, trying to coax the tamer ones to them. Hank met me at the fence and helped me to the top rail. Julia said she had to go home first, she had to check in with her mother, but she would be down later.

A group of yearlings sped by, ignoring the people on the fence.

"Where are the younger ones?" I asked.

"They're on their way to California, to prisoners who will give them a wise handling."

"And the rest?"

"I kept them all."

I was exhausted hearing how it took the wranglers all day to get the horses in the trailers, back to the ranch, and then weed out the youngsters, how Susan and the vet wormed and doctored wounds, how tomorrow they would geld the colts and separate out the yearlings and two-year-olds, hoping the mares might come around better with fewer distractions.

I asked if I could stay home from school and help, but Hank said no, that there would be plenty for me to do on weekends, and didn't I have assignments tonight? I told him I needed Askay's journal, that we had to bring some kind of writing from a family member, something of a literary nature.

Hank clapped his hands at a couple of mares who were squealing at each other and warned me to stay on the fence. I watched the boys doling out piles of grass hay mixed with a few flakes of alfalfa. Some of the horses came quite close to the wranglers. The animals were all thin, and their feet were in bad shape. It would take a long time to get them fit for adoption. One frail buckskin kept getting chased away from the sweet feed. I hopped down into the pasture before Hank could stop me. I picked up a handful of long stems, heavy with timothy, and then climbed back out. I went along the perimeter waving the grass until I got the horse's attention. He watched me. I stuck my arm through the rails. The sand-colored colt could not resist and stretched his neck out for the gift. Ty set a pile of hay out just for him and waved off the other horses.

On the way back to the house, Hank said to me, "Are you sure you're not related to my Grandmother Helen?"

After dinner, I closed myself in Askay's room and searched for the perfect lines for my Honors English. There seemed to be a theme, a metaphor of the sun, running through page after page. I typed up the best selections, but it didn't look as remarkable as it had in Askay's hand.

I found Hank in the living room reading the paper and asked him if he could print a copy of Askay's words right from his journal so anyone who wanted to could see them in his handwriting. They seemed more like poems to me then, and I couldn't wait to read them to the class. I hoped I wouldn't stumble over the sad references to his children and to Julian and Serena Rose.

The next day, Mr. Seavey didn't call on me. After the first two kids read, he talked about the literary as opposed to the sentimental value of the works, which I thought was a great lesson. Two of the Lakota Sioux students related Native American legends—one about ravens and another about horses.

Seavey explained after class that he hadn't called on me because I was far from home and perhaps couldn't get the required material.

"I have a surprise for everyone," I said. "But I want to tell you that I loved hearing what literature different students were raised with. It helps us know and respect each other, have things to talk about, and make friendships."

"You are the first one to appreciate that aspect of the assignment," he said, "and I've been doing this since I came here five years ago."

I caught up with Marci Sloman, who had read a poem about a panther in a small cage, by Rainer Maria Rilke, a German-speaking poet. I told her it reminded me of the captured wild horses that were being kept on the ranch. Marci said her grandparents were born in Germany and that her parents still spoke German at home. I told her about the Heinricksons who sold one of their coffee plantations to my father and that Mr. Heinrickson had taught my father German.

"It's a shrinking world," Marci said.

I admired her flowing yellow hair and eyes that were bluer than Mr. Glen's.

"Do you like horses?" I asked her.

"I don't know much about them," she said, "but I think they're inspiring creatures. They have so much spirit, you know, something intangible."

"Like the panther," I suggested.

"Yes! Exactly. So what do you do with horses?"

"I've always had horses around me, riding lessons, and experts to learn from. I see the way horses teach humans, and I have a passion for that."

"That would be so interesting. Maybe you can show me," Marci said.

"Oh, I'd love to!"

We parted at a row of lockers, and I went to Biology.

On the bus later, I regaled Trace with my new insights about language. "What if poetry could heal conflicts? What if the only words we could say to each other came from metaphors? What if, instead of insults, we offered a line from a great poet? Or our own poetry?"

"You are a dreamer," Trace said, just as a wadded piece of paper hit me on the back of the head. When we flattened it out, it read: "Why don't you go back to Africa and take the homo with you."

"I guess it will take a lot of poetry to change people like that," I said. Then, I stood up and faced the boys that had thrown the missile. " 'It seems to him there are a thousand bars and behind the bars no world'."

The bullies clapped their hands over their ears and tried to ignore me.

"Where did you get that?" Trace whispered when I sat back down.

"It's from a poem Marci read in English. It's the only line I could think of right then. I had to say *something*."

" '*Behind the bars no world.*' Wow. I'd like to read the whole poem," he said.

"I'll get it for you. What do you think it means? Do you know who's looking through the bars?"

"I have no idea," he said. "A bully? Something trapped? A broken heart? A lost child?"

"A panther," I said dramatically.

"Oh man! Metaphors upon metaphors."

The bus pulled up to Trace's corner. As he went down the aisle he slapped one of the bullies on the back of the head playfully and said, "There's *my* poem!"

I had a hard time getting to sleep that night. My mind was exploding with things America was demanding of me—touching wild horses, making friends, sharing my great-grandfather's words with strangers, opening myself up to the African priest, keeping the secret about Liana, drawing the blue dresságe horse, and learning a new language.

"Miss Farley, would you be first this morning?" Mr. Seavey asked, after everyone settled down in Honors English the following day.

I went to the front of the room and began:

> *sun take its time here*
> *long moments of gold and*
> *scarlet and purple a sky that*
> *won't let go its dreams*
> *of filling us with light*
>
> *how can I see this sun*
> *and not remember Iyeala Tanal*
> *my children in a distant land*
> *where this same sun stays*
> *only a moment before their eyes*
> *just as I their father stayed*
> *only a moment*

one time sun gone
darkness came in day
as if end of world
but life goes on under shadow
as I go on in a land
not my own

when friends take final breath
that lightning own
sun hold out longer than ever
not want to leave them in dark
remember when they watched together
from porch
all the hues compete
colors pretend to be painting
pretend that if sun never release
its light
into the places they call night
they would not die

Hands went up in the air.

"There's no punctuation!"

"Is that poetry?"

"Who wrote that? Is it an American author?"

"I'll never look at the sunset in the same way again!"

Mr. Seavey let students have their reactions and then turned to me. "Can you tell us more about these lovely words?" he asked.

I felt as if I had been born for this moment. "Many years ago, out on the Rancho del Cielo Azul, there lived a Maasai gentleman from Tanzania. He had been brought there from Africa to help Helen and

Henry Rose. He cooked for them, raised a garden and prize-winning roses, helped with their children, and became a shoulder for everyone to lean on when many tragedies struck. He kept a journal until he was ninety years old and could barely hold the pen."

I paused, swallowing my rising emotion. "His name was Askay, and he was my great-grandfather."

"That is so awesome," Marci said.

"The personal story is beautiful, but let's look at it as literature. What do you think?" Seavey asked the class.

"It's definitely a poem," someone said.

"What makes it a poem?" the teacher asked.

"The form?"

"The double meaning for things?"

"The metaphor!"

"Which is?" Seavey asked.

"The sun," a boy offered.

"Death," another said.

"Well, can it be both?" Seavey asked.

"The sun is life! It holds back death!" Marci cried.

"Pretty good, kids," the teacher said. "What else makes it poetry?"

No one answered, so he continued. "How about imagery?"

"Oh, yes," one of the Native Americans said. "All those colors and the way those people watched them from their porch."

"Good, Daniel," Seavey said.

"But having no punctuation was an accident," someone noted. "The African wasn't expert in writing English."

"Does it matter?" Seavey asked.

"I don't think so," Marci said. "It's the words that count anyway, the story within a story, the African comparing his own brief sundown with what he's witnessing in America."

"I don't get that part," a boy in the back said. "What's a brief sundown?"

"Kivuli?" Seavey seemed to want me to answer. I didn't even know how Marci knew such a thing.

"Near the equator, where my great-grandfather came from, there is no twilight or slow sunset. It's very bright and then, suddenly dark. We don't have the long shadows, so the shadows became a metaphor for Askay, a sign from God maybe, since life goes on when there is an eclipse of the sun, which creates the biggest shadow of all."

The bell rang. No one moved.

"What my great-grandfather didn't know was that I would be named Kivuli—the Swahili word for shadow."

There were a few appreciative murmurs as kids filed out, and Mr. Seavey stopped me at the door. "Kivuli, how many of these writings are there?"

"About forty years' worth. But many of the early ones are in Swahili. I chose from the more recent ones because they tell things that tie my family to the Americans—the Roses."

"How have they survived this long?" he asked.

"Mr. Rose has most of the journal. Some pages he sent to Africa with Thomas Sentinel, and that's how my family learned about Askay. His daughter, my grandmother Iyeala, never knew what happened to him, just that he went to America when she was a baby."

"Well, I thank you for sharing those lines. But wait, what happened to those people who watched the sunset together, who died?"

"They were struck by lightning."

"I was startled by that line but wasn't sure if it was literal. A difficult story to contemplate," he said. "I think your great-grandfather told it in an extraordinary way. May I keep this copy in his handwriting?"

"I'm glad for you to have it," I said.

At lunch that day, a boy with his dark hair in a ponytail approached the table. He hesitated, so I invited him to join me. I thought I recognized him from Seavey's English class.

He spoke right up. "My grandpapa knew your great-grandfather."

"Oh, my gosh! How?"

"He used to be the school gardener. He and Askay planted all those roses along the front sidewalk. I'm Manuel Ramirez. Manny."

This was so incredible I hardly knew what to say. "Maybe I can meet your grandfather." This might be a connection to my great-grandfather no one else had—a view of his life away from the ranch.

"Maybe. He's pretty forgetful. He talks a lot about the old days. Maybe if I read him some of those poems, he'll talk about Askay."

"Oh, Manny, please tell me everything he says, will you?"

"Okay. I'll meet you right here tomorrow, if you want me to."

"I can't wait!" I said.

In World History, Mr. Glen opened the class with a surprising announcement: "I've ordered an old book called *Inside Africa* by John Gunther. It was first printed in 1953, but it has detailed information about what was then called Tanganyika. I could only find a few copies, so you'll have to share and be extremely careful with them."

I couldn't wait to read such a book because most of what I knew about Tanzanian history had come from Granpa Farley, and when Gunther wrote his book, I calculated that my grandfather was only eleven years old. It would be interesting to have an alternative perspective on Africa. Mr. Glen didn't say why he had added some African history to his lesson plan, but I began to pay more attention to him.

Sunrose picked us up that day so when we got to the ranch, I was bursting with all the news to tell Hank and Susan, but Dancing Horse was in the round pen with a recently gelded colt. I raced to my room to change my clothes. I met Hank on my way out.

"Okay, missy, do not go in that pen," he said.

I gave him a quick hug and made my way to the small arena. I climbed up onto the top rail as quietly as possible. "Will I bother you, Henry?"

"Bother all you want. He needs to pay attention to me. You'll be the least of his worries when he's out in the world."

"I've been missing you, Henry."

"Oh, yeah? You've got school, your young friends."

"But you are in a class by yourself."

"I try."

The colt spun around and got wrapped up in the rope Dancing Horse had slung around his neck. He let the horse figure out how to straighten himself out. Then, he helped the gelding track around him with less and less fear. Soon the attractive Appaloosa was turning and stopping and walking up to Henry. He flipped the rope off and asked the horse to go again, left and then right.

Finally, he said to me, "When he slows down by you, reach down and stroke him. Don't pet, just caress."

"Hank told me to stay out of the pen."

"Well, it'll just be your *arm* in the pen."

Dancing Horse worked three more of the wild geldings until they didn't seem so wild, turning them out when they mastered a particular challenge, which meant he had to hike up to the pastures behind the barn and back each time. I saw he was getting tired. He finished the last horse, an albino with pink around his blue eyes, and returned to help me off the fence.

"Why don't you stay and have dinner with us, Henry?"

"Hmm. I might. What're we havin'?"

"I think I smelled fried chicken earlier."

"Susan's is the best," he said. "I might be tempted. You'd better go see if it's okay. Don't you have homework?"

"Yes, but you can help me. In history we're looking at the ways native populations adjusted to colonizers. Right now we're studying Tanzania, but I might do a report on the Americas."

"Well, that's an ambitious thing. It might be easier to break one of these starry-eyed colts."

"What *is* going to happen to the horses?"

"The youngsters need to grow a bit. The ones who develop a good winter coat will stay outside in those new escape-proof turn-outs with shelters. Some of the older mares and geldings might get a stall in the main barn where they'll be treated like the rest of 'em, maybe learn by osmosis. They'll get groomed and blanketed and let out some days. We'll figure out who's ready for more and use them with the cattle. I've noticed a few of 'em acting like 'well, now we're caught, might as well go back to work'."

We walked to the ranch house and then sat down in the mudroom to remove our boots. As I opened the inner door, Susan came out of the kitchen with a huge pan of fried chicken. There was already frybread on the table and an array of garden vegetables.

"Henry, I hope you're here to eat!" she said.

"Yes, ma'am. I just don't think I could take another step without a piece of that chicken."

"Well come on, you two. Hank's working on some new barn stalls. He's worried about the predicted hard winter this year. Might be a while."

I waited until Henry had enjoyed three pieces of chicken before I tried to get his opinion about aboriginal peoples and the explorers or armies who claimed their land for kings and queens thousands of miles away.

"Well, I have a friend—I should say 'had a friend'—who used to say all those Indians or Africans, or whoever, were conquered people, they should get over it. What do you think of that?"

"I think I should put that in my report! Where did that person grow up?"

"Right here in the USA. Unfortunately, he's not alone in his opinion," Henry said, and took a long drink of his iced tea.

"That's just wrong. Think what the conquerors could have learned from the native people?"

"Yes. And those are the aspects you should put in your report. All the blame and sorrow won't fix anything. Moving on doesn't mean getting over it. It just means moving on."

"I'll have to consider that, Henry," I said. I put my fork down and looked into his eyes. "Sometimes I think we're talking about two different things."

"Sometimes we are, Kivuli-from-Africa. Sometimes we are."

The next day, I waited for Manny at the same table, but I was half way through lunch when he finally sat down across from me.

"Hey, Kivuli. Sorry I'm so late. Littlefield kept me after class. I had some shortcut to solving the algebra problems he didn't like."

"There are shortcuts?"

"Apparently not," Manny said. He pulled chips from a bag and crushed them into his tuna sandwich.

I sipped my chocolate milk.

"I read Grandpapa those poems last night," Manny said finally. "He brightened right up and started talking about Askay, how they planted those roses and shared a vegetable booth at the fair for several years. He remembered some Swahili words your great-grandfather had taught him. He also knew Askay had left two children back in Africa, but he was helping raise two American children, so he was happy."

"Oh, that's such good news," I said.

"Then, he got worried. He said Askay was afraid of some crazy woman that was hurting one of Mr. Rose's boys—Hal…Harm?"

"No. He must have meant Hank."

"Anyway, Grandpapa wanted to know if the bad woman ever came back. He got pretty upset, and we had to give him one of his tranquilizers."

"I'm so sorry. Tell him the woman is in jail, if he ever asks again, okay?"

"How do you know that?"

"I ask a lot of questions."

That conversation pushed Liana right back into my sights. On the bus on the way home, I asked Trace if he could drive yet. He said he'd get his license next week but still ride the bus to save gas money and asked me why I wanted to know.

"There's someplace I need to go. And I'll need someone to drive me."

"How far is this place?"

"I'm not sure, but I have money for gas."

"Is this something dangerous?"

"Maybe, but not for you. You're just the driver."

"Uh-huh. That's what the bank robber's get-away man said."

"I can't explain it right now. You'll have to trust me," I began. "It's just that a tragic thing happened to Hank's family that my great-grandfather might have been able to prevent. I know it sounds impossible, but if I could be that savior—maybe that's too strong a word—maybe put myself in Askay's shoes and do what he should have done all those years ago, then my coming here would mean something.

Something beyond just thanking the Roses for loving my great-grandfather, which was my father's original idea. I have other reasons. It's all mixed up with something my mother did. Can I tell you about that later?"

"Sure," he said. "But I don't want you to get in trouble. You could get hurt, couldn't you?"

His expression was so apprehensive, I hesitated about getting him involved. Maybe I should ask Tyrone. No. That didn't seem right either.

"Probably I could get hurt, but my great-grandfather only wanted to keep the Roses from being hurt, so I have to take a chance."

"Okay. Who am I to argue with a beautiful woman?"

He grabbed my hand and held on until the bus stopped on the Martin's ranch road and he had to leave me. I thought of all the homework I had to do, the plight of the captured horses, Manny's grandpapa, the way the Roses trusted me and the ways Liana had betrayed them.

On the final section of highway Julia came back and sat with me. "Trace Martin has two dads," she said. She scribbled hearts on the cover of her notebook.

"I know. I'm going to meet them soon."

"Do you want to go riding when we get home?" she asked.

"I'm supposed to help Dancing Horse in the round pen."

"Oh, those wild horses! I like *broke* horses myself," she said, and she went back to drawing her wildly-shaped hearts.

On the way up the drive, I could see Hank leading two mares to the training pen. Dancing Horse was coiling some ropes and tossing saddles and blankets onto the rails. I had worn ranch clothes to school that day so I could see what Henry might want me to do the minute I got home. Hank tied one of the horses to a post outside the arena and handed the other one to Henry.

"Give me a few minutes with this one, Kivuli, and then you can come in," Dancing Horse said.

"Do not put her on that horse, Henry!" Hank called to him.

"Don't worry. I have my eye on one in the herd for her, but that will be next spring."

I almost forgot my mission for Liana when I heard that. I felt tugged in a hundred directions, but I gathered my courage and sat down next to Hank in a small spectator box that overlooked the round pen.

"Mr. Rose, something came up at school today. A boy in my Honors English read those lines from Askay's journal to his grandfather. The old man has some memory loss but became very excited when he heard Askay's name. He remembered doing things with him years ago, but then he got very upset about a mad woman that Askay told him might hurt your family. Who was that?"

"Must've been…the woman who stole our daughter," Hank said. "But Askay didn't live to see Sunny abducted. He couldn't have known how unhinged that woman was."

I took in a sharp breath. *But he did know something.* "I told the boy the mad woman was in jail. How far away *is* the prison?"

"Less than two hours from here. Not far enough, in my opinion."

The mare in the round pen kept stopping by the place where the other mare was hitched outside. Henry got after his mare with the flag.

"How long will she be there?" I dared to ask.

"Forever, as far as I know," he said.

"Have you ever seen her?"

"God, no!"

"Do you think she's sorry for what she did?"

"I think she's sorry she got caught," Hank said. "I frankly don't care what else she's sorry for. The damage was done."

I was afraid to look at Hank. His voice had that strain in it that always told me when to back off, when to delete the next three questions from the conversation.

"Okay, girl, get in here," Dancing Horse called to me.

"Thanks for trusting me, Mr. Rose," I said.

He must think I mean about working with the wild horses.

On the bus the next morning, I told Trace the drive was about a hundred and fifteen miles from school and that I wanted to go the day he got his license.

"You are a strange girl," he said. "But a long drive with you can't be all bad."

Strange or not, I was going to see that kidnapper, if not for Sunny or the Roses or for myself, at least for Askay, who could not take the "stab" himself. *I* would take the stab, if Liana still had the power to unleash it. I hated the idea of Liana but longed for the moment I would stand before her.

Finally, on Friday, in art class, I turned over my sketches of the glass horse and examined them. All week, they had been face-down in my folder. Miss Collins said to put the first drawing next to the last drawing, telling everyone the lesson would be self-evident. The blue horse crouched in his *levade* in a startling replication of the statue, the final sketch so different from the first they could have been done by two different hands. I had seen so much more to draw by the time the fifth day had come around—the roundness of the haunches, the bend at the hocks, and the balance of the horse's forelegs in the air. It looked alive.

23

first contact

In October, when everyone was preparing horses, pies, and prized bulls for the County Fair, I got in Tim Long's car the day after Trace got his license, and we drove straight to the Womens Prison. He told his dad he was going up to Elko to a huge mall parking lot to practice turns and such. He told me he liked secrets and wouldn't tell anyone what we were doing, "Whatever that is." I knew, however, that he did not like to lie. He had a pile of books to read while he waited, but I thought I might be back in five minutes.

"Should I worry about you?" he asked, as I opened the car door and hesitated at the sight of the stark and forbidding place.

"You can say a little Indian prayer, if you want to."

I entered a building marked VISITORS, and a large woman with dreadlocks asked for my identification. She stared at the passport photo and then back at me.

"Who you here for?" she asked.

"Liana," I said without hesitation.

"You related?"

"I'm the granddaughter of her step-sister," I told her, looking at her directly.

"You the first ever to ask for that one."

"I've been out of the country. No one else wanted to come."

"Well, it's no skin off my back. Have at it," the woman said. "There'll be a guard in the room. Right through there."

She pointed at a sign over a heavy, steel door: 20 MINUTES ONLY/NO PACKAGES/NO TOUCHING. I went in and sat at a bare table attached to the floor. The guard looked at my visitor's pass and said, "Oh, boy." Then he called someone and said, "Can you bring number 56400816 up to visitors?"

The man shook his head, and I sat up a little straighter. I was aware of a wall clock ticking and wondered when the twenty minutes started.

"I hope you know what you're doing," the guard said.

"I'll be fine."

An inner door opened, and a thin woman shuffled toward me. She had chains around her legs and one holding her arms that looped around her waist. I was shocked. The woman could hardly move. I wouldn't want to be like that for two minutes, much less twenty. And then I had a horrifying image: my own mother wrapped in metal, her eyes trapped and dead. I stood up.

"Does she have to have those chains?"

"I'm afraid so," the guard said.

"I don't mind," Liana said. "But thank you, *granddaughter of my stepsister*. How is the old bag?"

"She'll live," I said, playing along.

The guard moved to the side and ignored us. There was no one else in the room.

"That was a good one," Liana whispered. "How'd you think of that?"

"I tried to think of something reasonable that they couldn't check," I whispered back.

"Smart girl, but who the hell *are* you?"

"I don't know where to begin."

"Start with your name."

"I'm Kivuli Safina Farley from Dar es Salaam, Tanzania."

Liana shook her head. The chains rattled ominously.

"Did you read about me way over in Africa?"

"Sort of," I said.

"Sort of? Either you did or you didn't. We only have twenty minutes here, and this is about the best thing that's happened to me in a long time."

"Okay. I read a page from my great-grandfather's journal. It said that he had received a letter by accident meant for Hank Rose. It began 'I will stab—'"

Liana made a strange sound and twisted in her steel chair. Pieces of her hair, tied in a reddish-gray bun, fell loose. Her eyes narrowed.

"I know what I said. But who the hell is your great-grandfather?"

"Askay Joseph...who worked for the Roses for most of his life."

"Oh my god," Liana said. "That old African never gave it to him?"

"No. Askay died. I'm not sure where the actual letter is. I only saw what he wrote in his diary. My great-grandfather wanted to take the 'stab' himself, to save Hank. When I learned about the kidnapping of the Roses' child, I imagined only the kidnapper could have written the note. When I got to America, I asked the first person I trusted to tell me your name. So here I am."

"No! No! No!" Liana almost screamed and brought her chained hands down hard on the table.

The guard came over when he heard the commotion. "Calm down, Red," he warned.

She stared at me. "What good does it do to tell me this now?" she said. "It doesn't change anything. I stabbed him good, didn't I?"

"The worst stab of all."

I stared at the prisoner. *Oh my God. I'm looking into the eyes of Sunny Rose's kidnapper, but I have no idea what she did to the child or why.*

"Do you know these people? The Roses?" Liana asked, bending closer to me.

"I'm living with them at the ranch...for a year. Everyone's busy now, getting ready for the fair, not paying much attention to me, so I came here to see what I could find out."

"What? Are you doing a term paper or something?"

"Not exactly."

"Man, you like to be vague," Liana said.

"I'm a kid."

"Yeah, a nice-looking kid," she said. "I like you."

"Time's up!" the guard said.

"No, wait," Liana cried. "I've never had a visitor all these years. Just give me ten."

"You better mind your manners!"

"Thank you, officer," Liana said, and then wiped her mouth as though the words had burned.

"I don't think I like you very much, but you can tell me things," I told her.

"Like what?"

"Like Sunny saved your life but she didn't forgive you. Would it change anything if she forgave you?"

"I doubt it. Besides, it would be too easy for that *nun* to forgive. It's in her blood. But her mother? I'd take that pretty little Indian's forgiveness any day. That would be some forgiving."

"Susan would probably ship me back to Africa if she caught me here," I said. "But I don't think Sunny's over you. How could she be? She avoids talking about you like the plague. It's like she's haunted."

"A haunted nun. That's rich!"

Liana's eyes lit up in a mean-spirited way that gave me pause.

"You don't understand," I said, recoiling from Liana's words but wanting to make everything clear. "She's no longer a nun. She's married and has a daughter."

"No way. Who'd she marry? How could there be anyone better

than God?"

"She married a Native American named Thomas Heart-of-the-Hawk Sentinel."

"Don't know him. Tell me about their girl."

"I don't think I should."

"Oh, come on. Just give me something to dream about," Liana said. She ran her tongue over her lips.

"You wouldn't!"

"Probably not. After Sunny saved my life, I got help…for my mental problems. That drug just takes away my appetite for little girls. Most of the time. Anyway, if I was still into that, you wouldn't have lasted two seconds in here. Why *are* you here?"

"I thought I might want to be your friend," I said, and immediately regretted the way that sounded.

"You should run away as fast as you can." Her face twisted into a kind of leer.

"You don't scare me,"

"Yeah, well, you should see me without chains."

The hands on the clock moved, but I couldn't leave the chair. "There are so many things I want to ask you."

"What else you got, Africa? Hit me."

Still, I could not release the turbulence in my heart.

"You come see me, I'll answer all your questions. I'll take my meds regular and stop ogling that new chick who's already into girls. Half my job is done, but too bad. I'll give her up."

"My mother likes girls," I blurted out. "One woman, anyway."

"God damn, you are somethin', Africa. Why are you tellin' me that?"

"She committed a crime too, like you did. Not an abduction. Something worse. It's hard for me to understand, to talk about.

I thought, who better than you for me to say things I've never said aloud?"

"I am a captive audience, after all," Liana said.

"That's not why."

"Why then?"

"To make a difference," I tried to explain, "for the people you hurt. Maybe for you."

"Are you crazy?"

"Probably," I said, still guarded. "But what do you see when you look through the bars?"

"I see nothin'!" Liana jerked on the chains again. "In here I see a purty African girl. But the world? I don't see it no more."

Marci's panther in the flesh.

"Okay, Liana, let's go. You'll have to think about the world back in your cell," the burly guard said.

The prisoner looked panicked for a moment. She sat like a stone in the chair, and the man had to physically lift her to her feet.

"You'll come back?" Liana asked. Her back was slumped and her eyes had a hopeless glaze.

"Maybe. I can't promise anything," I said, as Liana was led away.

I had every intention of coming back and shouldn't have left Liana with "maybe." A person on the outside with an arm through the bars of a prison cell should offer only good things, no matter how bad the prisoner had been. Otherwise, what was the point?

Back in Trace's car, I curled up in the passenger seat and banged a fist against my thigh.

"That bad, huh?"

"Just harder than I imagined."

"Do you want to talk about it?"

"No. I'm sorry, Trace. It's very boring family stuff."

"Somehow I doubt that."

We rode along in silence. I could see, in my mind's eye, the last withering look on Liana's face. What had I imagined? More defiance? More bitterness? More readiness to stab when I least expected? But Liana seemed eager to know why someone would show an interest in her. I had to examine my own motives. It was beginning to seem less and less about my mother than about Sunrose and her growing despair.

I was four hours later than usual getting home from school. The Roses met me at the front door.

"You should have called us, Kivuli. We're responsible for you," Susan said, struggling to keep an edge out of her voice, it seemed.

"I was with Trace Martin, a boy from the debate team. We were talking and forgot the time. He's kind of my only friend, and he's Lakota Sioux. You'd like him."

The irony was not lost on me that I was asking them to trust a boy who had taken me to see the person they trusted the least in the world.

"How much do *you* like this boy?" Susan asked.

"A lot. He reads and is on the honor roll. He doesn't swear or gossip, and he's very tolerant of people, even bullies," I answered.

"He's bullied for being a Native American?" Hank asked.

"No. He's bullied for having two dads."

"I just don't understand people. Two dads are better than no dads."

Hank went out to check on a colicky horse but said he'd talk to me later about something he wanted to give me. Susan said she'd heat my supper and sit with me. What was it Liana had said? *Sunny's mother is the only forgiveness that means anything.*

Susan put a bowl of tortilla soup and a salad of butter lettuce, spinach, and yellow tomatoes in front of her. "So what do you and Trace talk about?"

"Forgiveness," I said before I could stop the word from coming out.

She shook her head as though a teenager couldn't possibly know what that meant. "What did you decide about such a grandiose subject?"

"We thought forgiveness meant different things to different people. Trace thought some people didn't deserve forgiveness—forgetting maybe, patience for their remorse maybe. I think it should be offered to everybody," I said. I took a bite of spicy meat and white corn so she wouldn't have to say anything more right then. But she did.

"I agree with Trace."

I stopped eating. "My question is who should do the forgiving? The person who was hurt the most? Relatives or friends of the victim? A priest? God?"

"You do ask the hard questions, don't you?"

I ate my soup and thought about how to keep this conversation from going too far.

"I'll bet you surprised Father Zenwa with your questions," Susan said.

"Maybe," I admitted. "What surprised me was he didn't have quick answers or Catholic answers. He treated me like a thinking person, not just a backward foreigner or a heathen in need of saving."

"You may be a lot of things, Kivuli, but I don't think you're a heathen in need of saving."

I scooped some meat out of my soup and put it on the salad the way I liked it.

"I know Catholics in need of saving, but that may be just my opinion. I guess I'm trying to find out if my opinions have any value, besides to Trace and my World History teacher." And Sunrose, I should have said.

"Oh, I'm sure they do, dear. Just don't let your opinions get you into trouble," Susan said.

"You sound like my mother. It was more than opinions that got *her* into trouble," Kivuli said.

"I'm not going to ask you about your mother."

I was glad Mrs. Rose didn't want to know more right then. I liked just sitting there with this sensible, uncomplicated woman who smiled more than she frowned and treated me like an adult, not like an overly inquisitive teenager who would be gone in a few months.

"What are you doing with Dancing Horse these days?" she asked.

"Oh, he's so challenging," I said. "He made up a dresságe pattern, to some glorious Native music, for Lazo and me for the fair, but that horse tries to do it like a western pleasure horse! I don't think there's any hope for *dresságe* happening. Besides, I'm not competitive that way…with horses, I mean. I like to learn from them, not show them off. But debate team is a different matter. I'm very competitive there."

"Do you like your teacher?"

I glanced down at Mr. Glen's next assignment, his bold handwriting that praised my prep for Private Property vs. Government Sovereignty. "Probably more than I should."

Susan looked at me with the first sign of disapproval and said she'd be back with dessert.

24

Little demons of doubt

I had a lot of homework, but I pulled my biology text out of my stack of books and opened it to the place I had left a bookmark at the chapter on DNA. Though it was technical, I was especially interested in that section because of the references I had read in the news article about Mvua. From some sweat and blood on the gray tape that had been used to wrap Mvua's body, lab technicians had found matches to her mother's DNA and that of a long-disappeared Shanga gardener. How could that be? What did it prove? My breath stopped in my throat just thinking about the answers, the ones I knew and the ones I didn't know.

Who was the Shanga art teacher's mother? There was no name or other identification, just that a mitochondrial match was in the system. Had the mother been arrested? Had she worked someplace that required a DNA test? There was a fingerprint on the body that matched the gardener, but that didn't mean he killed Mvua. The killer could have left no trace. The killer could be hiding in plain sight.

Hank came in and sat next to me at the kitchen table. Pass curled up between our feet. I couldn't tell if Mr. Rose was still upset with me for being out with Trace so late, but in a few minutes, he started talking in a normal voice, telling me about the captured horse that was having a difficult time adjusting to real hay after who knew how many years on sage and bunchgrass. Susan brought him a dish of apple cobbler, and he poured cream over it and ate three bites before he spoke again. Then, he said something I wouldn't have imagined in a thousand years.

"I was thinking you should have one of Helen's paintings to take home. Not the one in the barn, but any other. Your choice." He went on stirring the cream into his apples like it was his last meal.

I wondered if his sudden melancholy was because he was giving up one of Helen's watercolors or because he was remembering the sad journey of the one with the bad bronc and his grandmother's arm.

"I'm honored, Mr. Rose. Do you know if Askay had a favorite?" I thought of his "sun" poems I'd read in Seavey's class, a possible image close to my great-grandfather's heart. Maybe I would hang different paintings in my room to see which one I couldn't live without. But I was doubtful Hank could let any of them go.

"I don't think I can take one of Helen's watercolors from you," I said.

"Well, you choose, and I'll see how I feel. I just imagined you'd like the symbolism of the exchange. Helen brought Askay from Africa, and now his great-granddaughter will take one of her watercolors back."

"It's perfect," I said. "And Hank...if I can help with the horse, come and get me, okay?"

Susan cleared my bowls from the table and put a dish of cobbler in front of me. She brought Hank a cup of fresh coffee for his potentially long night in the barn. My lie had estranged me from them, and yet the gift of Helen's painting came like an arm through the rails to soften my unruliness.

Finally, I gathered my books and one of Helen's sketches off the wall in the hallway and returned to my room. The drawing was of a cowboy carrying a calf through a blinding snow storm. I didn't know who the man was—maybe Julian or his brother, maybe Henry Rose—people all dead and buried, but I loved the atmosphere of it, the tenderness. I placed it by a window where soon real snow would be falling outside.

I tried to do some algebra but couldn't concentrate. I went back to ask Hank where all Helen's paintings were, so I wouldn't miss any of them in choosing the one to take home. I could hear the Roses' voices but stopped in my tracks when I heard the word "lesbian." Susan had said something like "living with lesbians."

"Well, we don't mind that," Hank said.

"No, but I think Kivuli does. She's talked a lot about forgiveness and God and trying to figure out what redemption means, especially *Catholic* redemption. You don't think she believes her mother needs to be forgiven for being gay, do you?"

"No, I don't," Hank said without any hesitation. "But there must be something troubling behind that t-shirt she wears that says 'Forgiveness Warrior.' "

That should have been enough for me, but I didn't move.

"I told her I wouldn't ask about her mother and the woman who lives with them," Susan added softly, "but it must be confusing for a young girl. It would be natural for her to wonder about her own sexuality at this age. Doesn't her father live at home with the family?"

"Yes, he does. He said once in an email that he was comfortable with his marriage arrangement and that their rough times had nothing to do with his wife's and Safina's affair."

"We had our own rough time. Did you tell Askari about that?" Susan asked.

"I told him we spent eight years trying to find our kidnapped daughter. I didn't tell him not to tell Kivuli."

"Do you think that story scared her? And now, with some uneasiness over her mother, she doesn't feel safe?"

"It could be. But she was surprised when I told her Sunny had been gone from us so long when she was growing up. I guess Kivuli could be feeling we aren't very good at keeping children safe."

"Even though we've kept Sunny and her own daughter safe for

many more years," Susan said in a defensive tone, "sometimes it doesn't feel like enough."

Neither one spoke for a moment, and then Hank said, "I was so critical of Sunny when she first came home. I expected her to be a like the four-year-old we knew, just older, but she wasn't. It's my fault she didn't recover in a better way."

Susan's voice, as clear as a desert spring, allayed any guilt I might have felt, listening in. "We have a second chance here, with Kivuli. We can listen to her and accept her, no matter who she is or what she needs. And love her, no matter what."

I headed back to my room to consider what they had said. But I had learned one thing: these were people who would want the truth. About me. About their daughter. About what I wanted for the "mad woman," Liana, and what I wanted for my mother, Suzanna.

I crawled under the covers and thanked whatever god might hear me that I was safe in the house of Hank and Susan Rose.

25

going the distance

On the opening day of the fair, I rode Lazo in the Grand Entry. He was so jazzed by the crowd and the Indian drums, he moved out like a dresságe horse, but I had already withdrawn from the dresságe suitability class. I carried a Tanzanian flag of green, blue, yellow, and black that Susan had made for me. Mr. Rose and Henry Dancing Horse loped side by side in front of me, the Indian bearing the Nevada State banner and Hank raising the American flag high into the air. The crowd in the grandstand rose to sing the national anthem. I didn't understand the meaning of all the words, but I loved the diversity of all the people singing "the land of the free and the home of the brave." Where in the world was this truer? And how would I have come to believe this if my great-grandfather had not taken a chance on the good will of people and a culture he knew nothing about.

After we had circled the main arena several times, we returned to a row of portable stalls and settled the horses in to wait for their next events: Hank would be competing in calf roping and Dancing Horse was performing a bridleless riding exhibition. Julia had a costume class, but Sunrose would not be there to see it. I drifted away to immerse myself in this American ritual that was like the best of a Maasai Market in East Africa.

The Nevada fair-goers seemed joyful and contented, as if they had left family troubles behind, but when I walked through the 4 H livestock barn, I saw Susan standing by a lamb pen, staring down at the ground. A man rushed by and bumped into her, but she didn't react. I said her name, and she turned slowly.

"This is the exact spot that woman took my child."

Her voice sounded stricken as though she had swallowed poison. I put my hand on her arm. "Oh, Mrs. Rose, why did you come here?"

"I've come every year since Sunny was found. I stand here and remember the moment she disappeared. And then I try to comfort myself with the fact that it's not true anymore. Sunny's safe, she's alive, she's not gone forever as I had imagined that day. I feel peace returning somewhere deep inside. It helps me recover…to have that feeling. If I believed in Sunny's god, I would thank him for allowing me that feeling."

I looked down at the lambs in the pen, separated from their mothers for 4 H projects and grim-faced judges. What would Liana do if she came and stood there? Would she decide not to kidnap the four-year-old? Would she decide the "stab" was too great? I shivered and glanced around. Susan was gone. The noise and smells faded as I imagined being the four-year-old with my hand in the hand of an unfamiliar woman jerking me along toward a new and strange life. All at once a hand clutched my shoulder. I tried to pull away, but it was only Trace, who held on as if fearing I might fall.

"Hey, Kivuli, why are you so jumpy?"

"Oh, Trace, I just found out this is where Sunrose was abducted by that…mad woman."

"What mad woman?"

"You didn't know? I mean about the kidnapping?"

"I knew about the kidnapping, vaguely," he said. "It was a long time ago. Nobody ever talks about it."

"It's *supposedly* behind everyone now," I said impatiently.

Trace stared at me, trying to take in the meaning of what I was saying.

"No, wait! The prison! You went to see that woman!"

"Do you think I'm reckless?"

"I think you're insane. Why would you want to do that?"

"I'm trying to understand something that happened in my own family. I thought the kidnapper, of all people, could help me. And maybe, I could help her."

"I think there's a reason she's locked up, Kivuli. I think she's probably beyond help."

We were out in the sunlight now. The Ferris wheel turned against the sky, and a man on stilts made his way through the crowd. The scents of fry bread and cotton candy assaulted us as our emotions were piqued by how close we were to the place of the kidnapping.

"I just wanted to see if that kidnapper could respond like a bronc in the round pen," I continued. I wanted Trace to see the whole picture.

"And did she?" Trace asked.

"No. But I'm going back, whether you drive me or not."

"Oh, of course I'll take you, if just to keep you out of trouble. What are friends for?"

Julia cantered by in the warm-up arena, flashing her Second Place ribbon. Tom was waiting at the out gate—no Susan, no Sunrose.

"Let's go catch the Indian Relay. It's the state finals. Should be good," Trace said.

"What's an Indian Relay?"

"Just about the wildest horse race you'll ever see," he said.

At the end of the day, when Trace and I found the Sentinel's truck, there was a pile of blue ribbons and a few gold ones. Susan's vegetables and pies had taken firsts and thirds, and one of Askay's black roses had won Best Bloom in Show. I whispered to the ghost of my great-grandfather, "You are still touching America with your African hands."

The scent of roses filled the cab as I said goodbye to Trace and climbed into the backseat. After a few miles, when Julia fell asleep,

Susan reached over and squeezed my arm.

"I'm sorry I left you like that in the livestock barn. I couldn't stay."

"That's okay. It made me appreciate more intimately what happened."

"You'd think a person could get over it."

"I don't know," I said. "Some things are harder to get over than others."

"Sunny will be pleased with all these ribbons," Tom noted, as if that would give her a voice in the events of the day.

Julia slept on with her red ribbon in her hand. The sun was already down. I had missed the sunset. In the Nevada darkness, we passed the fields full of white cattle, rows of late summer corn, the rough patch at the Crossroads, and finally drove under the ranch archway. Hank had taken the horses with his truck and trailer, so I went to the barn to help him unload and put all the tack away.

I wanted to call home, but it would be too early in the morning in Africa. In another hour, it would only be seven in Dar es Salaam. I followed Hank around, sorting bridles and grooming buckets, and then got up the nerve to ask if he was sad that Sunrose wouldn't ever go to the fair.

"Not especially," he said. "I was sad when she went to the convent. It was the saddest I'd been since she was abducted."

"I've been sad, mostly when people die. At least Sunrose is still alive."

"But dead for eight years."

I hung the bridles under the horses' name tags on the headstall hooks. I'd clean them in the morning.

"Do you think it was all bad?" I asked, as politely as I could.

"Yes, I do."

I glanced at the painting on the tack room door, at the wound marks Liana had made on the canvas and the frame. She could still do damage to whatever she touched. Hank and I walked back to the ranch house in silence. By then, I didn't feel like talking to anyone back home. The Nevada drama had won me over. I couldn't keep leaning on my mother or father to sustain me.

On my way through the house, I chose another of Helen's paintings to hang on the wall at the foot of my bed. This one was a vibrant impression of a Nevada sunset. This might be the one—a view so different from the phenomenon in Tanzania that it would constantly remind me of my year in America, a reliable bridge to Askay and his metaphor of the sun.

A week after the fair, I asked Trace to take me to the prison. He didn't resist, just made me promise not to do anything I couldn't take back. A thunderstorm enveloped us on the way. Little cells had been passing over the countryside all day, and I had gotten drenched tracking across the field to World History. I was still shivering, maybe more from going to visit Liana again than from the storm.

"An omen?" Trace asked when lightning struck a telephone pole off to our left.

"I don't believe in omens," I said. "If I did, I'd be a Catholic."

"I can tell you about Catholics," Trace said.

"You can?"

"My dads are Catholic, but they can't have communion because they're married."

"You mean if they weren't married, just secret lovers, they could take the body and the blood of Christ?"

"That's about it," he said.

"Well, they need to move to Africa. My mom's priest gives everyone the Sacrament and never asks the details of relationships."

"I guess the African Church is more progressive," Trace said.

I did not let another mile go by before I pushed the subject. "Does Father Zenwa refuse your dads this Sacrament?"

"He's the one who told them they'd have to break up before he could offer them communion."

"Maybe he's afraid of losing his job, his parish. I like him a lot."

"You know Father Zenwa?"

"I've talked to him a couple of times. He's very open to new ideas."

"Maybe there's hope for him."

"Maybe there's hope for Liana," I suggested.

"Oh my god, now I know her *name*," Trace said.

"Yeah, well, that's what you get for being my friend," I said, punching him light-heartedly in the shoulder, but in my heart I felt the weight of Liana's contemptible crime.

To the west, the clouds were lined with molten gold, and a few thin rays of light reached the ground. I wondered what Trace's dads would say if they noticed the mileage on the odometer, but I didn't want to bring it up. The prison appeared out of the shadowy gloom.

Liana was surprised to see me. Her hair was clean and curled a bit, and there was color on her lips. She was still thin but said she had been exercising to keep her heart strong. I didn't want to to be as late getting home as I was the last time so we had cut our last class to gain an hour. I started right in.

"I need to ask you something, but I want you to think about it before you answer," I said.

"Okay, shoot," Liana said.

"If you were in the livestock barn where you grabbed Sunny, would you take her or leave her alone?"

"Oh, I don't have to think about that. I'd take her in a hot minute!"

"That's what I was afraid of." I rose to go.

"Wait, listen. I wouldn't take her again just to hurt Hank. I'd take her because I *liked* her."

"That's worse!" I cried. "I thought you were sorry. I thought you'd never do anything like that again!"

I had raised my voice so much the guard rushed over. Liana's hands were unchained this time, and she reached out to me. I stepped back from the table.

"Wait! Tell me why you asked that," Liana demanded.

"Every year at the fair, Susan Rose goes and stands in the exact place where Sunny vanished. Every year."

"Why would she do that to herself? Not that I care."

"Why did you do it to *her?*"

"I didn't consider the mother. I just wanted to stab Hank when he least expected."

"Well, you did that, and everyone is still feeling the shock."

"Why do you care so much?"

I hadn't decided how deeply I would go into Suzanna's life, what did I have to lose? I lowered my voice.

"My mother killed someone. I'm almost sure she'd do it again. She is not in jail. I think, but I'm not sure, she's been absolved by her priest. I can't talk to her about it. I should have known I couldn't talk to you, but I so wanted to know someone who would never repeat her crime, if given a choice. Do you want me to come back? Do you want me to find something about you to like?"

"Maybe. But first tell me about your mom. Who'd she kill?"

"A very bad woman, as bad as you." And then, I felt ashamed of myself. When had I gone from admiring Mvua, longing for her to be my teacher, regretting the way her father had tortured her and the way my mother had ended her life to reviling her in a thoughtless moment?

Liana put her head down on the hard table. Some muffled words came out of her mouth.

"I have to go now," I said.

The prisoner looked up. "Can I tell you the truth?" she said.

"I hope so."

"I was real good to that girl the last few years. I didn't hurt her. I bought her books, put her in fine schools, let her have the dog, for heaven's sake. She didn't run. Lots of times she could have run. Ask Sunny about *that*."

"I might. But first I'm going to get some advice from a priest I know."

"Oh, don't get those Catholics involved. They'll make a mess of things."

"It can't be any worse than the mess you made. Aren't you sorry at all?"

The smirk faded from Liana's face, and she spoke with some gravity.

"I'm sorry about the dogs."

"What dogs?"

"I guess they didn't tell you everything. I killed two of Hank's dogs and stole another one. Yeah, I'm real sorry about the dogs. And Africa, I'm sorry about Sunny. I didn't mean to hurt her, only Hank. But she was such a handful and asked too many damn questions."

I remembered Dancing Horse saying something about burying the dogs Liana killed. "But the dogs. How did you kill the dogs?"

"With rat poison."

I slapped my hand to my mouth, and tears filled my eyes. Liana stared at me, making the connection before I could recover.

"Your mother used rat poison, did she?"

"No. Her best friend used the poison. My mother wrapped the

woman in tape...while she was still breathing."

"Oh, my little African, I think you're the one who needs a friend. I'm here for you, Kivuli. You can count on me," Liana said.

I felt the seduction, the complete change of character in the woman in less than a minute. I closed my heart. If I had ever wondered what an arm held out to a person like Liana would mean, I had just gotten my answer.

An alarm rang, and all the prisoners had to go to their cells for lock-down. I was relieved. Liana exhausted me. Just when I thought I saw a glimmer of something good in the kidnapper, like remorse or gentleness, the woman would ruin it. Dogs! She poisoned dogs! It seemed that whenever I got close to my own story with my heart's questions, Liana would lead me down some dark trail of her own choosing. I should forget this miserable person and concentrate on school and the family who loved me.

I hurried out to the car, trying to control my emotions. Trace started the car and drove out of the parking lot toward the highway. The storm whipped colorful leaves against the windshield and buffeted the car now and then as we sped back home.

The twilight miles rolled by. In between towns, the desert was empty. It was so like East Africa: the flickering ranch lights of Nevada like the lanterns of scattered tent camps, the cries of coyotes like the strange calls of hyenas across the plains. *We are not so different, you and I, America. We are all thankful for the comfort of a friend in a darkening night on a long road.*

Luckily Trace had me back to the ranch a couple of hours earlier than the last time we'd gone to the prison. But I had a lot of homework, and I asked Susan to let me take my dinner to my room, mostly because I didn't have the time or the energy for a long conversation.

My debate topic was "gay marriage." Mr. Glen always gave me the most controversial issues, but this time he didn't know my mother was bi-sexual or that I was seeing a very "out" lesbian in a Humboldt County lock-up.

When I discovered the massive amount of information—social history, legal history, praise and repudiation of gay marriage, as I sat down to work at my laptop, with three coconut shrimp and a glass of milk—I felt overwhelmed, and right then and there, decided I couldn't do the subject justice. I might, in the bizarre twists and turns of my life, venture to discover the attraction two women might have for each other, or two men like Trace's dads, but it was something I only wanted to discuss with Father Zenwa. Mr. Glen would have to miss my argumentative skills on this one.

The next morning, Trace wasn't at the bus stop. Half the day passed and he didn't appear. I had forgotten my phone and had to borrow one from a senior girl who was the lunchroom monitor. There was no answer at the Martins. When I gave the phone back, the girl touched my hand.

"You like that Indian, don't you?" she said.

I started to protest, reacting to what I perceived as a racist comment, but the girl smiled.

"Oh, Trace and I go way back, almost to diapers. I know his folks—well, *knew* his biological parents, and of course I know Tim and Stuart. They're good friends with my dad. And they're gay, like me."

I didn't know what to say. "Are you Catholic?" *Might as well get everything out in the open.*

The girl's instinctive laughter filled the room, which I took as a polite *no*. The lovely senior's eyes sparkled, and she held her hand out. "I'm Avery, and I've been wanting to meet you."

"Really?"

"Oh, don't worry. I've got a girlfriend. She's not here today either. Sit with me on the bus later, okay?"

"Okay," I said. I watched Avery straighten out a squabble at a table full of third graders. The girl was lanky, with short red hair and a confident, kind manner. I was surprised I hadn't noticed her before, but then, Trace and I usually kept to ourselves on the bus.

After World History, I stopped at Mr. Glen's desk. He didn't look well, and I almost changed my mind about the debate, so as not to disappoint him. He didn't stand up as he usually did when speaking to students. He'd loosened his tie and opened the collar of his shirt. There was a drop of sweat in the hollow of his throat.

I wanted to touch him, but it scared me. Maybe he would think that too familiar, or maybe he would think I wanted something from him. I hesitated.

"Kivuli, I'm sorry…can't talk right now…migraine…"

"Oh, no. I can help you."

I had watched Safina heal people with her hands. I knew it was possible. I got a bottle of water out of my purse and a piece of sweetened ginger. I told him to eat the ginger slowly and take a sip or two of water. I pressed my fingers to the acupuncture points for pain. I poured some water on my scarf and twirled it in the air until it was icy cold and then wrapped it around his head.

After a few minutes that seemed like forever, Mr. Glen put one hand over one of mine and said, "You should go. I'll be all right," while seeming to hold tight to whatever aid I was giving.

"I can't do the gay marriage debate," I said hastily. "I approve of gay marriage. I just don't want to debate about it."

He looked up at me. "I didn't mean to pressure you, Kivuli. I'll change your topic." He took his hand away. "How did you know… how to help me?"

"My family lives with a Maasai woman who is a healer. I've learned some things. No one yet has trusted me to try them."

"But I shouldn't have let you, Kivuli. It was against every rule I can think of."

"Sometimes it's hard to keep track of all the rules," I said. "I didn't like to see you suffer."

"I won't…forget."

I left him sitting at his desk, his head in his hands, his hands still entwined in my scarf.

26

hearts on a wire

I was still thinking about Mr. Glen when Avery found me on the bus and sat down next to me. "Have you ever broken a serious rule?" I asked her.

"Well, yeah. My whole life is breaking one big rule."

"Never mind."

"What's up with you?"

"How can I fit in this Nevada life when I can't fit in my own life?"

Avery sighed and dropped her books on the floor.

"But that's what I want to talk to you about. Your horse life. You fit here all right. One of the wranglers out at Rancho Cielo has a kid in my Economics class. He told me his dad is so impressed with you, that you're riding with Dancing Horse and can handle just about any horse they put you on. Everyone respects Henry Dancing Horse around here. I want to come watch you guys work the wild horses. My dad and I have horses, but we're not very competent. What do you think?"

"I'm still learning, Avery, and Henry is kind of shy about visitors while he's with the horses, but hey, I could come to your house after school and show you a few things."

"Donna will have a fit, but I'd be so pleased. I'll pay you."

"Oh, no, I couldn't take your money, but maybe I could talk to you about…you know, gay stuff."

"Well, that's weird. I wouldn't ask you about straight stuff."

I leaned back against my seat and stared up at the ceiling of the bus. "You're right. I never know when to keep my mouth shut. But what would you say if I told you I lived with my father, my mother and her uh, female lover?"

"Oh boy," she said, looking at the ceiling herself. "How much time do you have?"

"Not much. Where's your stop?"

"Coming up. God, Kivuli, what do you call the woman?"

"Mostly Safina, to her, and my mom's girlfriend to anyone who asks."

"Do you like her?"

"Yeah. She's very sweet and a healer, if you know what I mean," Kivuli said.

"Like a shaman or something?"

"Not a pagan healer. She's Catholic."

"Well, that's not so simple," Avery said.

"Complicated seems to be my middle name."

The bus was slowing down.

"You can just get off here with me one of these days. My dad will be so happy to see I have friends besides Donna."

"Because you're gay?"

"Because we're *young*."

I had so much to learn.

"Okay, kids. Treasure Road," the bus driver called.

Avery gathered her books and sauntered down the aisle. She tousled Julia's hair, and I heard her say, "Hey, little Injun, looking good!"

Susan was waiting at the Crossroads' turnout. Julia talked about Avery the minute they got in the car. "That girl is always so nice to me. I don't mind her calling me an Injun."

"What girl?" Susan asked.

"Someone I just met who gets off at the stop right before the Crossroads," I said.

"She's really pretty," Julia added.

"Uh-huh," I agreed. "She's a senior, and she invited me over."

"I like to see you making friends," Susan said.

"I seem to have trouble with boundaries though." *Like putting my arms around Mr. Glen.*

Susan reached over the seat and squeezed my hand. " 'Just stay grounded in the simple things,' my Iroquois grandmother used to say."

The long sundown was beginning already, filling the truck windows with amber light, and masking the desert life around them.

"There's nothing simple here, in Nevada," I said. "But I can understand why Askay stayed. This life demands your attention, your whole heart."

I thought of my complex feelings for Mr. Glen, the only man I had met in America that I would choose to touch in the way that I did him. Even if I hadn't touched him, there was an intimacy I couldn't deny.

"You are a good girl, Kivuli. Don't let anyone stand in your way when you've decided to do the right thing."

"I won't."

Later that night, Trace called. He was full of apologies, but I was so relieved he was all right, I forgave him immediately. His dads had noticed the increased mileage and were not pleased. He told them he was showing the girl from Africa the country north of Elko—the extraordinary Jarbidge Wilderness area. "In case they ever ask you what you thought of it," he added.

"I don't like you having to lie. I'll tell your dads everything."

"Okay, but here's why I didn't make it to school. Stuart said if I was going to put so many miles on a car, it might as well be my own! We spent the day in Winnemucca and just now got home. Wait 'til you see what they bought me!"

"Oh, my gosh, this is like buying you a Whopper after you ran away!"

"I thought it was a terrific idea," Trace said. "I mean the car."

"I *was* worried about you."

"I'll make it up to you."

"Oh, yes, you will. We might have to see some country more often in your new ride, if you get what I mean."

"Yeah, I get it," Trace replied.

But I didn't see the surprise vehicle right away. All he told me was that it was red, and we decided arriving together at school every day in a red car might call attention to a relationship we didn't have…yet. And I knew Sunrose would rather have me on the bus with Julia every day. I was a little bit worried about the car, being alone with all that extra time. I liked Trace a lot but wasn't ready for the other things I was informed most boys wanted. I think he had figured that out.

We rode the bus. We talked on the phone. We did not go to the prison.

It was two weeks before I had time after riding and doing my ranch chores to consider going to Avery's. I was hoping to ask Susan to take me, but she was off with Hank and Thomas and a few of the other wranglers, driving the cattle southwest into the winter range. So I walked up the hill to the Sentinels and asked Sunrose. Julia was coloring while she waited for her piano teacher to arrive, and Sunny asked, "Where does the girl live?"

"Not too far down Treasure Road."

"Sure. I think I can make it out there and back before Julia's lesson is over. I never want her to be alone. And beyond that, I need to know where she is and whom she's with," Sunny explained.

I thought, but didn't say, how a child might rebel from such a tight rein. In the round pen with an already resistant horse, it could be a disaster. But I knew this would be a very difficult release for Sunrose to give.

Julia looked up from her coloring book. "I can take care of myself!"

"Of course you can, sweetie. Momma just wants to make sure you're safe. Someday when you have children, you'll understand."

"I'm never going to have children," Julia said.

"But why?" her mother asked, straightening a few second-year piano books on the music rack of the baby grand.

"They might not like me."

"Julia, everyone likes you. That won't change," Sunny told her.

"Do you like me?"

"I love you."

"Okay," Julia said and bent over her uncolored pictures.

The doorbell rang, and Sunrose ushered the teacher in, informing him she'd only be gone for thirty minutes and please not to leave Julia alone.

"Fine, Mrs. Sentinel. You needn't worry," the instructor said.

Sunrose and I headed out for Treasure Road. We drove along in the golden glow of sundown. There were other ranchers herding their stock toward better cold-weather habitat. A few riders waved when they recognized Tom's truck. At first, Sunny and I talked about the debates I was working on and the fate of the wild horses. Then, Sunny said she was sorry she had missed the fair, seeing Julia win her ribbon, and cheering for an Indian Relay team. "Did you know my dad met Dancing Horse at a Relay race when they were kids?"

"No. What happened?"

"Henry was riding a Piebald stallion, and my dad was cheering for him as if his life depended on it. He had informed everyone in no uncertain terms that he needed a Native American friend, and he had chosen Henry, partly because they had the same name—the 'Henry' part anyway. They hit it off from day one, though Henry was several years older. Dancing Horse won the race, of course!"

"That's a great story!" I said.

"If you could stay here longer than a year, you'd have stories like that to fill your heart," Sunny said.

"Oh, I've a few plots developing!"

"Should we worry about any of them?"

"Probably. I think I get in trouble because I like to fix things and to learn things about people. It's why I made friends with Avery. She's gay."

Sunrose slammed on the brakes but released them and turned down Avery's road. After a silence, she pulled over and stopped this time. "Kivuli, I can't let you do this."

"Do what?"

"Spend the afternoon with a lesbian."

"She already has a girlfriend. Nothing to worry about."

"But I do worry. It could be risky for you."

"Why?"

A pair of cows wandered across the road in front of them. Sunrose waited longer than necessary. "What if she…seduces you?"

"Not possible. I'm not gay."

"You could still like her."

"I already like her. I like gays. That doesn't mean I am one."

"She could trick you."

"Why would she?"

"Because you're smart and attractive and passionate."

"Sunny, I am mostly passionate about horses and…several of my teachers. I'm having a love affair with America. I'm not trying to prove anything. I am passionate about having some diversity in my group of friends. I want to know the hearts of Latinos and whites and Native Americans, gays and priests and felons, to name a few. I'm not afraid to dive into life, and I'm not afraid to spend the afternoon with Avery."

Sunrose moved again down the lane.

"Besides, didn't you have any gay friends when you were my age?"

"I loved my gay friends, it's true, but they had lots of problems, sometimes with no way out. Things were different then. Hidden. I pretended to be my friend Tim's girlfriend to keep him from being beaten up."

Oh my god. "Tim Long?"

"Yeah…how do you know that?"

"Tim and Stuart Martin are my friend Trace's dads."

"I had no idea they stayed together! I was cheering for Andrew, Tim's first boyfriend. They had some of those "problems" I was talking about. If you get too close to gays, there can be trouble."

"Sunrose…do you not know my mother is gay?"

This time when she slammed the brakes, she didn't start up right away. It was so dark I couldn't see her face.

"Kivuli, really, I didn't know. Please forgive me."

"Well, you're right about the trouble anyway. But I still need to go to Avery's. She's expecting me. Please don't worry. Her dad will bring me home. It's just a couple of houses down. I'll walk."

I got out of the truck before she could say anything else, and when I turned in at Avery's gate, Sunrose was still sitting there. What I thought was so odd was that Susan had not told her about Suzanna.

After I went through Avery's front door, I wasn't as sure of myself. I wandered around Avery's interesting house, decorated with Native American beaded hides and pottery and exquisite photographs of desert landscapes.

"You're pretty quiet today," Avery said finally. "No more questions for your favorite lesbian?"

"My questions seem to get me in trouble."

"Not with me," Avery said.

"What I want is everything good to come under one big heading: love. Everything bad to be labeled 'not love.' I guess I don't have a perfect word for 'bad', because that takes some kind of judgment. I don't feel qualified to judge."

"God, you must win all your debates!" Avery said.

"Almost," I said. "But I can't win the debate with myself."

"I can solve your problem right now. Come here."

I went reluctantly to the sofa where Avery waited.

"Come on. I won't bite," the willowy, tight-jean-clad girl said.

But when I sat down on the edge of the couch, Avery quickly took my face in her hands and kissed me. She opened her mouth slightly and moved softly against my lips. I pulled away as fast as I could, not entirely disgusted. "Avery!"

"Well, did you like it?"

"I didn't hate it, but I'm pretty sure I'm not gay," I said. "There *is* someone I'd like to kiss, but if I tell you, you have to swear with everything in you not to repeat it."

"I promise."

I got up from the couch and went to look out the front window. A storm was gathering. I felt it in my heart, but I faced Avery and whispered, "Mr. Glen."

"Jesus, Kivuli! I'd kiss him too. He's a doll!"

"I don't know what's wrong with me."

"I'd say go with your gut, but you could get him in big trouble."

I gust of wind hit the window, and I jumped. "Sunny would kill you if she knew you kissed me!"

"Sunny? Sunny Rose?"

"Yes. She lives at Rancho Cielo. I stay with her parents, Hank and Susan."

"Yes, I know the Roses slightly, but I didn't know Sunny still lived on the ranch. I assumed she and her husband and Julia had moved to town. Of course, I know who she is. You can't live here very long without hearing *that* story."

"That's exactly what Hank Rose told me."

"That's why I give Julia special attention, help her with schoolwork in the cafeteria, and buy her coloring books and stuff—normal things that have nothing to do with what happened to her mother. Is that stupid?"

"No, Avery, it's very sweet."

The front door blew open, and a few knickknacks flew off the shelves. Tumbleweeds skittered across the yard. The lights that Avery had turned on flickered in the growing darkness.

"Looks like the horse adventure is out for today," Avery said.

"It wouldn't be fun," I agreed. "Let's just talk."

Avery got up to close the door and make me come back and sit down. Then she went to the kitchen and brought back milk and cookies.

"I baked these in all my spare senior time," she teased.

I ate half a cookie, and Avery dipped one in her milk. The wind screamed outside, but the scanner in the room wasn't reporting anything serious. I tried to calm down.

"Do you ever wonder how that kidnapper feels now?"

I had trouble swallowing and put the other half of my cookie back on the plate. "I can tell you how she feels. She says she *liked* Sunny and would steal her again."

"Oh my god, how do you know that?"

"I went to the prison to meet her. I wanted to see if she had any remorse, if she wanted forgiveness or a visitor once in a while. She's so contradictory it makes my head spin."

The lights went out and stayed out.

"Maybe I should get home," I said.

"Oh no! You can't drop a bombshell like that and then just leave. Give it up, girl."

"I first went because I imagined the woman might need a friend. A life sentence is a long time. I've been three times. She likes that I come, but she always says something to scare me. Then, I started seriously wanting her to be sorry so Sunny can maybe forgive her and get past the whole thing."

"You don't want much!"

"I know it sounds hopeless, but I can see something decent in Liana waiting to break free. If a person like that can show regret for criminal behavior, then there's hope for my mother."

"Hope that she'll be straight some day?"

"Oh, no, Avery! Oh my gosh, no. Hope that she'll be sorry for a crime she committed. That I can find a way to forgive her, even if she doesn't want to be forgiven."

"Well, of course I want to hear more about that, but now I'll tell you something. My mother left when I came out. Blamed my father. Said he didn't raise me right. Said she couldn't stay in a home with a… well, she couldn't say the word 'lesbian.' I won't tell you what she did say. I think they were having problems anyway. It was just an easy way for her to escape," Avery explained. "And I don't forgive her."

The lights flashed on and off again. Through the large front window, I could see Avery's dad plowing a field backed by lightning-laced black clouds west of the highway. The storm would be over the Roses' ranch soon. Avery called his cell phone, and he got off the tractor and headed their way, unlatching gates as he leaned into the wind.

He reached the house and stuck his head through the kitchen door. "Can you girls help me get some stock in?"

Avery's dad had a weathered face and graying hair. His jacket hung loosely on his lean fame, and from where I stood, his eyes seemed self-assured and friendly.

Avery and I went out as rain began to pelt us from all directions. Two geldings were already at the barn door and a few milk cows were wandering about close by. We crowded the animals as Avery's dad swung the door open. He grabbed halters to go after the reluctant mares. Chickens scurried in behind the small herd, and we spread hay and scratch in the animals' accustomed places. Soon, Avery's father led the other two horses, who were white-eyed and shaking, into the shelter.

"Why is it the females always give you the most trouble?" he mumbled, and Avery and I crashed into a pile of sweet straw in fits of laughter.

27

turning point

The first real cold began to seep into the cracks in the house chinking and in the barn at the edges of windows. The horses grew shaggy with winter coats; down jackets and insulated work clothes lined the hooks on the outer wall of the tack room. Hank informed Susan and me at the dinner table that he couldn't take the remaining guests that had signed up, admitting he was exhausted handling the wild horses and gathering cattle from the high pastures that were already threatened by snow. Susan got up and massaged his shoulders, saying he worked too hard just like his father had, that she remembered Julian weeping with fatigue during the last year of his life.

"I miss my father...so much," Hank said, and he put his head in his hands.

I thought instantly of all the years my father had searched for his father and had grown up without him. And my mother, of course, had never known her father. So many years without fathers who might have saved them some grief. I looked at Hank and asked him what I could do to help. He told me I could be in charge of blanketing five of the horses when the temperature dropped below zero.

A few days later, I rushed to the barn after school as the gauge plummeted. I did Lazo and Tom's gruella mare; they were easy. Then, I struggled a bit with two of the spoiled dude horses, but I got it done. The last horse was a challenge. He was not mean or scared, just determined not to have that *thing* on his back. I would sling it over his shoulders, and the gelding careened to the back of the stall, leaving the blanket on the ground. Finally, I tied him up. He pawed and carried on until there was a huge hole in his bedding exposing the lowest beams of the paddock.

That's when I saw the marks in the wood. At first, I thought they'd been made by horses' hooves or the pitchfork, but when I knelt down to get a closer look, I felt faint. There was a crudely-etched heart with these words scratched inside: Hank and Liana forever.

Oh my God. Oh my God.

I pushed the straw back up against the stall wall and leaned against the horse. He seemed to empathize with me and let me finish buckling the blanket which I had finally gotten on his back. I felt stricken. It was just a long-ago scribble, a forgotten inscription, but the consequences still stabbed at us all. Then, I wondered if Hank had ever seen it. Maybe it was just another fantasy of the woman who took his child. How could I sit at the dinner table that night with Hank and Susan?

But I did. I blamed my shivering on the severe cold and the time it took to get the horses blanketed. I felt a little better after a couple of Susan's Indian tacos. Later that night, I laid out a black turtleneck, jeans without holes, and my new black boots to wear the next day. I piled two quilts on Askay's bed and wondered if I would ever get used to such bitter air or the discoveries of secrets that didn't belong to me.

The week after that, the debate team was scheduled to travel to Reno for a four-day event. Before I left, I asked Thomas to blanket my five horses. I clutched his arm in a pleading way and said, "It must be you, Tom. There's a reason." He promised he would do it.

The topics at the event were hard for me, and I stumbled on an aspect of immigration. The life of undocumented immigrants was a tragedy in the whole of Africa where hundreds of thousands of refugees constantly streamed across borders ahead of terrorists, revolutionaries, and the next drought. How could choosing a new, friendlier country, if there was such a thing, be illegal?

My emotions got the best of me, and I couldn't speak very convincingly. My team lost that round.

"Hey, Kivuli!" Trace said, as he caught up with me for the lunch break. "Cheer up. The next topic is gay marriage!"

But I had already declined to debate that topic. Trace won with personal testimony about his life with Tim and Stuart. It seemed more convincing than anything I could say. At the end, Ochala High had enough points to make the state finals in January. Mr. Glen said with emotion that it was the first time his team had done that. He hugged the boys. He didn't seem to know what to do with the girls, or maybe he was just being respectful of the rules. A few girls shook his hand. I hung back, unsure of myself. Mr. Glen and I had hung back from each other since that day in his classroom when I had pressed my hands against his pain. My heart raced a little thinking about it. I had not expected there would ever be this much feeling between us.

In the hallway of the hotel later, he said, "You are still my star."

The night I got home from Reno, it was minus thirteen degrees. I made it to the barn and saw that four of my horses were already blanketed. The fifth, in the stall with the illicit heart, was not. I tied the horse and managed to place the blanket on him with the first try. With my boot I kicked away the loose bedding and looked down at the bottom board. It had been sanded clean.

My confidence rose. The stab could not go on forever wounding everyone it touched. The only way was for Liana to show remorse and give Sunny a chance to forgive her. I believed if I got Liana that far, Sunny might consider taking the final step. A week later, I finally got to see the red truck—2010 super cab 4 x 4 Ranger—when Trace drove it to school. We were cutting our last class again as it was very hard to explain spending time in the surrounding wilderness areas in the freezing dark of late November.

Trace waited in the outer room at the prison, and I slipped through the metal door for maybe the last time.

Liana was already sitting at the bare table. She was handcuffed. "You just don't give up, do you?"

"Too much pressure for you?"

"You are an interesting child," she said.

I pulled out the hard chair and backed it a bit further away from the place where Liana sat glaring at me with eyes as hard as the furniture. I sat down. I didn't want to be interesting. I wanted to be provoking. "Since I've seen you, I've kissed a girl," I said to get her riled up so she'd feel the seriousness of my intentions.

Liana's eyebrows went up, and she folded her shackled hands together on the gray steel. "You are a surprise a minute."

"Well, don't get excited. I didn't like it much."

"Was it a pretty girl?" Liana asked. Her mouth softened and her eyes glinted.

"Yeah. But she has a girlfriend. She was just trying to prove a point."

"Which was?"

"I'm not gay."

"I could've told you that," Liana said. "You mean you didn't know yourself?"

This was not the conversation I wanted to have, but I guessed I had started it. "I knew. But Sunny didn't want me to go to the girl's house."

"What'd Sunny say?" She suddenly sat up straight, and the whites of her knuckles showed in her clenched hands. Liana always became anxious when I mentioned Sunny.

"She was afraid the girl might hurt me," I said.

"But you might have had some fun."

I felt frustrated and tired. "I think I'm losing the battle here. I had so many ideas of how things would go when I first came to see you, and none of them are helping anyone."

Liana drummed her fingers nervously on the table. She seemed to have a catch in her throat, but she managed to say, "You're wrong, Africa." She paused again and glanced at the officer. "You're helping *me*."

"They must have upped your meds."

"Actually, they reduced 'em to see if I could handle regular therapy. I think I can only handle being me because I know a real good person like you hasn't given up on me. A person who was willing to kiss a girl to figure me out better. Oh, I know, I know, you were trying to figure yourself out…and maybe your mother, right? But I'm still the missing piece to one of your puzzles. And I 'preciate it, Africa. I've never been anyone's missing piece."

I wondered if Sunny had ever seen this side of Liana—conversational, placating, almost reasonable. But the child Sunny would not have known how to parry back, and I did.

"There's something else. Speaking of missing pieces," I said. "I had one of your stabs deleted. Just for the record."

"What're you talkin' about? I can't throw a stab too far from here."

"But you left one in the barn at the ranch. Won't hurt anyone now."

Liana's eyes widened, and her face blanched. She tried to stand, but one arm was cuffed to the table. The guard yelled at her to sit down. She collapsed in the steel chair as if she had been deflated from the inside out.

"You got me, Africa," she said. "I thought that little ol' heart would last longer than any of us, longer than my real heart, for sure." She actually smiled then as if she didn't mind that the joke was on her.

"I wish I had erased it, but I didn't," I told her.

"Who did it then? Who cancelled the best part of my whole life?" Liana asked, some of her fire returning.

"Thomas Heart-of-the-Hawk Sentinel—Sunny's husband."

"Hah! Serves me right, I guess. Better than justice, I guess."

"*I* thought so. But I believe the best part of your life is ahead of you, Liana. What do you think?"

She looked me right in the eyes, maybe for the first time. "I think I'm going to prove myself to you," she said.

"I don't think I'm the one you need to prove yourself to."

"Well, I'll start with you and see how it feels."

Liana and I stared at each other across the divide of age, the choices we had made, and the locked cuffs.

I spoke first. "If I was sure there was a god, I'd ask him to help you."

Liana laughed sharply. "Oh, there's no god, just a little ol' African girl who lied to get herself in here," she said.

"Blessings have come from stranger things."

"Well, aren't we a pair—damned and holy at the same time."

"It seems so."

The guard came to get Liana. I stood up and turned toward the exit.

"I wouldn't do it again, Africa," Liana said to my back. "I mean, take the kid. She was so scared. Sometimes I was glad I had Dog to help her through."

"Dog?" I faced her again. I knew who Dog was, but I wanted Liana's story.

"My shepherd, a not-too-distant relative of the puppy I stole from Hank. But that wasn't the dog's name. His name was *Paraíso*," she said. "After another shepherd I used to know."

I went back to the table and stared down at her where she was trapped by the handcuffs. "You killed Hank's first shepherd with the merle stripe! You killed the female *Paraíso!*"

"I told you once I was sorry about the dogs! What else do you want from me?"

"Liana...I want you to be sorry enough for kidnapping Sunny that you will ask her to forgive you! All the other forgivenesses might come later, but Sunny is going through some turmoil all these years later. She needs to hear you say you're sorry, and she needs to forgive you."

"Is this *her* idea?"

I reached over and broke another rule. I touched her hand that was clasped by metal to the table. Her hand was colder than ice. The guard was reading a magazine. She flinched, but I didn't let go. "This is *my* idea. I don't know how it will ever happen, but I'm not going to give up. It's because of my great-grandfather that you had the chance to abduct Sunny. I don't know any other way to make up for what he did."

"I'll think about, okay, Africa?"

"I have to go. I have chores. And homework. I don't know when I can come back. Half my year in this country is already gone." I let go of her hand, and I swear I saw tears in her eyes.

Trace had gone out to warm up the truck. I climbed in beside him. "Something has changed," I said.

28

the crux of the story, edited

Father Zenwa's gray Volvo turned into the ranch drive and went up the hill to the Sentinels. I was on the front porch wiping mud from Pass's feet and stood up, but the priest went on by. We hadn't spoken for a while. I went in the house with the dog and called Sunrose. "Is everything all right?"

"Yes, dear. Father's here to plan our Thanksgiving mission to the Res."

"Oh, good. Would you ask him if he has time to drop by the ranch house on his way out?"

"Do you want to come up? Hank and Susan are here too," she said. Her voice was strong, amiable.

"Thanks, Sunrose, but no. I'm grooming Pass. He got in some mud."

I got a towel and tried to dry the shepherd's paws better. The merle stripe was slightly hidden under his rich winter coat, but I put my hand there and thought of his recent ancestors—the dogs Hank had loved, the dog Liana had called Paraíso who was Pass's sire—and suddenly I saw my way clearly. That Paraíso was something Liana thought she had lost forever. *I will put True Passion in her hands! I will do that before she says she's sorry!*

I curled up with the shepherd on a warm rug on the kitchen floor and waited for the priest.

Father Zenwa knocked at the front door two hours later. I had forced myself to get up and work on my algebra equations. They were not as easy as in the beginning chapters. I was glad for the break.

"Father," I said, as he came in. I shook a light dusting of snow from his overcoat and offered him some coffee.

"Oh, I've had plenty at the Sentinels. The Roses are staying a while longer. I suppose that's your preference."

"Well, I guess I shouldn't expect you to be my personal confessor."

"Do you have something to confess?"

We sat at the kitchen table, and I closed my math text. Maybe those problems would be easier than talking to Father Zenwa. I didn't think I was his favorite person—too alien to his dogma. I would see whether or not he judged my words as a confession. "I've seen Liana."

He didn't look shocked at all, but kept his eyes on mine. "How did you manage that?"

"It's a secret," I said.

The priest sighed and straightened a piece of his garments, and I was almost sorry I had told him. He probably had been hoping Liana was a distant memory, that maybe I wouldn't be able to visit her in the prison. But he asked in a resigned voice, "What did she say?"

"She said she'd never kidnap a child again. I don't know if I believe her."

"You should be careful, Kivuli," he said, more sternly this time. "I think you're playing with fire."

"Like half the people I know!"

He sighed and clasped his hands on his golden cross. Maybe he was going to ask God what he should do with me. "Ah, Kivuli, I am so sorry, but do you think you may be trying to reconcile people to God whose sins are not yours?"

"I think I'm trying to reconcile people to each other."

"Bless you, my dear, but know that even a priest cannot do that. I will keep you in my prayers."

"Thank you, Father."

He seemed to be bent over some as I walked him to the door. True Passion walked along with us. Zenwa leaned down before he went out into the night and put his hand on Pass's head. "This is such a beautiful dog."

I could see the headlights of the Roses' truck coming along the lane. The next day was Thanksgiving.

That night, I dreamed about Chui the leopard, who had died when I was seven and living in Dar es Salaam. The leopard's son, Jumanne, still hung around Shanga. In my dream, both leopards cavorted down the coffee tree rows. Rabbits bounded everywhere, but the cats didn't kill them. In the background a smoldering slash pile flared up. The leopards began to pull something from the edge of the pit and stretch it between them like a rag doll. A ghostly Mvua shook off the gray tape that wrapped her, some of it hanging in strips from her burned body, and struggled to her feet with a savage cry. The cats slunk away, and the woman wandered off into the eucalyptus grove beside the plantation.

Winter sunlight broke through the window. I shook off the dream and thought about the coming day. I could smell celery and onions and sage. I could hear pleasant voices drifting from other parts of the house. The Roses were going to have their traditional meal without me because I was going to the Martins.

When Trace invited me for dinner, he had said, "I've told my dads so much about you, they said they wouldn't believe any of it until they saw you in person!"

"Did you leave me anything to say about myself?" I had asked.

"Well, a *lot*, as you can imagine," he'd replied.

I dressed in black tights, a flowing silver blouse and shiny silver boots. When I went into the living room, Sunrose was sitting quietly on the couch, not taking part in the preparations. Maybe Thanksgivings in her frightening captivity were especially melancholy.

"Are you going somewhere today?" she asked.

"To her boyfriend's! To her boyfriend's!" Julia cried, running in from the kitchen.

"Oh, that Indian boy, Trace," Sunrose said. "I remember, back in high school, being hurt when his dad Tim broke up with his first boyfriend."

"Why did that hurt *you*?" I asked.

"I don't know. Changes of any kind upset me. And relationships were confusing to me. I wanted them to be permanent, stable, and unquestionable," she tried to explain.

"Yeah, me too," I said. Nothing very stable in my parent's and grandparent's lives. "I thought you might have seen Tim and Stuart at St. Mary's, although they haven't gone in a while, Trace told me."

"Are they married?"

"They call themselves married. I'm not sure of their legal status."

"Well, they're committed to each other," she said. "They're heeding their heart's calling."

"That's a nice way of putting it, Sunrose," I said.

Sunny's face lit up at that. I thought maybe the woman just needed to be appreciated more.

"Turn around. Let me check you out," she said.

Julia sighed and said, "I can't wait until I have a boyfriend."

"Don't think about it for about ten more years," I warned her.

"Why?"

"Don't ask for about five more years."

Julia put her foot up next to one of the bright boots and shook her head as if realizing it would be a long time before she could wear them. Sunrose looked as though she never wanted to see that day.

The doorbell rang, and Susan opened the door to Trace standing there with an armload of flowers—chrysanthemums, gladiolas, carnations, and tulips—all white. He entered with a flourish, dressed in pressed jeans and an indigo silk shirt with yellow, green, and black ribbons sewn in vertical stripes down the front. No one had the image that was in my head—the Indian Ocean tossing the colors of the Tanzanian flag across its blue expanse.

Susan took the blooms. "You are a sweet boy," she said. "I saw you at the fair, but we weren't formally introduced. I'm Susan Rose. I can't believe you found these flowers this time of year!"

"They're from Stuart's greenhouse, ma'am," he said.

"I will have to meet that man! Sometimes I give up on the greenhouse in the winter. Now, Julia, come help me with these."

Sunrose held out both hands to Trace's and grasped his warmly. "I am one of Timothy's best friends from high school. I'm sorry to say we lost touch after I joined the convent. I lost touch with many things, thinking I only needed God," she said in a surprising intimate voice. "I'm Julia's mother, Sunny Sentinel."

"Maybe you could visit sometime," Trace said, as she released his hands. "We're just up the road on Adobe Lane."

"Yes, I would like that."

A frosty wind blew the door back against the coat rack as Hank and Pass came in from morning chores. The shepherd headed straight for Trace and nearly knocked him down.

"Do I know you?" Trace asked the exuberant dog.

Hank laughed after containing Pass. "How long have you lived with Tim and Stuart?"

"About six years."

"No, you don't know each other, but if your dads still have the female, Miner, Pass is one of hers!"

"Oh, wow! Miner's still with us, almost eleven. Tim was just saying the other day how bad he felt about losing track of her puppies. He'll be excited to know you have this one."

"I'll call him. I have an idea I want to run by him," Hank said.

Trace and I said our goodbyes and went out to the red truck. We didn't say much going down the long drive to the highway and turning north toward the Crossroads. I looked east toward the Ruby Mountains. The light in the canyons broke out onto the desert in a watercolor wash of ochres and pinks and lupine blue, what I was learning in Miss Collins class aligning with reality, with everything I was feeling—the layers and layers of colors that made up my life.

Soon, we pulled onto a gravel lane that led to a white-washed, sandstone house with a muted, red tile roof. I cried, "Oh, Trace, it's so like our house on the coffee plantation in Arusha!"

"It's a good desert house—warm in winter, cool in summer."

"If I lived here, that's the house I'd want."

We parked on the street in front of the house and approached a sturdy gate. Four big dogs leaped up against it, and I felt a little skittish, being raised with complacent leopards. The canines were intimidating in large numbers. Trace assured me they were well-mannered, and the dogs proved themselves by backing away from the gate as we went through. They sat perfectly still, waiting for introductions.

The largest German shepherd, Trace called Gabriel, lifted a paw as I bent down. "Well, hello," I said shaking the black paw. The next dog was Miner, beginning to wiggle a bit and push her nose into my hand. The next was a female, with one blue eye and one brown eye and a dark grey coat. She gazed right into my eyes but was panting as if afraid of a stranger.

"This one's part wolf," Trace said. "My dads were breeding for a certain shepherd bloodline with Gabriel but fell in love with a neighbor's captive female wolf and couldn't resist crossing the two. Ariel is from that breeding. She's a very good wolf-dog, but the poor thing doesn't know who she is. We had to build this high fence to keep her in. She's escaped through the gate a few times when people aren't careful coming and going."

"But what is a wolf-dog, anyway? Is that like a farmer's or hunter's dog mated with a hyena or a jackal?"

"Kind of. I think wolves and dogs are probably more closely related than dogs and hyenas. It's a controversy anyway, mixing the breeds—maybe a good debate topic."

Ariel calmed to the sound of Trace's voice and rested one paw on my boot.

"I knew she'd like you," Trace said. "She's good with people usually, but she's already killed a little rat terrier someone brought into the yard, not knowing there was a wolf there who was picky about who came through the gate. It's a hard life for a half wild animal who doesn't understand her boundaries."

I had overstepped those boundaries myself recently. Maybe I was half wild too.

The fourth dog, who had been waiting patiently, also a female, Trace said was from Gabriel's last pairing. Her name was "Out for a Lark." Stuart had sold her as a two-year-old, but the couple who purchased her had to move to a place that didn't allow big dogs, and they gave her back. She was elegant.

The dads came out on the front porch. "Hey, we live here too!" one of them called out.

I noticed one man was quite tall with short brownish hair and a welcoming smile. The other had wavy black hair and an athlete's body. Both were lean and fashionably dressed, I supposed, for desert-dwelling dads. The dogs jumped around them.

The tall gentleman leaned down and kissed my cheek. "I'm Tim," he said, "and this is my husband, Stuart." We shook hands and moved into the house.

"Come on in, girl from Africa," Stuart said. "Remind us of your name."

"Kivuli."

"Does that mean anything special?" Tim asked.

" 'Shadow', in Swahili."

"Nice," Stuart said. "I'm betting it doesn't quite suit you."

"You'd be right," Trace said.

In the living room were three gorgeous cats. Two hid immediately, but the third, lounging on the couch, rolled onto its back to reveal dark spots on a pale gold belly.

"Oh, you are a little Jumanne!" I cried, putting my face in the clean-smelling fur.

"Who's Jumanne?" Stuart asked.

"A leopard I grew up with."

"A wild leopard?" Tim and Stuart said at the same time.

"Oh, yes, but there were two of them. The first leopard that came into the Shanga compound where I first went to school was called Chui. He died a few years ago, and his son, Jumanne, took over as *mlinzi*."

"Mlin...zi?" Stuart queried.

"Swahili for 'guardian'."

"A leopard guarding humans. I would like to have witnessed that," Tim said.

The cat purred and stretched out, half upside down. I caressed the feline. I didn't think people who had domestic cats could understand what those leopards had meant to me. I told the dads my mother always bragged about how the older leopard would block the porch steps of the plantation house to prevent me, as a toddler, from tumbling down.

Stuart said, "Tell us more about your African life while we serve dinner."

Trace and I pulled chairs up to a walnut table set with red and gold square china plates, gold utensils, and tall drinking glasses etched with three gold horizontal stripes. There were yellow, red, and white carnations in a milk-white pitcher and white linen napkins. It was so artful and surprising I could hardly speak.

"If I were in the rural parts of my country tonight, I'd be eating on an oil drum under a grass-thatched roof. I might feel a raindrop on my face. I might be sitting on a stool made from woven leather scraps. If I drank from a glass, it most probably would not match the one next to it. Nearby would be sleeping hammocks with nets to block out the mosquitos. The dinner plates might be tin but sometimes ebony, if the tourists hadn't bought them all that day."

Tim filled the square red and gold china bowls with a mixture of baby greens, yellow tomatoes, cucumbers, green onions, pieces of avocado, crumbles of white cheese, and dried cherries. Stuart offered a choice of dressings that matched the decor—red wine something and yellow-gold honey mustard.

"This is a fantasy," I remarked, wondering what the main course would be.

We ate our salads. A sudden wind rattled the windows and then died away. The three shepherds barked outside, and Ariel began to howl in her unique way. Tim got up to see what had disturbed them. He came back and told us it was just a runner with a headlamp.

Stuart loaded our plates with garden vegetables, chicken dipped in egg and coconut bits, cornbread, and honey from local hives. The two scared cats reemerged and circled under our feet. I couldn't resist putting small bites of chicken on the floor, and the cats rubbed on my legs. I thought again of the leopards and the way they bumped their heads against people's legs for food treats. No one seemed to want to break the silence.

"Tell us how you like American school," Tim said finally.

"It's good. I like all my teachers, although I didn't start off well with Mr. Glen because he didn't have Tanzania on our study guide. I think he liked that I was outspoken about it, because he quite favors me," she said. "Put me in lead position on the debate team, although I have let him down a couple of times."

"He's *my* stiffest competition, for sure," Trace told them.

Trace didn't know I preferred my easy relationship with him. I didn't need the complication of a crush on a teacher, especially one who seemed to like me back. But it was what it was. I took a few bites of cornbread with the golden honey and tried to relax. Being with two men who were married to each other was so new for me. They were extremely attractive and complemented each other in such a natural way.

"I'm supposed to say hello from Sunny Sentinel! She's glad you're both happy," I said.

"Sunny Rose," Tim said. "I haven't talked to her in ages. We were very close in high school, and I spent many weekends at the ranch. She taught me how to ride and let me hold her hand at school so no one would guess I was gay. I missed her a lot when she went off to St. Mary's Convent, but I understood why she did it. We had our theories about what she had suffered with that odious woman."

I didn't mention I had been visiting that odious woman and that Trace was driving me to the prison. I didn't tell them about my mother and Safina. Perhaps I would before the year was over, but right then, I wanted to leave the African part of myself, with all my own family drama, far from these lovely men and their settled life.

I ate slowly, wanting to draw out the meal and the conversation with Tim and Stuart. They asked me so many questions that it was easy to do. Then, it was time for dessert. Stuart dished up homemade vanilla ice cream with strawberries from the Farmer's Market, grown in someone's greenhouse. He gave each cat a dish with some of the ice cream. The leopard-looking cat tried to push the others away, and a few hisses erupted under the table.

"They won't fight, will they?" I asked.

"Oh, no. Their whole life is one big game," Tim assured me.

After that, the dogs were allowed in, and we all moved to the living room with our second helpings of dessert. One of the dads had built a fire in the fireplace, and the room glowed with soft light. Trace got me talking about horses, but the dads were interested in my mixed heritage, so I had to allow Africa back into the room.

When I started to tell them the simple story, that my father is Maasai and my mother is British, Tim broke in with, "Oh, that's not nearly enough." I felt trapped. There were so many twists and turns that even I had trouble keeping it straight. And I was so far from everyone I loved, I might slip and not get something right and damage my family in the dads' opinion. So I just said my father had looked for his father for half his life, because his mother wouldn't tell him who he was, but on the day I was christened in the Catholic Church, the man came forward and claimed my father and the Maasai woman he had loved for thirty years. I revealed that that man was my white granpa, Fulsom Farley, and his story was way too complicated to go into right then.

The only sound was the clink of spoons in the china dishes. Stuart got up and piled more logs on the fire. It blazed up, and I was grateful for it. I was feeling chilled, maybe from the ice cream, maybe from the convoluted past I was choosing to omit.

"But how on earth did you end up here, in Nevada?" Tim asked.

"The Maasai woman, my grandmother, had said goodbye to her father, Askay, who was going to America with Henry and Helen Rose. I'm following in his footsteps to finish something he started but didn't live long enough to do, if he was ever going to do it."

"More and more mystery," Stuart said.

And they didn't know their son was in it. I would have to tell the rest of the story sometime. I had promised Trace I would. We didn't stay too much longer. The dads said not to worry about the dishes, for Trace to drive carefully and come right back as the storm seemed to be building. The dads hugged me, and I told them it had been the best night I'd had in America.

Trace and I rushed through the sharp wind and climbed into the cold truck. By the time we reached the main road, the heater had warmed us up, but we hadn't said anything.

"You didn't tell them about your mother," Trace said.

"No. Did you tell them? The day you met me?"

"It was not my story to tell."

"I left out a lot of 'my story,' I guess. And I didn't admit my forgiveness plan for Liana. I don't know the whole of it yet…but I'm working on it."

At the ranch, a light was still on in the kitchen. Hank had waited up for me.

"How'd it go?" he asked.

"Those dads treated me like a princess…and you wouldn't believe how they can cook! Their dogs were so beautiful, and smart, and the wolf-dog intriguing. But to be honest, Mr. Rose, I am haunted by the dogs with the merle stripe, and the *two* Paraísos—one yours, and the one Liana used to lure your daughter into her van. I want to make sense of it, make something…honorable."

Hank looked at me as if he trusted me not to be just a kid anymore. Then, he went to the coat rack by the front door, and came back with a black leather collar. He handed it to me. Engraved on a smudged, bronze nameplate on the frayed loop was the name "Paraíso."

29

sea-glass prayers

On Monday in World History, Mr. Glen began lecturing on the slave trade that had occurred in East Africa and the island nation to the east, Zanzibar. I hated that part of my own history and barely listened. I caught phrases like "Arabs noted for their viciousness to captured blacks" and "a slave could be sold for less than the price of a goat." It made me think of the collar Hank had given me last night and how, when I laid it on my nightstand, the ghost of Liana's Dog lingered, the dog that had known everything and seen everything, that had lived in the hole in Sunny's childhood. Maybe there were ghosts of enslaved Africans all over the world where they had been towed by collars to do whatever white men wanted them to do.

My mother is white. My grandfather and my great-grandfather that Dakimu Reiman killed were British military. That is half of *my* history. Then I heard Mr. Glen say that the British were the first Europeans to try to end the slave trade in Tanganyika. My Granpa Farley had never told me that!

"Kivuli! I asked you a question," Mr. Glen said. "This is your country we're talking about."

"Sorry. I was thinking about the sea-glass rosaries I brought with me. All the pieces came from the shore of the Indian Ocean where you can still find relics from slaving ships," I said, hoping to contribute to the day's lesson.

"All right. Maybe you could you bring one in for us to see."

"I'd like to."

The bell rang and saved me having to answer the question I didn't hear. But it didn't keep me from being hurt that Mr. Glen had been so short with me. I wanted to be special to him, but what he probably wanted was for me to listen and learn something from his class more than anything else.

Biology caught me off-guard too, and I floundered in the discussion of gene expression and mutation. To me, the field was too vast and unknowable. My mind drifted to a line I had read in that book Mr. Glen had brought to the classroom, *Inside Africa*.

"Kivuli? Are you with us?" Thea Bell asked.

"I was thinking about *coelacanths*."

"Oh. Okay," Mrs. Bell said and left me alone.

Sometimes I got A's for my quick thinking, but other times I barely passed quizzes because they were not on the facts or the theories I cared about. What did the reproductive life of protozoa matter if there was no forgiveness in the world?

Trace slipped in beside me on the bus going home. "Someone told me you liked me," he said.

"And who might that be?"

"Well, Avery."

"Oh, yeah, that." I hadn't told Trace the latest with the sometimes intense girl.

"What?"

"She sort of said she had a crush on me, and I said I liked *you*." I closed my eyes for a moment. I saw two women in a tight embrace—my mother and Safina. They were so enticing, but I couldn't see myself in either place. "I like you all right," I went on, "but you're not liable to come to Africa for the rest of your life."

"I might," he said. "Girls like you are hard to find."

"You are a 'sweet-talker'," I said. "I just learned that word at lunch. Some girl said she could sweet-talk her dad into anything. So naturally

I asked what it meant."

"Well, I just say what I mean anyway," Trace assured her.

The bumpy, sundown-filtered miles passed. White boys threw erasers at Indians who threw balls of paper back. I wondered when they were going to grow up and thanked the universe for the day Trace Martin sat down next to me on the bus.

"Boys like you are hard to find," I said.

Trace put his arm around me. "Maybe you'll stay in America."

"In zero degrees? I don't think so."

"I could keep you warm," he offered.

"Trace! That makes two propositions in one day!"

"Avery and me?"

"Yes."

"I thought she and Donna—"

"Oh, they were…are…I don't know. I can't worry about their love life. I'm still confused about my mother's."

"Why are you confused? Gay is gay."

"I know some smart, courageous gay women and ones that have committed crimes," I countered. We had lowered our voices considerably.

"Aren't those criminals smart and courageous too?"

"Yes. Actually, they are. I just can't get over the crimes. It has nothing to do with their being gay, except that their passion got out of control," I said.

"Does your mom know how you feel about this?"

"Are you kidding? She hardly knows how I feel about hair styles. I'd be afraid to tell her half of what I've told you and the Roses. And Dancing Horse. Sometimes it feels like I came to America to have someone to talk to, someone I could…well, *heal* is too large a concept maybe."

"Not too large a concept for you, I think." He moved his hand along the top of my shoulders. "But I don't understand why you're so set on helping these *adults*. Maybe you should be healing *me*."

"What's wrong with you?" I asked, suddenly worried.

"Heartache? Something like that," he said.

"Trace, you are my best friend. I wouldn't be making it here without you. It's not your fault my heart is divided into a hundred pieces…well, maybe not a hundred."

"I get it, Kivuli. If you didn't have your passions, I wouldn't be attracted to you. I for sure wouldn't be driving you to the prison. I'll be in such big trouble, you know, even though I'm driving my own car, and we're not going to the Jarbidge."

"I'll take all the blame," I said, as the bus slowed to a stop. "Here's your lane."

"Darn."

At the ranch, Tom and Sunrose were leaving a crying Julia with her grandparents for a couple of hours. Sunny grabbed my hand and took me into a nook in the kitchen where Julia couldn't hear. "We're going to see Father Zenwa…for counseling. We told Julia for a church meeting, but she's already upset so we just left it at that."

I asked her to wait a minute and went to get one of the rosaries from my bag. I rushed back and put one of the most unusual ones in her hands.

"Oh! What's this?" she asked.

"My mother and I make these from pieces of glass and metals we collect at the beach. I meant to give them out sooner, but I got busy with the horses and then school. I have a few more of them, but I'm waiting for the right Catholics," I said.

"This means a lot to me, Kivuli. Sea glass from Africa."

"A sea glass rosary is special. I know it's a Catholic symbol, but why couldn't it bring all kinds of broken hearts together?"

"Oh, if it were only that simple," Sunny said.

"Come on, hon, we're going to be late," Thomas called.

After they left, I found Julia curled up in Hank's easy chair. "What happened, sweetie?"

"Daddy yelled at Momma."

"Oh, honey, I can't believe that," I said, tucking a nearby fleece blanket around her.

"But he did," Julia wailed.

"What did he say?"

"He said 'Stop! Stop! You will do no such thing!'"

"What was he talking about?"

"Momma said, 'If someone takes Julia, I'll kill myself'."

"Julia, your father was raising his voice because he *loves* your mother, not because he was angry with her."

"But what did Momma mean? Who would take me?"

I had to think for a minute. My answer might change everything. It would have to be the truth but not scare her. It could not be the part of the truth that I myself knew.

"Listen to me, Julia," I began. "You know that doll that had a sad childhood? The one you don't like to play with? When she grew up and became your Momma, all those bad times were erased. You will never be like that doll. The children of sad mommas…are safe. But that doesn't mean the momma can't worry about them. And sometimes the daddy is just trying to shake that worry right out of her."

"Is that why daddy yelled?"

"Yes."

Julia uncurled a bit. "Did someone take Momma? Did someone make her a sad little girl?"

"I think you know that, Julia. But look at you! You are so happy. You live with your momma and daddy and your grandparents. You have that special guardian Medicine Hat pony. You have friends who love you to pieces, like Trace and Avery and Dancing Horse. And me. We're not going to let anything happen to you or your mother. Okay?"

"I wish I could believe it," she said.

Oh, God.

The next day, I passed another of the sea glass rosaries around my history class, and when the bell rang, it was in Garrett Glen's hands. I wondered if he might be Catholic because of the way he touched it with reverence.

"Would you like to have it?" I asked, when I reached his desk.

"I'd love to have it," he said. "I've fallen away from the Church in recent years. Now I have two reasons to go back, and they're both African."

"Both?"

"This rosary and Father Zenwa," he said.

"You know the priest at St. Mary's?"

He hesitated but held up the sea glass to the light from the west window, as if searching for the right words.

"Father says the odds are I'll find God's path for my life…if I leave it in His hands."

" 'It will be a sight or a sound that has no other explanation,' " I quoted from the words of Father Amani of Dar es Salaam.

"Who said that?" Mr. Glen asked.

"A Tanzanian priest I know."

"Three reasons," he said. Then he looked at me seriously. "Maybe four."

30

unquenchable ties

Manuel Ramirez and I sat in the lunchroom together the day school let out for Christmas vacation. We barely touched our macaroni and cheese, after he told me his grandpapa wanted to meet me.

"Maybe in January because my family celebrates Christmas with friends and relatives from all over the country," Manny said. "A meal can last three days!"

I didn't answer right away thinking about this first Christmas so far from my family—how I would have snow and they wouldn't, how I would be blanketing horses and they would be riding them, how I would be hearing Zenwa's Mass and they Amani's, or I would be staying home with the Roses and my Africans would be lighting candles.

"The first of the year then," I finally said. "He could come to the ranch, and we could sit in Askay's garden, if it's not too cold."

"I guess we'll have to hope for a warm day and a day he's in his right mind," he said. "Also, he doesn't speak English."

We picked at our food, and I tried to shut out the noise of scraping chairs and hyper voices.

"I can practice my Spanish, and you can translate if I need help," I suggested.

"Good idea."

I looked out the lunch room window at a golden eagle perched on a dead jack pine. The eagle turned his head from side to side slowly, as if willing a varmint to appear. The school ground was empty and silent as a jail yard during lock-down.

Manny went on with a somber look on his handsome, brown face.

"You see," he said, "my grandpapa doesn't believe in you. Says I am fooling him. When he says it in Spanish, it comes out I am making a fool of him. So I said 'I will bring you the girl'."

"*¿Cómo se llama?*"

"Hernando."

"Hernando Ramirez," I repeated. "What a lovely sound. I wish I could learn the language, but I don't think I'll be here long enough."

We both watched the eagle soar away from the snag. The sun was already inching toward the horizon, and the bird disappeared in the amber sky.

"*Muchas gracias*, Kivuli," Manuel said, and he stood up with his tray and nodded a goodbye.

I stayed for a moment. How would I converse with the old man about Askay? There were so many things I wanted to know, but it would be nearly impossible in the grandpapa's language. How had the two men managed in Swahili and Spanish with very little English between them? How much could Askay have told Hernando about "the mad woman?"

Later, on the bus, I looked to the east where storm clouds threatened, thick and black, but through the window to the west, the sun still gleamed in its liquid golden path toward the edge of the earth. I felt molded to that place, heading south toward Rancho del Cielo Azul, caught between the brightness of my dreams and the darkness that was Liana.

Then, just before Christmas, on Julia's seventh birthday, a day that snow fell hard in the high country and a bitter wind swept down from the canyons along the Ruby front, I opened the ranch house door to an older but very attractive woman asking for Kivuli Farley. Pass, whining for attention, seemed to like her immediately.

"I am Kivuli."

"Yes, I see the resemblance. I met your mother once in Dar es Salaam when she was a bit younger than you."

"Do you know her now?"

"No. I wish to, but I haven't been back to Tanzania in many years," the visitor said. "I'm Reena Stone."

I was sure I had heard that name but couldn't think where. I opened the door a bit wider and asked, "Why are you looking for me?"

"A few weeks ago, I spoke to a long-time friend of mine in Arusha, Dakimu Reiman, and he told me close friends of his had a daughter in the states. Maybe I could go see how she's doing. He said I'd find you with the Roses on Rancho Cielo Azul south of Ochala Junction in Nevada. So here I am."

"Well, come in then. It's bitterly cold today. Mr. and Mrs. Rose are out taking care of some horses that get blankets in this kind of weather. I'm helping their granddaughter with a school project," I said, warming up to this unusual woman.

"Oh, don't let me disturb you. I'll just watch you study, if I may."

But Julia appeared at Kivuli's side. "Kiki, please, let's stop for a while," she begged, and then she edged closer to the visitor. "Hi. I'm Julia. I'm seven today!"

"My name is Reena, Mrs. Reena Stone," the woman said. "Today is your birthday?"

"Yes. Which shall we call you?" Julia asked.

"I don't mind Reena," she said. "Mr. Stone is…his ashes are scattered in a special place in Africa."

"Oh, show us on the map!" Julia cried. "We were just now writing descriptions of places we want to go in our lifetimes. I picked Tanzania, of course, because Kiki makes it sound special."

"It is special, Julia. I hope you can discover that for yourself one day. Now, show me this map," Reena said.

I retrieved it from the desk, and Julia and I spread it out on the coffee table in the living room.

"Show me where *you've* been," Julia said to Reena Stone.

Mrs. Stone placed her hand on the continent of Africa. A subtle change came over her, as if she wished for the continent to come alive under her fingers. She took a deep breath but still seemed unable to speak. We waited politely beside her.

"I have been many places. Here." She pointed to Johannesburg. "And here." Her fingers brushed Ethiopia. "But the best places in the world are here, in Tanzania." She touched the area at Huzuni and said, "This is where I met Jim Stone…and many years later we were married there. And here, in the lush forests of Manyara, Dakimu and I laid him to rest."

"It still saddens you," I said.

"He had a very big heart and loved Africa with all of it, especially Tanzanians," Reena replied.

"Have you been to Dar es Salaam? Where Kiki is from?" Julia asked.

"Yes, I have. I lived there for a while."

Julia set small, toy animals on the places Mrs. Stone had shown. I considered how much I should say to this lady.

"I've never been to Huzuni, but it's where my mother met my father. She was riding her horse on a dangerous trail to be reunited with her best friend," I told Reena.

"Her best friend? Safina?" the woman asked with some surprise.

"Yes."

"They are still close?"

"You could say that. Safina lives with us in Dar."

Julia looked up. "Show me Dar!"

Mrs. Stone's hands and mine met on the map where the name of the seaport town was printed on the edge of the Indian Ocean. Then the older woman said, "The same week I met Jim, I met Dak, right here in Dar es Salaam. We…went through some tough times together…but loved each other, the three of us. I guess that sounds odd."

"Not to me," I assured her.

Reena looked up from the map as if the memories of those places daunted her.

"So Safina didn't marry that boy she liked at the Light of the World School?"

"I've never heard of a boy," I said. "As long as I've known her, she's liked *girls*."

"Oh, dear Lord," Reena said softly.

Julia was talking to herself, telling little stories about the towns and places Reena had shown her on the map.

I asked right away, "Are you Catholic too?"

"No. But I've called on the Lord many times. When I was sixteen, I was a Christian missionary at Huzuni."

I felt comfortable saying a little more. "Practically everyone I know is Catholic. Dak and his wife, their daughter Safina, my mother, and my Granpa Farley and, of course, my great-grandfather on my Maasai side, Askay. He's the reason I'm here, to see where he spent his life."

"Your great-grandfather lived on this ranch?" Mrs. Stone asked, again surprised.

"He came here with the original owners of the ranch. He left his wife and two children on the rim of the Ngorongoro Crater. His daughter was my Granma Iyeala. His son, Tanal, killed himself after one of his sons died in a mine in South Africa."

"I didn't know any of this. I don't suppose I would. How tragic for your family."

"Yes, but Askay is still caring for this family who loved him, through my friendship with them and my hopes for them," I told her.

"And what might those be, my dear?"

"It's kind of a long story."

"I like stories," Julia broke in.

"Well, right now, I think we should get Mrs. Stone something to drink!"

"Then will you tell the story?" Julia asked.

By way of an answer I reached down and hugged her shoulders. Julia moved the horse to Dar es Salaam.

Reena and I went to the other room and poured glasses of mango juice for the three of us. Mrs. Stone took a sip and said, "I have never forgotten the joy of this taste. I always think of the women at the mission offering me this juice as a gift before I knew how to thank them in their language."

"The Roses like to find things that make me feel more at home, like mangoes or plantains and seasonings I'm used to."

"How thoughtful. I can't wait to meet your American family."

Before we returned to the living room, Reena said, "Safina and Suzanna. They were not much older than Julia when I saw them last."

"Yes, well, they never got over themselves," I said.

"Does it bother you?"

"Sometimes...but they, and my father, seem very happy. Who am I to judge?"

"You are not a Catholic amongst all those Catholics?"

"Not really. The only Catholic I understand is Father Amani, back in Tanzania."

"Yes. He was the light at the end of a very dark tunnel for some people I loved," Mrs. Stone said.

Just then the Roses rushed in from the frosty day, huddled in their down clothes with wool scarves wrapped around their faces. Pass trotted around them in circles. Julia abandoned her map as Reena and I walked out of the kitchen. We had to set the glasses full of juice on the dining table when Susan turned from the coat rack and reached out her hands.

"Oh, I know you! Don't I know you?" Susan cried.

"There's something familiar about you too. I'm Reena Stone."

"Reena! Reena Pavane. I am Susan Sun!"

The women embraced with expressions of disbelief.

"Gramma! You know this lady?" Julia asked, wide-eyed.

"Yes, I do! She was my best teacher when I was your age and lived at the orphanage in New Mexico."

"You lived at an orphanage?" Julia asked, amazement showing plainly on her face.

"Oh, Julia, I'm sorry you don't know everything about your gramma. It was so long ago. But I never forgot Miss Pavane," Susan said. "What on earth are you doing here?"

"I know that!" Julia piped up. "She's here to see Kiki. She knows her family in Africa!"

"Oh, my," Susan said. "Your other life. I knew so little about you back then, but I remember you were in love with Africa."

Mrs. Stone still had a hold of Mrs. Rose's hands. Hank stood close to them but had not said a word. He looked curious and amused—the way I thought my father looked when the women in his life had the stage.

"I was in love with many things, my dear Susan, and after I found them, I never looked back. And you have found a good life I see."

"Yes, I have," she said. "This is my husband, Henry Rose. I see he's still speechless. Hank, come take the hand of a woman who changed my life."

Hank put both of Reena's small hands in his large ones. "I'm pleased to meet you. You can stay a while, can't you? We have guest cabins, mostly empty this time of year, and there's Sunny's old room here in the main house."

"Sunny?"

"My mother," Julia said. "The girl who was kidnapped."

A silence fell over the room. Julia went back to tracing the map of Africa with one finger. "I thought everyone knew about *that* girl."

Reena sat down on the couch next to Julia and turned the girl's face toward her.

"I do remember reading about a child who was abducted in Nevada years ago. I recall her mother's name was Susan Rose, but I didn't imagine it was the Susan Sun I'd known at the orphanage."

Susan leaned against Hank and said, "Sunny married Thomas Sentinel, whom she's known since the year she was rescued."

"But first, she was a nun," Julia added.

Oh my gosh. Oh my gosh. Please don't let anyone say anything about Liana.

Hank said, as though trying to abate the turn in this conversation, "Sunny and Tom are coming down later for Julia's birthday dinner."

"Come help me, Reena. We can get caught up," Susan said.

But Julia grabbed Reena's hand. "No! I want her to show me where else she's been in Africa. Please?"

"Okay, Julia, but be careful what you say at dinner. There are things your mother is trying to forget."

"I know, Gramma. I just don't know what those things *are*," she said, stamping one foot on the hardwood floor.

Reena looked uncomfortable, but she let Julia lead her back to the map which was now covered with horses, cows, antelope, and the odd zebra and lion that Julia had found in a toy store. I shrugged my shoulders at Susan and followed the visitor. Hank volunteered to work on the birthday dinner.

"Have you been to the rim, what's that place called? Where Askay was born?" Julia asked.

Reena took Julia's hand and made it follow the huge, jagged edge of the crater. "The name of this place is Ngorongoro," she told her. "Askay was very brave to leave his home there and come to America. I think he was a good *mlinzi* for your family."

"I know that means 'guardian'," Julia said. "But what was he guarding?"

I glanced at Mrs. Stone with a question in my eyes. *Can I trust you?* Then I picked up a horse Julia had stationed in Dar es Salaam and galloped it through the city, over the savannah, across rivers, and up, up the outer slopes of the crater to a place on the rim that had not been marked, and said, "The Roses…from all the people who tried to hurt them, to make false claims on their love."

Mrs. Stone stroked the horse. "Stories within stories," she whispered.

Susan came back in to pull the drapes closed against the increasing cold and suggested I show Reena around the house. "Julia, come help me set the table now."

Reena and I left the map to wander through the rooms. Mrs. Stone admired the bronzes and shelf upon shelf of leather-bound volumes, the garden just out the back door, mostly frozen now, the ample greenhouse next to that, and Sunny's old room where she had agreed to stay for a few days. Then, we went to Askay's room and sat on the edge of the bed. There were a few of Helen's paintings on the wall, a stack of books I had borrowed from Father Zenwa, and new color in the curtains from threads of African silk Susan had recently sewn into them.

"Susan's right about one thing," I began. "I, too, have things that are hard to forget. The Roses have been so wonderful, but the only person I can talk to honestly is the local priest."

"Probably a good choice, since your feelings are safe with him."

Mrs. Stone reached down and took a book off of the top of the pile. *Christianity Must Change or Die.*

She looked at the title thoughtfully. "I was just sixteen when I was forced to go to Africa. I didn't want to be a missionary. As it turned out, I wasn't a very good one. I abandoned my people when they needed me the most, when the country was falling apart, when there were tribal wars—blacks against whites, villages burning, and many betrayals," Reena said.

"But didn't you love many Africans after that?"

"I did. I helped make it possible for Safina to know her father."

"Wow! That's a big thing. Have you and Dak been friends a long time?"

"I've known Dakimu since I was about sixteen. He's part of who I am."

I noticed Mrs. Stone still had on her wedding ring, but she seemed to be lost in some memory of Dak Reiman.

"Safina's father is married to her mother now," I said. "Her name is Reena too."

The visitor's face clouded over, and she turned the ring on her finger absent-mindedly. "Yes. I know Reena. She and I were good friends once."

"Aren't you still friends?"

Reena hesitated again and put her hand over the word "Christianity" on the black cover of the book she was still holding. "We have an understanding," she said. "We share some secrets and have forgiven each other for…mistakes."

I admitted my secrets were the worst ever, and she asked me to tell her one, promising that it wouldn't leave the room."

"It's in this room that a disturbing secret was kept…by my great-grandfather."

Reena put the book down and looked at me.

"Not long before he died, he read a letter that was meant for Mr. Rose. It was from the woman who kidnapped Sunny. It read, 'I will stab you when you least expect.' Askay wrote this in a journal, some of the pages of which found their way into many different hands in Africa. The point is, he didn't tell anyone. He suspected who the writer was because she had made a lot of trouble on the ranch when Hank was growing up. He thought he would take the pain, whatever it was, to spare Hank and Susan. But, of course, he couldn't. He didn't live long enough to know this woman actually abducted Sunny."

"And how do you know the letter was from the kidnapper?"

I had gone this far. All I had left was the truth.

"I went to the prison where she's been all these years, and I asked her, though I had pretty much figured it out from things people told me after I got here."

"You are very brave," Reena said.

"Or out of my mind."

"Well, we all do crazy things in this world. That's another of your secrets then? That you have been to see this woman?"

"Yes."

"Did you learn anything?"

"Not anything that would make a difference to the Roses. Everyone here just wants to forget what happened. I tried to be Liana's friend. No one would understand that."

"And I'm having a hard time."

"But there's more," I said. "I don't think you could possibly know this. My mother and Safina committed a crime. They think I don't know much about it, but I do. I found a news article my father had hidden in his tool chest, and one night, my Granpa Farley had been drinking a lot of whiskey, and he told me things that were not in the paper."

"What did they do, Kivuli?"

The winter wind banged rhythmically at the windows as if to say, "Don't tell, don't tell, don't tell." I had told no one the whole story, just small pieces to Dancing Horse, Father Azenwa, and Liana to see what it felt like. Here was this Mrs. Stone, who seemed sympathetic and would be gone in a while. No need to worry about what she knew or what she might say.

"Safina gave her lover poison, but the woman didn't die," I said in a lowered voice. "She probably would have died anyway, but my mother found her and buried her alive…well, not exactly buried her, wrapped her up in gray tape."

"Dear God!"

"And left a slit for her eyes…and for her mouth."

"Jesus! How could you know these details?" Reena asked, still with a horrified expression on her face.

"My granpa told me he hid the rat poison for Safina, and also the poison her lover had been feeding her for months, and after…the body…turned up in the burn pile, he got rid of the stuff. I wish he hadn't told me. I'm sure he was drunk."

Mrs. Stone seemed very disturbed, and rightly so. "This is the darkest secret I've ever heard. I would hardly have believed those sweet little girls I met when they were in the third grade could be capable of such a thing. But what does it have to do with the woman who kidnapped Sunny Rose?"

I got up and paced around in front of her. I had to say this just right. I was shaking. I pulled a drawer open and laid my "forgiveness warrior" t-shirt in the place I had been sitting on the bed. Reena stared at it.

"My mother and Safina are not paying for their crime. They have each other, my father, and family who love them. I imagine their priest has absolved them, but I don't know for sure. It's certainly something I've never asked. So I wanted to know what the kidnapper felt, locked away with no one who cares about her, as bad as she is. I wanted to know if forgiveness or absolution or just friendship would make any difference in the years she has left."

"What did you find out?"

"Not what I wanted to hear. Liana says she would never take the child again, but she has a reputation there for molesting young female prisoners. She says the only forgiveness that would mean anything would be Susan's, not Sunny's. She thinks forgiveness is too easy for Sunny because she's Catholic and was a nun."

"She's probably right," Reena said.

"But Sunny saved her life once. Did CPR on her in the yard when Liana was having a heart attack, but that's not like forgiving her for messing up eight years of her life. If Sunrose forgave the kidnapper, I'd know it was possible. And if *I* could be the one to make this happen, no matter how much trouble I got in or how the Roses hated me, it would be like taking the stab that my great-grandfather couldn't."

"Honey, I don't think life usually unfolds that way," Reena said, her hand smoothing the letters on my shirt.

"But listen. Tyrone, one of the wranglers who's been here forever, told me about a grave out on the ranch where a crazy woman was buried, but she had been forgiven for her crimes against the family!"

"One of those hidden stories," Reena said.

"It's what I want for Liana, and for my mother and Safina. It's a way of forgiveness, or maybe just second chances for enemies and even unruly horses, a way that all the Roses have known. Wait a minute! I know how to explain it to you. There's a painting in the barn. Can I show you before you have to leave?"

"Of course, my dear. I'll look forward to it."

Susan opened the bedroom door. "Oh, Miss Pavane, don't let Kivuli wear you out. She is full of questions."

"I don't mind. I think we shall be good friends."

Then, Susan took Reena's arm and pointed to the diamond ring on Mrs. Stone's left hand. I followed them as they started down the hall.

"Did you marry the man of your dreams? The one you always talked about?"

"Oh yes, Susan. When I left you all at La Casa de la Paz, I found that he was in New York City. He'd been there most of the years I taught at the orphanage."

"And you're still together?"

"In a way," Reena said, "but he died many years ago. He's buried in Africa, near Manyara. Julia has put a lion on the place on her map."

Susan seemed not to know what to say. She stopped in the hallway and gripped her former teacher's shoulders. "Did you have a good life?"

"We adored each other and never lost faith in our bond, no matter what we faced."

"You never fell in love again?" Susan asked.

Mrs. Stone hesitated. She twisted the ring on her finger and glanced back at me.

"There is a man I've loved as long as I loved Jim. It was a different kind of passion, one I could never allow myself. Jim was everything to me. The other man married us in Huzuni and then had his own complicated life. We are great friends still and sometimes wonder what our lives would have been like if I'd not met Jim first."

Reena looked at me once more, and then, I was sure.

"Oh, but who is he?" Susan asked

"I can't say, really," she answered.

Dakimu Reiman. Safina's father.

31

the gift

Before they got to the living room, where the voices of Thomas and Sunrose could be heard as they came in the front door, I took Mrs. Stone's arm and whispered in her ear, "Thank you for confirming that secret—a story within a story."

"I thought I owed you one," Reena said.

We didn't rush, as though wanting to share those secrets a bit longer. But soon we were surrounded by the Sentinels being introduced to Mrs. Stone. "How wonderful to meet you both," Reena said, but to Sunny she added, "Your mother was one of my best students because she was full of questions."

"Just like two other young girls I know," Sunny said, glancing at Julia and me.

Susan retreated to the kitchen where she was dishing up the meal.

Thomas hugged the visitor and said mysteriously, "The woman on the bench."

"Do I know you?" Reena asked.

"No, but when I was in Africa last, my friend Dakimu told me about a white woman who met his leopard by the creek at Shanga and whenever he sat there he dreamed about that woman. When Susan said you've known Dak for a long time, I thought that woman might be you."

I had a hard time not gasping, but Reena was very cool.

"Yes. That was many years ago."

"He had not forgotten it," Tom said.

"Well, I'm glad of that. He's very dear to me."

That image swept into my head—Dakimu and Mrs. Stone and Chui together, watching the clear stream that wound through the *vibanda*, a lost painting from another world.

"Show me the creek," Julia pleaded, grabbing his hand and drawing him to the map. "Does it go through a village?"

Thomas picked up a porcelain leopard and set him on the bank of the stream that ran through Shanga. "Someday I'll take you there, Julia," he promised.

I thought it was odd he didn't say "we," meaning "your mother and I."

"Dinner's on the table now, everyone. Let's sit down," Susan said. She was carrying the last platter of fried chicken.

I sat by Mrs. Stone, and Julia scrambled to her other side.

"Jim and I never had children. I feel very blessed by these two girls," she said. "Questions or not."

"Speaking of blessing, perhaps we should have one," Hank said.

"I can't do it. I'm not Catholic," Julia said.

"Oh, she doesn't know what she is," her mother noted.

"I'll say it," I offered, "with the words my great-grandfather often wrote at the end of his diary notes."

After everyone's heads were bowed, I pronounced the words very slowly, "*Kyrie…eleison…Christe…eleison.*"

"Good enough," Thomas said, and reached for the hot fry bread.

I raised my head and thought about the unquenchable ties between Africans and Americans. I thought Thomas had loved Safina, and, of course, the Roses had loved Askay; Julia perhaps loved me a little, and their guest, Mrs. Stone, had surely loved Dakimu. *I didn't bring Africa to America. Africa was already here.*

"Daddy, can you help more with our map project?" Julia asked. "You've been lots of places in Africa. We need to write descriptions, and they can't be out of a book."

"I'd love to help you girls. Have you marked Dodoma yet? It's the capital of Tanzania," Thomas said.

"No! You've been there?" his daughter asked.

"I certainly have," he said. "It's where I missed your mother so much I had to fly back to the States and talk her into marrying me!"

"Oh, that's a perfect story!" Julia cried.

"You may *not* have all the details, Julia," her mother said.

If there had been hidden tension, it was now gone. We ate in silence mostly, commenting now and then on Susan's incomparable fried chicken. I dropped True Passion a few pieces and took extra Indian fry bread for myself. Hank got up once to put some wood on the fire as the wind picked up outside and the chandelier lights flickered. Pass jumped up on the couch, his tail sending a few of Julia's animals flying off the map where it lay spread out on the coffee table.

"Grandpa, do you think someday I could have a leopard like Kivuli has," Julia suddenly burst out.

"I do not," Hank said. "This is not Africa. A leopard would last about a week here."

"Well, it would be the best week he ever had!" Julia shot back. "And it would be the best birthday present too."

In all the commotion of company, the rising storm, and Julia's map, we seemed to have cast her big day aside. Susan told her to be patient and winked at Hank. Sunrose smiled. I thought another secret was about to be revealed.

Soon we were eating chocolate birthday cake and Julia was opening a few presents. Mrs. Stone removed a beaded bracelet from her arm and handed it to her. Then Hank slipped a handwritten note under her last gift—a book about training horses by GaWaNi Pony Boy from Henry Dancing Horse. Julia looked at all the color pictures on every page before picking up the envelope beneath the book. She opened it slowly.

"Read it out loud," Hank suggested.

" 'Tim Long and Stuart Martin invite True Passion over to play with our shepherd, Out for a Lark. Miss Julia Sentinel will get the pick of the litter for her seventh birthday!' " She shrieked. "A puppy! I get a puppy?"

Everyone cheered, and Pass made a few soft woofs in response to our enthusiasm. Little did he know.

Reena spent Christmas and New Year's with us. It snowed a foot, and she taught me how to cross-country ski. I thought it was the best thing next to riding my horse. We got as far as the Cliffs one day, and I told Mrs. Stone about the plane crash, the heartbreaking way Hank's dad had lost his parents.

"That must have been doubly hard on Hank never to know his grandparents and then to lose his daughter," she said.

"And then, Hank's parents were killed in a lightning storm just before Sunny was born."

"Oh, how grim!"

"Is there something that's been doubly hard on you?"

She didn't hesitate a second. "Losing my husband and then, saying goodbye to Dakimu."

I edged my skis sideways down a steep incline and tried not to fall at the bottom. "I don't think I've ever had *two* sad things at once," I said.

"You're a lucky girl," Reena said, and we skied on.

The white desert glistened under a weak sun. All the beautiful wildflowers were gone, and the cactus blossoms had turned in upon themselves. Hawks still circled for unwary jack rabbits, and three or four ravens called to birds or coyotes in the vicinity, identifying a dead deer.

"I've looked at that watercolor in the barn," Reena said, when we stopped to sip from our water bottles. "I saw it was painted by Helen Rose."

"Askay came to America to help Helen and Henry, but he couldn't catch that plane falling out of the sky."

"But he was there for the next generation, and the next," Reena said.

We turned around at the base of the Cliffs.

"I just want to fix Askay's mistake," I admitted, as we glided off toward the ranch.

I waited for her to discourage me, but she didn't.

"When we get back, I'd like to hear what you think of the painting," was all she said.

We had five miles to go. When we could find snowmobile tracks, the going got better, but we didn't see any machines. The silence hovered around us. Our cheeks filled with tears, but whether that was from the brisk air we created skiing through the twilight or from the moments of sadness we had experienced in our separate, other-world journeys, neither of us would say.

Liana would never have a friend like Mrs. Stone. Reena would never be with either man she loved. Maybe there was a small chance with one of them, but the odds were against it. Hank and Susan would never have their little girl back, not the one they had lost anyway. But all the good outcomes were still open for me. I understood the desire to give credit to something bigger than myself. That I should be out here in this stark and glorious landscape with a woman who had met Suzanna and Safina as children seemed beyond miraculous to me.

The steep roof of the barn appeared in a cloak of falling snow, still a mile away. Reena and I slipped our yellow goggles on to capture the last of the light and pushed on in silence. The skis made rhythmic whispers along the grooved track to the safe haven ahead, a scene for Helen's brush. No one met us; no animals responded to our approach. We could have been the only two people in the world.

We stepped out of our bindings and clomped around inside the barn in our stiff ski-boots. Finally, warming our hands on cups of hot chocolate a wrangler had made for us, we stood together before the painting. For me, it had new life every time I studied it.

"I see one thing," I said. "Forgiveness. The colt has been bad. Look, there are broken railings. The cowboys are mad. They have whips and spurs and are going to teach him a lesson he'll never forget. But wait! Here is an offering, a hand with a carrot or sweet grass— it's not clear. 'Just give a tiny bit, horse. Just reach out for me, and I'll save you. I'll forgive you. I'll give you another chance.'"

"Who's doing the saving?" Reena asked.

"That's the great thing! Helen Rose painted her own arm in the picture. She was showing the horse and the boys on the rail a different way, a better way. It could be forgiveness…it could be trust…it could be love," I said. I put my hand on the bronc's rough-looking coat. "But what my mother needs is forgiveness. What Liana needs is forgiveness."

"But, Kivuli, you can only offer that arm when the naughty colt has hurt *you*. If *you* aren't threatened by the colt, your forgiveness or love or friendship or whatever you intend to give doesn't mean as much."

"I know. I'm glad you see it that way. It seems that each person who gets farther away from the painting understands it less and less. Some people don't see the arm through the rails."

"Who do you think understands it?"

"I wish I knew. Sunny won't have one of Helen's paintings in her house and for sure hasn't held out her hand to her kidnapper."

"What about the CPR?"

"That was a good deed. I don't think it's the same as forgiveness. The painting is faded and cracked, the colors blurred, the meaning dying with the people who once knew what it meant. Askay wrote about the 'way' with horses, and that page was given to my mother. She told me she only knew her stepfather's way with horses, and she was too old to learn a new way. Granpa Farley always rode with spurs and a long whip. But to his credit he always said to me, 'I'm going to show you ten ways to praise for every one way to punish'."

Reena sat down on a bench close by and rubbed her sore ankles. I stayed by the painting, lost in thought.

"What could you do with that painting now?"

"I could show it to Liana and ask her if she still needs that arm with the sweet grass to be Sunny's. Of course, she's seen the painting before, but she sold it before it taught her any lessons," I answered. "As far as I know."

"You are a determined girl," Reena said. "Whatever your mother did wrong, she surely did right raising you."

Sunrose had said something like that to me, but Sunrose didn't know I'd been to see Liana.

"Dancing Horse thinks I'm a trouble-maker. I respect him so much. He's like having my father in my ear. He says Indians forget and move on, and that's a way of forgiving, and maybe he's right. But I want to go home and hold out my hand to my mother and Safina, unless I can find someone better who is willing to do it."

"Who might that be?"

"Someone who loved the dead Mvua. She was someone's child!"

"Kivuli, this is upsetting you. Let's go back to the house," Reena suggested.

"It's funny, Mrs. Stone. I wasn't upset until I figured out the painting and realized how difficult it was going to be for the people I love in Africa, and now in America, to grasp its true meaning."

"I think the long-dead Helen Rose and your great-grandfather Askay are still speaking to you, and that is a beautiful thing. I'm not so sure about you visiting Liana in that prison. What if *you* had been kidnapped and molested by that woman?"

I sat down on the bench next to her. All this time, I had never put myself in Sunny's place.

"I don't know. One time Liana would tell me she adored girls and flirt with me, and the next minute say she'd never touch a child again. Sometimes I think she was trying to scare me away, but I kept coming back to see if there was a part of her that just wanted a friend, someone to talk to, someone that would see her beyond her crime."

"Do you think you might make things worse?"

"There's always that chance. If I was sure about God, I'd ask him what to do, but you showed up first."

"I would not presume to speak for God."

"Neither would Dancing Horse or Father Zenwa," Kivuli said, "and they are a lot closer to God than I am."

We wrapped up in our warm powder pants and down jackets, and left our skis propped up outside against the front of the barn so they would maintain the cold temperature and skim more easily across the snow the next time. Back at the ranch house, Susan had made spicy chili and corn soufflé, not unlike my mother's corn pudding, and I ate two helpings.

After dinner Hank relaxed in his father's easy chair and oiled a pair of boots. The two women and I sat close together on the couch and paged through photograph albums. We found a black and white shot of Susan and Reena on the porch of the orphanage in New Mexico, another of Hank's first Paraíso, one from Dancing Horse's wedding, and several of family birthdays and trail rides. No one said anything about the absence of pictures from Sunny's lost eight years.

"I'll be leaving tomorrow," Mrs. Stone told them. "I have some work in New York I need to get back to."

"Oh, I have cousins in New York," Susan said. "I might go there someday. We could meet up again."

"I'd love that!"

"I hate goodbyes," I said.

"It's very hard," Reena agreed. "The hardest times for me have been when I had to leave Africa. It feels like that now, Kivuli, having to say goodbye to you. I hope it won't be goodbye forever. But I'm going quite early in the morning. Let me hug you now."

As they held onto each other for a long moment, Reena whispered in Kivuli's ear, "I will keep your secrets safe."

"And I yours, Mrs. Stone."

Then Reena and Susan went into the kitchen for their own final conversation.

"You two got along great," Hank said, when they were alone.

"She loves the same people I do," I said. "She met my mother when Suzanna was nine years old, and has known Safina's father, for—oh my gosh—fifty-some years! I hope I can know Trace that long or—"

"Or who?"

"Oh, never mind. I need to ask you something...unrelated."

"Anything," he said.

"I'd like to borrow the painting that's in the barn."

"Helen's painting?"

"Yes. There's someone I want to show it to. I'll take good care of it."

"Sure. It's had a life of its own. One more person can't hurt," he said. "Are you taking it to school? To art class?"

I thought this was a terrific idea so I said yes. There might be more eyes than Liana's that could benefit from the art of Helen Rose. But I would not take the painting off the tack room door until I knew exactly what I was going to do with it. Who could know what might have happened in the round pen of the painting? Maybe the bronc snatched the gift and kicked another board out. Maybe a cowboy jumped down and beat the horse. There was no guarantee in this world that the gifts of love and forgiveness would make any difference, but I was not going to rest until I found out for myself. The hand through the railing was something to believe in, as powerful as a sea glass rosary, as necessary as breathing.

32

eres un fantasma
January, 2014

A chinook wind came up the day school resumed after the holidays and almost obliterated the snow. I caught up with Manny after Honors English and asked him if he wanted to bring his grandpapa over soon.

"He's afraid to go out. I'm sorry, Kivuli. He thinks we want to take him to a rest home or a hospital to die. Some days he forgets who I am. He'll say, 'Where's Manny? Where's my little boy?' and when I come near him, he says, 'No, no, my *little* Manny.' It's no use. He might scare you, or you might scare him."

"I could come over with a gift, like my coffee beans from Africa. Maybe hearing the word 'Africa' might remind him of Askay, and the conversation could begin," I suggested.

"Okay. That sounds like a good idea. I'll ask my mom. She has a gentle way with him."

The meeting was arranged for the following weekend. It couldn't come fast enough for me. Tyrone helped me with the Spanish I might have to use to communicate with the grandpapa, but I was worried the old man wouldn't understand me. And then, the temperature plummeted and a storm threatened, but I promised Manny I was coming.

That week, the heating system failed at school, and we all had to huddle in our down garments. My fingers froze trying to write an essay for Mr. Seavey, and Mr. Glen cancelled debate practice, "until further notice," he wrote in a shaky hand on the board, even though we had state championships at the end of the month. He had seemed depressed since the first of the year, but when I passed him going out the door, he gave me an upbeat smile.

On Saturday, Trace and I drove to the Ramirez home on the other side of Ochala Junction. Manny met us in the driveway and asked Trace to go around to the back door and wait in the kitchen so his grandpapa wouldn't be overwhelmed or confused by more than one stranger. Manny took me through the front door. I carried a sack of coffee beans and a few pages from Askay's journal that Hank said the old man could have.

Hernando was slumped in a wheelchair next to a cluttered table that held a glass of water, a vase of hot house roses, and a few books.

"He just looks at the pictures," Manny explained. "Sometimes I translate the words into Spanish."

I stood in front of Hernando, but he didn't look up. Manny brought a chair over so I could sit facing his grandpapa.

"Abuelito, aquí está la niña de quien te platiqué, la niña de África. Es la bisnieta de Askay. Se llama Kivuli." Manuel told him that here was the girl from Africa, Askay's great-granddaughter, and that her name was Kivuli.

"¡Véte! Eres un fantasma," the grandpapa said in a frightened voice.

I glanced at Manuel.

"He thinks you are a ghost."

"No un fantasma, Hernando," I said softly. *"Soy real."*

Hernando put one hand over his eyes and raised his head.

"Tengo algo para usted de mi bisabuelo. Son unas palabras de Askay." I told him I had something for him from my great-grandfather and held up the thin pages to show him the words.

"¡No, No! Es imposible," the grandpapa cried, still holding his hands over his eyes.

"Shall I read them to you?" I asked him and then looked at Manny for the Spanish. He whispered in my ear, but I spoke the words. *"¿Se los leo?"*

Hernando shook his head but dropped his hand to his lap. The light was dim in the room, but I saw him change when he looked into my eyes.

"¿Qué ves, Hernando? Acércate." I asked him to come closer.

The old man bent over and searched my face, my eyes. At first, he said nothing. Then he said, *"Veo una niña bonita blanca. Viniste a llevarme."*

"He thinks you are a very pretty white girl but that you came to take him away," Manny explained.

"No, Hernando, soy una niña negrita de Africa. Mírame otra vez," I said, telling him I was a black girl and he should look again.

"Veo ojos oscuros."

"He sees your dark eyes," Manny whispered.

"Si."

"Veo ojos que acuerdo," Hernando said. I was sure he said, "I see eyes I remember."

"Si," she responded.

"Déjala leer las palabras de Askay, Abuelito." Manny asked him to let me read Askay's words.

But I was insecure translating them exactly and wanted Hernando to know their meaning.

"Manny, could you read them? The Spanish is harder on this."

He took the page from my hand. The English was broken. He tried to make the translation smooth and clear.

"Hernando...amigo mio...no nos entendemos nuestras palabras pero conocemos nuestros pensamietos...nuestros corazones...mientras que florescan rosas...estaremos juntos...seremos amigos."

The old man reached for the paper and held it up where he could see Askay's handwritten English words:

Hernando my friend we do not understand each other's words but we know each other's thoughts each other's hearts as long as roses bloom we be together we be friends

"Te llevaré a ver las rosas en la primavera, cuando estén en flor las rosas otra vez, ¿está bien?" Manny promised to take his grandpapa to see the roses in the spring.

"¡Sí! ¡Sí! Las rosas. Iré a ver las rosas, y Askay estará allí." I'll see the roses, and Askay will be there.

Then Hernando slipped a marker out of one of the books on the table and gave it to me.

"Esto es para ti, bisnieta. ¿Qué ves?" Hernando asked. This is for you, great-granddaughter. What do you see?

I took the slick, worn photo from his hand. It was a picture of my great-grandfather and Hernando, side by side at the fair, holding up a blue ribbon and I looked at last, almost not believing it, into Askay's eyes.

"¿Qué ves, niña?" the old man repeated. What do you see?

I stared for a long moment at the photo, the curve of Askay's face, the strong, lean body, his gardener's hands that had briefly touched his own children, the dark, unfathomable eyes.

"Me veo," I said. "I see me."

On the way out to the car Manny said, "This means a lot to me, Kivuli. Grandpapa needed something to live for. Now he has spring and the roses."

"This is the only photo of Askay that we know of. Hank and Susan haven't been able to find any in their albums or in any of the things

Askay left behind. Now his African family can look into his eyes. We'll always be grateful to your grandpapa, to Hernando Ramirez."

"You did great with your Spanish," he said.

"Yeah? Tell Señora Alvear. I need all the extra credit I can get!"

As we turned out onto the main road, Trace said, "I'm so happy you got that photograph. It shows another side of your great-grandfather."

"It helps me know him in a way I never thought I would."

"He's in you. I know it. I'm thinking way in the future, but I would be so happy our children would be Askay's great-great-grandchildren," Trace said.

"You are a dreamer! I can't think that far ahead. Let's make a deal. Let's promise to meet again when I'm twenty."

"Can we kiss on it?"

"You are *imposible!*"

Trace left me at the house as snow began to fall. Inside a note on the kitchen table said Hank and Susan were in the barn blanketing horses as Ty was off that night. I changed into warmer clothes and walked up to help them. I glanced at the painting on the tack room door and went in and retrieved the blankets for Lazo and Dancing Horse's pinto. Hank had just finished the last two wild horses who had been brought in because they hadn't grown an adequate winter coat. Susan was topping off the insulated water buckets.

Then, we sat on some hay bales, and I showed them my picture of Askay and told them everything Hernando had said.

"It would seem that photo made your whole trip worthwhile," Hank said.

"It's an incredible gift to look into Askay's eyes…but what I want most of all is to *be* Askay, just once for you, before I go."

"What does *that* mean?" Susan asked.

I hadn't expected such a wary reaction and knew I had backed myself into a corner. Hiding the truth was getting harder than telling it, so I let it come out. "I know I'm just a kid, but I think my great-grandfather has only me to speak for him, and I know something that might…help you. If it doesn't help you, it will give you more truth to rely on."

Susan frowned. "Sometimes the truth is too much to bear…and Askay has been dead for twenty-five years. What could you know that we don't know?"

"I can't tell you, but Askay can," I said.

I dug into my coat pocket and brought out the page from Askay's journal that I had purposely kept close in case I ever had this chance. The paper was wrinkled and smudged from being crumpled in my jackets and jeans, but the words were still clear and devastating. I handed the note to Hank, and Susan read over his shoulder.

mad woman exists i know this hank not know how to tell him i open letter by mistake writing was poor it say 'Hank, I will stab you when you least expect' i only know what word stab means it means make pain why? why woman do this? i tell world now if woman comes i will stop i will take stab for hank he never have to know god help me

"This is not possible," Hank said.

"I didn't want to believe it either," I said. "I ask your forgiveness for my great-grandfather, who could not tell you."

Susan stared at me. "Do you know what this means?"

"Yes. I think Liana tried to warn you. She thought you knew she was coming, when you'd least expect, and would be prepared, be watchful."

"How do you even know that name?" Susan's breath seemed to be coming in short gasps.

"Mr. Rose told me her name because I asked. He didn't want to. But I found her myself," I said. "I'm so sorry."

"What do you mean you *found* her?" Hank asked.

I wanted to tell them everything, but I felt myself falling into a deep hole from which I could never climb out. I thought the truth would free them somehow, make them understand what happened in a new way. I looked at them with my last bit of confidence.

"I went to the prison to ask her something about my own family, but I got caught up in the story about Sunny. She wouldn't leave me alone about it. No matter what I asked her, she always came back to Sunny. She said she wouldn't…take her again, but I know that doesn't matter to you now. I wish I didn't know it. But not telling you what I'd done felt like lying, and I couldn't do it anymore."

Hank looked at me with what seemed like a sudden understanding. "You're taking Helen's painting to *her*."

"I thought about it. You told me she'd stolen it from you years ago and sold it. I wanted her to see it again, see it with her whole heart, and then I was going to tell you what she said."

"Oh, my God. Why would we want to hear anything that woman had to say?" Susan asked, anger flashing in her eyes, but then she softened, as if she realized I must be so naïve I couldn't know what I was doing.

Hank just shook his head and then got up and took the painting off the wall and rested it against some bales of hay where it startled the fading light in the barn, and they could all see it clearly. "Tell us the real reason you did this foolish thing," he said.

I knew this was the most dangerous time for all of us, that my more-than-foolish idea had come from wanting to know if my mother and Safina could be forgiven for the things they had done. I couldn't plan the words in that brief space of time. I had to hope whatever came out of my mouth would be enough.

"My mother allowed someone to die. She's never been caught or punished. She doesn't seem one bit sorry. She is like the unruly bronc, full of herself and unremorseful. Who will feel the death of that person and hold out a hand? Who will forgive her?"

"You want us to *forgive* Liana?" Susan asked, with an incredulous look on her face.

I hesitated. "Maybe just not hate her so much. Maybe give her a chance to be sorry, do something to redeem herself."

"Oh, girl, you are way out of line," Hank said.

"Well…maybe not *you* give her a chance, maybe Sunrose," I said, trying to deflect the whole concept of forgiving the monster from the two of them.

"You have no idea what that woman did!" Susan cried.

I pointed to the watercolor in front of them. "No one knows what the horse did either. Maybe he wounded someone. Maybe he killed someone. But there is that hand reaching through the rail. I want it to mean something. I want to experience it in my life, but it seems to have gotten tangled up in your lives, maybe only because we're tied by Askay's mistake."

Then, no one spoke. The only sound was that of the horses pushing their hay flakes around in their stalls and a steady wind against the side of the barn. A wrangler came in and checked all the stall bedding and re-buckled a couple of horse blankets. He left by the side door, and a knife-edge of winter slipped in.

"I do know some of what Liana did," I said. "She told me in remorseless detail. She tried to shock me…but I am kind of beyond shocked by the things people do. Mostly I just wanted to understand it."

"And did you? Understand it? If you did, you're smarter than any of the rest of us," Susan said.

"No, I don't understand it. I don't understand my own mother, but something is missing in her life. That hand with the gift. I want to feel what that's like, holding out that hand." I had tried to explain this to Hank once before. Now I said it again for Susan.

But Hank's eyes took on a wounded expression. "Did she tell you I once said I'd never forgive her?"

"No."

"Did she tell you how she starved my child? Made her do unspeakable things?"

"No."

"Did she tell you how they lived in motels and run-down trailers, how she threw all of Sunny's books out the car window because our daughter asked an innocent question?"

Susan gripped her husband's arm.

"Henry, stop," she said. "I think we should let Kivuli do what she wants. There's more to this now than just our feelings. Take the painting, Kivuli. Maybe you'll have your eyes opened at last."

"I'll bring it right back, I promise."

The worst seemed to have been said. The watercolor was almost blurred beyond recognition in the dim light.

"How do you get to the prison?" Susan asked.

"Trace takes me, but he doesn't know everything."

"But how did you get to see Liana?" Hank pressed.

"I lied."

Hank waved his hand at her as if not wanting her to divulge how she'd lied.

"Was she mean to you?" he asked.

"Sometimes. She's a wreck."

"Good," Susan said. "A taste of the wrecking she did."

"I'm so sorry," I said. "I won't go again."

"No," Susan said. "You go see her, but don't tell Sunny. It might be more than she can handle right now."

Mrs. Rose squeezed her husband's shoulder and went out into the frigid air. Hank hung the painting back on the tack room door and turned back to me. He didn't seem angry. He seemed resigned.

"Just tell us when you go, all right?" Hank said.

"I will," I said. But I felt, in that moment, as if I had cancelled out all the good I had done in the Roses' life.

"Are you mad at me?" I asked Hank before he could quite get out the door.

He turned back. "I should be," he said, "but you're not to blame for this situation." He hesitated as though not knowing how to finish the conversation, but finally said, "Just be careful, Kivuli. Don't get yourself in over your head. Come on. I'll walk you down to the house. That's a dangerous storm brewing out there."

As we made our way past the guest cabins, empty now, and the snow whipped against us like spray from ocean waves, something felt wrong. I grabbed Hank's arm and tried to make myself heard over the wind. "Hank! Where's Pass?"

He had to shout an answer. "I took him over to Tim's earlier!"

The relief I felt extended to bearing Hank's and Susan's disappointment in my unwise and selfish agenda.

33

champion

I sat on the school bus and stared at my topic for the state debate finals: "Church versus State." *Oh, god. How appropriate.* Not only did the whole idea of religion bewilder me, but I was distressingly cold. The new year chinook had been wiped out by a blast of arctic air—a bitter blizzard from Canada. As I shivered I made a mental note never to visit that country.

While waiting for Trace, I dreamed of the tropical winters of East Africa: wading in the warm, shallow tide pools of the Indian Ocean, and riding in a tank top over the sun-bathed hills behind the military post in Dar es Salaam. My minus-thirty-degree down parka was no comfort, and my hands shook as I opened a text on the problems associated with religion and the U.S. Constitution. Half the team hadn't shown up yet so I couldn't compare notes with anyone.

Finally, Trace arrived and took a seat beside me. I immediately told him I didn't understand my debate assignment because Tanzania's Constitution was so different. Trace offered to trade his assigned "Refugees or Terrorists," but I didn't think Mr. Glen would let us.

"How can I argue you should separate God from public institutions when I always thought this country was founded on some sort of religious freedom?"

"But separation of church and state has nothing to do with religious freedom," he said.

"See? Totally confusing," I said.

The driver started the bus, and the heater came on. I noticed Marci and Manuel sitting together a few rows in front of us. Marci had told me earlier she and Manny were preparing the same side in the debate on legalizing marijuana for recreational use. I knew much less about that. I only knew some of the medicinal uses of the substance from hanging around Safina.

"Anyway, I don't think I've been here long enough to take a side in Church vs. State."

Trace began to write down his ideas supporting the world's refugees, and I closed my eyes. During the ride on the winding, ice-heaved road, I saw clearly my path through the mire of American politics or rather what side was missing in the word "versus."

I listened to my teammates for two days and began to feel completely out of my element. Trace and Manny and Marci seemed so polished and sure of themselves. I made notes on the U.S. Constitution, but didn't understand how it worked in day to day life, especially for citizens who were welded to their faith and wanted their god in schools and public buildings and everywhere. I only knew how things worked in my own country.

So on the last day, over the noise of a restless and tired crowd, I spoke from my own experience:

"I was born in Dar es Salaam, Tanzania. My mother is a white Catholic, my father a Maasai pagan. There is no religious conflict between them. One's beliefs don't make the laws for the other's. In our country, the name of no god appears on our coins or in pledges to our flag, but our churches and mosques and synagogues are full. In school, when it is time to pray, the Muslims are excused to their prayer mats in the hall; Catholics may say their rosaries in every class, and Jews can have their food prepared according to their religious traditions. This courtesy is extended to tourists and missionaries, atheists and priests.

"What's important is why this unusual tolerance works. Many, many tribes in our history, especially after bitter conflicts, were encouraged and sometimes ordered to send their children to distant places to be raised by strangers with ethnicities and faiths often very different from what they would have had at home. And so, tolerance was born among them. Here, in America, it seems many people are afraid to see the Ten Commandments carved into the front of a public building because it might offend a non-Christian. The Christians are afraid if the words are removed, atheists will take over the country.

"It's not about church *versus* state. It's about giving individuals a choice for each one's religious and civil life and not making one rule for all. *One nation, under God*—a fine concept, but think: there is more than one nation here. There is the Lakota Sioux Nation. There's a Catholic Nation and a Socialist Nation. There's a Tea Party Nation and a Mine Worker's Nation, a Horse Nation and a Ponderosa Pine Nation. A nation of whales and a nation of plankton, a nation of monarchs and a nation of the homeless. Nations of soldiers and adopted children, gays and teachers and prisoners, a nation of addicts, a nation of healers. They can only kneel where their hearts are blessed.

"The state separated from the church makes no sense. They should not be adversaries but give equal value to all who come under their influence. If a Maasai can walk in the shoes of an Anglican colonizer, a fundamental Catholic walk in the shoes of a gay person, a law-abiding citizen walk in the shoes of the felon, nations embrace other nations, the world will only get better. Arguments will become meaningless. Church versus state will not be necessary."

There was a brief moment when no one reacted. I knew I had missed the point of the topic, but once I started, my notes seemed meaningless. I had wanted to please Mr. Glen and was so afraid I had failed him. But suddenly, everyone was standing. There were whistles and cheers. There was applause, and later the first place trophy for

Ochala Junction High. Garrett Glen held my hand through the entire awards ceremony. He was through with rules, it seemed. When it was over, he let me go but said, "Thank you, Kivuli. Just…thank you."

On the way home, Trace hugged me. "So now I'm going to have to get in line for you?"

"Don't be silly. I did say Lakota Sioux nation first!"

"And I say the Maasai nation took the day."

I didn't know if I could ever explain to anyone in Africa what those words meant to me.

34

second chances

Winter daylight lengthened, but the cold would not let us go. I began to dread going out to blanket my five horses that now were eight. Sunrose offered to remove blankets, if needed, in the mornings, saying she enjoyed that quiet time in the barn and that Thomas would get Julia ready for school. I wondered how Julia felt about that, but she was so excited about the coming puppies, she hardly cared about anything else.

One morning, before Julia and I left for the Crossroads, Sunny came down from the barn and wanted to know who had taken Helen's painting off the tack room door.

"Kivuli needs it for art class," Hank told her.

I sat right there in the kitchen with the watercolor in my backpack under the table. "We're supposed to bring a painting that's changed people's lives, if possible," I said.

"Do you know enough about this painting?" Sunrose asked.

"I've heard things from Dancing Horse and Tyrone mostly," I said, not to put Hank in a bad light for telling too much of Sunny's story.

"It's ancient history anyway," she said.

Hank glanced at me with a kind of warning in his eyes, but I swallowed my good sense and replied, "Sometimes ancient history holds a lesson for today."

Sunrose gave me an odd look but didn't question me any further and went out to the truck with a warm jacket for Julia that the girl had left at the Roses' house. I shouldered my backpack, but before I left, I told Hank in a shaky voice that Trace and I were going to the prison that day after school.

"Thank you for telling me," he said.

To make the lie about art class palatable, when I got there later, I showed Miss Collins the watercolor before class started. She studied it thoughtfully and held it up to the window for more light.

"I know this work," Faith said. "Not this particular painting but paintings of Helen Rose. Did you know there were some of hers in the County Library?"

"No. Mr. Rose didn't tell me about those. Are they ranch scenes?"

"Why no. I believe they are impressions from her time in Africa as a young woman."

I was startled. *Things she painted in Africa? The places she'd been and the people she'd met…seventy-five years ago!*

"Maybe the Roses don't know about them," I said, when I found my voice. "They would mean a lot to me."

"I'll take you to see them, maybe on a Saturday, all right?" Miss Collins offered.

"Yes. Thank you so much!"

When I got into the car with Trace after school, I was full of mixed emotions. The highway stretched dark and wet in front of us, and Trace decelerated on every curve. I traced the frame of the painting nervously with my fingers. I barely looked out the window.

"I found out something interesting about Helen Rose today," I told Trace.

"What's that?"

"Some of her watercolors are in the County Library. Maybe some she painted in Africa on the trip where she and Henry found Askay."

"Wow. That's cool."

"I have to go see them, of course. But right now I have to see if *this* painting can speak to a bronc wilder than the one Helen painted,"

I said.

At the prison, I walked up to the door with one hand in Trace's and the other clutching the painting as if it were alive. "I owe you," I said.

"I'll take a night in the hay loft."

"You wish!"

Inside the visitor's room, the security guard stopped me before I could sit down. The woman at the front desk had buzzed me in out of habit.

"What's that?" he asked.

"Just a painting. There isn't a backing, no place to hide anything."

The guard took it and turned it over and over, poking at the worn spots.

"I guess it's okay," he finally said.

I leaned the painting against one leg of the table where Liana wouldn't see it immediately. I sat on the hard chair. The prisoner was brought to the room in chains. She wore no make-up, and her hair looked like it had not been washed for a week. She shuffled to her place across from me.

"Hey, Africa, where you been?"

"Busy with family stuff. What'd you do, anyway?" I asked, indicating the chains.

"Kissed a girl…but I swear she wanted it!" Liana said. She raised her voice a notch. "You can't do nothin' fun in this place. Besides, they transferred my bunk mate for her final trimester, and she was the best in a long line of—"

I looked into Liana's clouded eyes. "I don't know why I bother."

"You like to see me suffer?"

"No, that's not it."

I picked up the picture and set it on the table between us.

"God…that old thing. Why'd they keep that? It's ruined," Liana said, as she leaned over it and narrowed her eyes. "I thought that horse treat would be rubbed out by now. Doesn't much work anyway, with the bad ones."

"You'd be surprised," I said.

"What'm I supposed to think, Africa?"

I didn't answer right away. It seemed as if the two of us were not speaking the same language.

"I just wondered, if someone held a gift out for you…like forgiveness, say…you'd give up the bad behavior, do something worthwhile with your life."

"It's too late for me. I told you once before."

"If I believed that, I wouldn't be here."

Liana stared at me and then tried to touch the painting with her shackled hands. "Are you sure you aren't the reincarnation of someone else? Like Serena Rose?"

"I wouldn't mind," I said. "She knew things none of us will ever know."

"She was a tough one. Didn't like me much. I was not right for her precious boy. I sure as hell wasn't right for Hank's daughter, now, was I? But Serena died. She was spared the freaky bronc that I was."

"Just tell me if you'd take the offering."

She glanced at the picture. She seemed a little afraid of it suddenly. "The sweet grass? The sugar cube?" she asked.

"Yes. Whatever was offered in good faith."

Liana took her time answering. She fiddled with the cuffs and stared at the wall above my head before looking back at me. "There was a time I would've said no, but I'm not sure now. You came half way around the world and ended up in front of me, your worst nightmare—Sunny's worst nightmare, for sure. I guess I'm in that painting now, and I'm damn sure I don't want whips and spurs!"

I pressed on. "If you couldn't have Sunny's forgiveness, or the Roses', what would you want?"

"Something I could ask forgiveness of and it wouldn't run away," she responded quickly.

Liana had made my decision for me. *But a puppy? Or True Passion himself?*

"Your wheels are spinnin', Africa."

I sighed. "I have four months left. I'll find something or someone that won't run away,"

"You know what, Africa? I hope you do. I'm getting tired. But I can't sleep. Sometimes after you leave, I get a little nap, but I seem to be always waitin' for something, but I don't think it's forgiveness."

Liana's head fell forward, but she jerked it back up.

"Sorry, Africa, I'm no good to you today. I'm real glad you brought the picture though. I kinda wish it could've done what Julian and Serena intended when they wanted me to study it an' hang it in my cabin at the ranch," she said. "I couldn't see past wantin' their boy. Then I couldn't see past wantin' Hank's baby girl. I was an unmanageable bronc. I sometimes think I'd like to start over. Maybe they'll release me into your custody and cuff me to you all the way back to Africa. Wouldn't that be somethin'? I'd show 'em perfect behavior for a chance like that."

I almost had to smile at that image. Had the woman ever managed "perfect behavior" at any point in her life?

"I think it's too late for your perfect behavior in Hank's life," I began, but Liana cut me off.

"He was crazy about me!"

"He was a *kid*, younger than I am now! What were you thinking?"

"I can't explain it, Africa. All I know is after Hank, I didn't like anybody…until Sunny," she said. "Now I can tell you—male, female,

I don't care. I just like messing with people. But I only got one choice in here."

"Is it the choice of these women?"

"Mostly," she said. "If not, they come around."

I started to wrap the painting back up, holding my tears and anger inside. "You're just a twisted bronc, lashing out at the world, at the rails that hold you in. You don't want the gift of sweet grass or a saving hand. You are beyond help."

"Now, wait a minute, Africa," she said, reviving a little. "Do you think that horse noticed that hand? Do you think he grabbed the treat the very first time? Maybe you should study that picture a bit more."

I picked up the splintered frame and studied every corner of the faded watercolor. And then, I gasped out loud. In the bottom right-hand corner there was something sketched in, something near the railing, behind the conciliatory arm: a few brush strokes of gold and green that could have been the surface outside the arena, but it wasn't. It was shaped like a pile on top of the ground. Beneath the thumb prints and the aging grays and browns of round pen landscape was the unmistakable suggestion of more of whatever was in Helen's hand.

"You see somethin', kid?"

"I see that you are right," I said. "A second chance for the crazy colt is not all there is."

Liana nodded as if she'd known that all along.

"What're you going to do, Africa?"

"I'm going to bring you something a lot better than this wrecked painting."

"Is it a surprise?"

"Yes. A very big surprise. It's going to amaze you. Just be as good as you can until then, okay?"

"Okay," she said.

The guard stood over us. Liana gave me a weak smile.

"You know what, Africa? I might take a piece of fresh hay. Whether it would mend my ways, well, that's a long-shot. Redemption? That's a mighty big word to put in a sentence with my name. But don't take your arm back, Africa. I'm gettin' kinda used to it."

The guard didn't help Liana to her feet or speak to her as she shuffled away.

"I'll be back," I called to her.

"I'll be here," she replied.

As soon as I went through the door, I fell into Trace's arms. He didn't say anything, just held me like an anchor would hold a floundering ship at sea. The matron reacted in a suspicious manner.

"Hey!" she said and started to come from behind her desk.

Trace waved her away. "It's been an emotional reunion," he told the woman.

"I don't like Liana stirring things up," she said.

Kivuli untangled herself from the comfort of Trace's arms. "I'm the one stirring things up, ma'am," I muttered.

When we got to the truck, I gave in to my despair. "It's just spiraling out of control. Whatever I do could have unthinkable consequences. I thought I could make things better. Who did I think I was?"

Trace waited to start the engine. "You are a girl who cares," he said. "You care about the victim and the victimizer. I respect you for it, though I don't completely understand it. Now tell me what Liana said that's got you so upset?"

"Liana actually used the word 'redemption', actually told me not to give up on her. I'm only upset because now I've made her consider something I honestly don't know she can have. And she saw things in the painting no one has noticed. It was strange."

"Like what?"

"Like more than one chance for the horse. A *pile* of chances."

"That's weird. I mean, doesn't she usually just think of herself?"

"Yeah. I hope she's not conning me." I leaned back in the seat and couldn't look at Trace right then.

"What'll you do?"

"I'm going to hear what she has to say to True Passion. That will tell me everything," I said. "I'll just have to figure out how to get the dog off the ranch and into the prison."

"That might be a good trick," Trace said. He turned the key so we could warm up and be on our way home. It was later than Trace normally liked to be on the road. "What if Liana doesn't say the right things?"

I took a deep breath. "I'll take the 'stab' my great-grandfather never got the chance to do."

White fields enclosed us in a bleak cocoon. I felt the cold right down to my bones, like the unrelenting cold of Liana's hand. The painting propped against the backseat told me nothing.

"Did she remember the painting?" Trace asked.

"Yes. First, she said she didn't know why the Roses had kept it. She didn't ask me how they got it back, which is something I don't know. Then, she said she wished the painting had done what Julian and Serena intended—for her to choose a better way. Those last words are mine, but I think that's what she meant."

The sun splashed its own watercolor on the sky behind us. It had dried the tarmac and sent its light into the snowflakes still clinging to the cactus and jack pine in the desert around them. Few cars passed from either direction. A coyote lunged across the road and disappeared. It might have been a Mexican wolf with its long legs and half-curled tail, but I didn't say anything. We rode on in silence. For me, words were the last thing I needed in our lonely crossing of the twilight world.

When Trace drove under the sign *Rancho del Cielo Azul*, I asked him to go to the barn so we could hang the watercolor back in its accustomed place. Thomas was just finishing feeding and blanketing horses, and he came over to where we stood, gazing at the scared bronc who might have been considering his own better way.

"How'd the school project go?" he asked.

"Better than I expected," I said.

"Good. Glad the painting can help someone."

I still had doubts about Liana but gave Thomas a positive spin. "I think Helen Rose could never have imagined the people it was going to help."

Trace left, and I walked back to the ranch house. I thought of my mother and Safina wasting away in a prison someplace, not being able to see each other, ride their beautiful Thoroughbreds, or kneel in St. Joseph's cathedral to receive the Holy Sacraments. I wished my Granpa Farley had never confided in me, and that I had never read the news article that stamped the horrors into my head.

A while later, I sat in Askay's creaky rocker, reading his journal. I heard a soft knocking and got up to open my bedroom door. Hank was standing there, an anxious look on his face.

"You know I want to hear what happened," he said, "but I don't especially want Susan to hear it...yet."

We each took a place on the chest at the foot of the bed.

"We said a lot of things," I began. "It wasn't easy at first because she'd been in solitary for a week and looked sick. But finally she told me she should have chosen a better way—the treat instead of the spurs, you know?"

"So now you think Liana should have *redemption?*"

"I haven't figured that out yet."

"Well, figure this in. That woman cost us eight years of unbelievable pain," Hank said. "And then, more than a decade for Sunny's recovery, if she's recovered yet."

"I'm not trying to be the judge and jury for that, Mr. Rose. I can't give back Sunrose's life. I can't give back Mvua's life."

"Mvua?"

"The woman my mother buried alive," I said, barely above a whisper.

"Her name was *Mvua?*" Hank said with a strange look on his face. "That's an odd coincidence."

"Why?"

"It was one of Sunny's favorite Swahili words we'd learned from Askay. A special word, a connection to the old man. I never thought I'd hear it again, especially in that context—a woman who was buried alive." Hank shook his head. "But you might as well say Liana buried my daughter alive! These women should be punished! I'm sorry, Kivuli. I don't know your mother, but Christ, she did a hideous thing!"

"So did my great-grandfather."

"No—"

"Yes. Maybe Liana would have taken Sunny anyway, but if Askay had shown you the letter, you would have known who kidnapped her, and you could have found her a lot sooner."

"So now, young lady, you propose to take the 'stab' for everyone?"

"Maybe just for you. It was meant for you."

Hank got up and went to the window. The Nevada sunset lingered in faint streaks of light across the solemn sky.

"Why do you think you have to make up for something your great-grandfather did thirty, forty years ago?" he asked. "We don't know how long ago Askay intercepted the note or where the damned thing is."

"Because the stab is still making a wound," I said. "I'm doing it for my father. And my mother too."

"But how will you know when your part is over and done with?"

I hesitated but gripped the closed journal of my long-imagined great-grandfather as if he could send me the answer from the grave.

"There will be a sight or sound that has no other explanation."

"Like that story your Tanzanian priest told."

"Father Amani. His name means 'peace' in Swahili."

"Yes, I know," Hank said.

35

mourning in spring

March would have been beautiful but for the ice. Two of the range horses had to be put down after severe leg injuries. We moved some of them into the indoor arena, and Hank and Tyrone worked tirelessly to divide the pastures into smaller areas so the horses couldn't get too rambunctious and fall. On one of those days, Ty had a stroke, and I never saw him again. It was then that I learned he was eighty-six years old.

Julia and I had been at school so we hadn't seen the ambulance come and go or the line of wranglers in their trucks following it up the highway. Ty was still alive then. I tried to hide my feelings when, a week later, we all learned that he had died. Hank was the only one who was with him at the end.

Susan let me stay home from school for two days. Near the end of the second day, we were making a salad for dinner, standing side by side at the kitchen sink. She pushed some hair out of my eyes with one hand and asked what was special to me about Tyrone. I was grateful for the question, but it was not going to be easy to answer.

"He trusted me. He was the only wrangler to consistently give me work with the horses or ask me to help insecure guests, teach them how to keep their mount's feet still when they got on or how to hold the reins properly. He was the only one to use my name or treat me like more than just a bothersome child."

"That's a lot," Susan said.

"It changed my life here."

She was silent for a minute and then said the most surprising thing.

"Kivuli, I'm going to do something you won't believe. I'm going to ask Sunny to trust you, and that you are going to show her something no one else has in all these years."

"Oh, Mrs. Rose—"

"I mean it. Maybe Hank and I were afraid we'd say the wrong thing. Maybe her priest too. Maybe a teen from Africa has the courage to say the right thing."

I couldn't speak, so I threw my arms around her.

The next day on the bus, Trace told me Lark's puppies were due in a few weeks and that the vet said there were five of them. He'd told Julia on his way down the aisle, and we heard her calling out puppy names. I squeezed Trace's hand and leaned against his shoulder. I was sad about Ty but also sad that my time in Nevada was getting shorter and shorter. I would not see those puppies grow up, and probably not Trace, ever again.

Ty's death was not softened by sunnier days or the glorious life of puppies to come. But the wrangler had had a fulfilling life with seven decades of Roses, their horses, and their unique way with resistant animals—and resistant humans. But he'd lost his chance, as had others, to put Liana in a round pen. I wished I had told Tyrone what I was doing.

Mr. Seavey noticed that I was subdued in class, and asked me what was wrong. I just said a death in the family, and then modified that to say a death in the Roses' family.

"I want you to write about it," Seavey suggested. "Fiction, non-fiction, poetry, an essay—however you can express your deepest emotions. Take your time."

I was fascinated by this idea and thought I would write as though Ty were my father and someone killed him the day before I was to be married and he was to walk me down the aisle. I already hated the killer but knew, as myself, not the writer, that I would have to work my way to forgiving the fictional woman who had put a knife in my father's back.

It took me a week to write the first sentence, and I was beginning to think I couldn't do it when my mother called as we were sitting down to dinner. Hank handed me the house phone.

"Mama! It's practically the middle of the night there. Where are you?"

"Oh, Kivuli! Safina and I just got back from Arusha. We drove all night. I just had to talk to you."

"What's going on?"

"We had to take Rim. He wants to go to school at Shanga. He hates Light of the World."

"Well, no priest in our family then," I said.

My mother let that go. "He'll stay with your father at the plantation during the week and with friends at Shanga on the weekends Askari comes to Dar, or maybe come home with Askari once in a while. Both my children separated from me!" she cried.

"But, Mama, is Rim okay? How can he live without *you?*"

"He was having a hard time living without his father. We'll work it out, honey. Please don't worry."

"You know I will. You're not telling me everything."

"Are you telling *me* everything? What about this Native American boy you're seeing? Your father mentioned him the other day."

"Trace? He's very considerate and smart. He has his own car, and he's showing me the country."

"What? Now you're scaring me!"

"I'm fine, Mama. I love America. I love the Roses who took care of Great-grandfather. I have good friends and good grades. What's to scare you?"

"Oh, Kivuli, you're just so far away, with people I don't know. The world is such a dangerous place."

"Yes, I know."

"What could you know, darling?"

My audacity leapt to my throat.

"I know what you did to Mvua." I had meant to say it a long time ago and not on a transatlantic call. There was such a marked silence that I thought we had been disconnected.

"It has nothing to do with you," my mother said finally.

"But it does, Mama. You sent me to find out more about Askay. Well, I found out he failed to stop a terrible thing from happening to the Roses."

"What terrible thing?"

"A vile crime, a hurt that can't be taken back, like what you and Safina did."

"Kivuli, please! We've all gotten over it."

I remembered Hank saying that very thing when we first spoke about Sunny's kidnapping.

"I don't believe that, Mama. Sometimes when you push too hard at a scab, the wound opens up again."

"What wound? What are you talking about?"

"The wounds in the hearts that are still alive," I said.

"Kivuli, please be careful," my mother said, as though the rest of the conversation had not taken place.

"I'd rather be fearless."

"What was that, darling? You're fading."

"I wish you were here, Mama," I said, raising my voice a little. "But don't worry. I'm bringing something from Nevada home with me."

Helen Rose's sunset painting? The horse savvy of Henry Dancing Horse? The photo of Askay with his friend Hernando? But Suzanna didn't ask. She was already gone.

At the end of March, when the crocuses began to push up through the snow in Askay's garden, etching the borders of the ground with purple and white, I felt as if my great-grandfather's very heart was opening up to the light. But I was torn between stepping into Askay's shoes for the Roses' sake and finding a way for my own mother to be redeemed. I buried the news article about the gruesome murder of the abusive Mvua deeper in my hand bag and admonished myself, *one stab at a time.*

On a Saturday, Tim drove down to pick up Sunrose, Julia, and me and take us back to his house to meet Lark's puppies. There were three males and two females. Two of the males and one of the females had bands of merle buried in their German shepherd coats. Stuart said to take as many as we wanted, that he and Tim were over raising dogs. Sunrose chose one of the merle-striped males that she said had her old Paraíso's coloring, and she called him "Paradise Found". Julia was clutching the largest unmarked female, whom she called "Pass's Flyer"—one of the many names she had been reciting on the bus.

"Kiki, you choose one now!" she cried.

"Oh, sweetie, I don't dare get attached to one of these pups. The leopard on my father's plantation might want to eat him!"

I picked up the other merle-marked male. He fell asleep in my hands. I was struck suddenly with the thought that I had not been born when Liana killed Hank's Paraíso and started the Roses down that long, unbearable path. I wanted this dog but could not let it show.

We couldn't take the puppies back to the ranch for several weeks, but Tim said we were welcome any time to come play with them and get them socialized. Sunrose said she'd bring Julia and me at least once a week. Julia cocked her spoiled seven-year-old head and suggested twice.

At home later, I pulled my cell phone from my pocket and called the prison. I asked the administrator who answered, without any preliminary explanation, if I could bring a dog for a prisoner to see.

"A dog? Which inmate?" the man asked with slight irritation.

"It's a long story. Liana raised the grandsire of this dog but got separated from him when she was sentenced to life in prison. I thought seeing him would bring her a little peace," I said.

"It's highly irregular. Who are you?"

"I'm the relative who's been visiting her, Miss Farley."

"Oh yes, I know who you are. But you'll have to give me a number where I can call you back."

I gave him my cell number and lay back against the pillows on Askay's bed. I let my imagination run away with the possibilities of Pass in the prison. It scared me a little. When the phone rang, I answered it with a quiver in my voice. The official had made arrangements for me to bring the shepherd to the yard during one of Liana's yard times a week from the following Friday. I asked him to please not let anyone tell her. He assured me he'd try but that he was not the boss.

"You may only get one chance to do this," he said. "Things are not going so well for Liana. She's been in the infirmary all week."

I sat up straight and could hardly find the breath to speak. "I'll be there."

When I told Trace in the morning, he said he hoped this was the last time, not that he didn't believe in me, but that so much could go wrong. "I'd feel better if you would tell Tim and Stuart, like you promised," he said.

"Okay. I'll get off the bus at your stop on the way home."

I was anxious about telling his dads everything. Would I have to tell them about my mother to explain my obsession with Liana? My morning classes dragged, and I felt shaky. At noon, I saw Manuel

Ramirez sitting by himself outside on the retaining wall by the roses. His head was down, and he was not eating from a sack lunch he was holding. I went over to him, not wanting to stay in the noisy cafeteria anyway.

"Manny, what's wrong?"

"Oh, Kivuli. My grandpapa died last night."

I dropped my books and put my arms around him. "Oh, no. Oh, I'm so sorry."

"He was old. At least he won't suffer like old people sometimes do."

"Hernando gave me such a great gift," I said, hugging Manny a bit harder before letting go.

"And you gave him one too. Don't be sad. He died thinking Askay had come back for him."

"How do you know that?"

"His last words were 'Askay, I see you', and that's why I'm sitting here. I feel them both, don't you?"

"Yes. I have just lately felt Askay close. And now I feel Hernando too."

We sat there quietly until the bell rang. I saw a tiny bud on one of the roses nod in the spring breeze.

After school, Trace and I perched on the edge of the couch in front of the dads. I told the briefest version of the story that I could, but Tim could not be convinced the Roses knew we had been going to the prison.

"But does Sunny know?" he asked.

"Hank said not to tell her."

"You don't understand, sweetheart," Tim said. "I told you when I was in high school, Sunny kept my secret that I was gay. She lied for me, pretended she was my girlfriend. I can't do something behind her back. I won't."

"Then I'll tell her. Tonight. I only have a week. The prison administrator already said I could bring the dog for Liana's yard time."

Stuart looked at Trace who hadn't said anything. "I think you have some explaining to do, young man."

But I jumped in. "Mr. Martin, it's not his fault. I didn't tell him where we were going or why until we'd been there a few times. He thought it was a debate assignment."

"I'm sorry anyway, Dad. I…I kind of got caught up in Kivuli's dreams."

Tim took my hands from where they were folded in my lap. "What kind of dreams would include that disastrous woman?"

I tried to explain how I dreamed of finding out more about my great-grandfather, to live in the place and with the people he gave his life to, but that I discovered right away he had not warned the Roses about a threat from Liana, and that Sunny might have been safer if they had known. I told the dads I had come here already struggling with something my mother had done, more monstrous than the kidnapping."

"I don't think you should tell us about that," Tim said.

"Okay, but I've learned sometimes the monster horses need more than one chance. Hank, the wranglers, Dancing Horse, Helen and Serena Rose before them, practice a special way of dealing with those horses. Serena worked those ways on troubled humans. So here I am, thinking Pass might help me try those round pen ways on someone like Liana."

Tim let go of one of my hands and grasped one of Trace's. "If someday you ever want to marry this girl, you have my blessing."

"Mine too," Stuart added.

At home later, at dinner, I pushed my food around on my plate.

"Something on your mind?" Hank asked.

I froze with my fork in the middle of my mashed potatoes and answered quickly before I could change my mind. "I have to tell Sunny I'm going to the prison with Pass. Tim won't let Trace take me if I don't."

"Good for Tim."

Hank picked up the phone. "I'll ask her to come down in a while—alone. I think you'll know right away how she feels, and maybe that will help you make the best choice. You'd better be planning the kindest way to bring this up."

"Yes, sir."

Susan cleared the dishes. A plate slipped out of her hands and broke against the porcelain sink. I jumped up to see if she had been cut and pressed a wet cloth into a small wound in her palm.

"It's nothing, Kivuli. Don't worry," Susan said. "I'd break every dish in my house to have my daughter in one whole piece. You do what you have to do for her mending. Nothing else has worked."

"I'll be careful," I promised.

36

the long-ago kidnapped child

Within the hour, Sunrose opened the front door. "What's going on?" she said. She removed her coat and snow boots and came over to where I sat stiffly at the kitchen table. "Are you in trouble, Kivuli?"

I shifted uncomfortably in my chair. "With you, I think. I've done something rash. You're going to hate me."

She sat down next to me. "I don't think I could ever hate you. You have been so good for Julia, and for me, too."

There was not going to be an easy way to say this. No excuses or reasons good enough to have interfered in Sunny's private anguish. I dreaded the words as they came out of my mouth. "I've made friends with Liana."

Sunny's eyes darkened as with sudden fever, and she clenched the edge of the table with both hands. "No. That's impossible," she said, in a suddenly cold voice.

Hank and Susan retreated to the living room, trusting me to make this right. I took that as a sign that I should follow my heart's instincts and be the girl in the footsteps of my great-grandfather.

"I only wanted to find out how to help my mother live with her own crime, pay for her crime, maybe be forgiven for her crime. But one visit to the prisoner wasn't enough to figure all that out, and then Liana said she felt like the bronc in Helen's painting, and I was the one holding out my hand—"

"Wait! That was your school project? Visiting Liana? Taking Helen's painting?"

"I didn't want to hurt you."

"I don't care about the painting. The lie is another thing. Why are you telling me this now?"

"I had an idea that if I could get Liana to break down and be sorry for what she did, from her heart, your family could forgive her." I whispered the last with great misgiving.

Sunrose got up and brought two glasses of cold water from the kitchen faucet. She handed me one and took a swallow of the deep well water from the other one. "You can't imagine how I missed this water all those years in California," she said more calmly, but the glass trembled in her hand. "How were you going to get to this…this *remorseful* Liana?"

"I tried everything I could think of. And then lately I imagined I could put Paraíso—his grandson, True Passion—in her arms."

Then, the dam broke. Sunrose gripped my shoulders. "Oh my dear child, you cannot imagine what—" She dropped her hands but went on in the same frantic voice. "I called that woman *Mommy*! She…hurt me. She pretended to care about me, then she wouldn't let me eat or read a book or ask where we were, for heaven's sake! But she let me make friends with the dog. That dog was all I had for years. He was the only living thing I was allowed to speak to until I was seven years old!"

I shrank back from her desperate words.

"One time, I saw a grey horse in a field, and I thought I knew him. Liana wouldn't stop the car. She sped away as if it pleased her to deny me this one thing—the touch of that horse. Oh, there are so many things I could tell you. Sometimes I couldn't eat. Sometimes I couldn't sleep. Just wondering what she was going to do next. But I could hold onto that dog. I could say 'Mommy' to that despicable woman and know she wasn't my mother. It was a nightmare. Eight years, Kivuli! Eight years of a non-life! And you *made friends* with her?"

Sunrose stared at me as if to drive her own desperation into my soul.

"This has been about your mother all along, finding a way for her to be redeemed. You don't believe in the Catholic absolution, and anyway, Liana doesn't qualify for that. You are hoping that if you discover a word, a gift, something dear to Liana, she might seek forgiveness from me or someone who loves me—my parents, my husband, my child!"

"Then, if forgiveness is possible, there might be a chance for my mother…someday," I admitted, trying not to break down myself. "I have to take the dog to Liana. I have to."

"Dear God, Kivuli," Sunny said. "I don't think I can let you do that without me."

"What?"

"I don't care whether she's remorseful or not. I should have my hand on the leash with the dog. Don't you see? She'd take the dog or anything from you—darling, sweet, African *child*. She'll have to think twice about taking the dog from *me*. She'll have to wonder why I'm there."

"You're not mad at me?"

"I should be. Are you telling me everything?"

I took a deliberate swallow of water.

"You don't know about the connection to Askay."

"To your great-grandfather? What could that be?"

"I only know because I found a page in his diary that…it's bad, Sunrose."

"Nothing's bad anymore," she said, her finger tracing a small circle on the polished oak.

"Liana sent Hank a note warning him she was going to stab him when he least expected. Askay opened it by mistake, but he never told your father. He said he would take the stab himself."

Sunny's face drained of color. She was already paler than her mother, her thin cheeks nothing like Susan's glossy brown ones, her lips compressed as though she was afraid of the words that might erupt. She put her hands together on the table. They were white against the golden oak.

"Oh, dear Lord, Kivuli," she finally said. "You have been carrying this all these months. Well, that's why I'm going with you to that prison. You are not going to take any 'stab' by yourself! When is this supposed to happen?"

"A week from Friday, during Liana's yard walk."

"And how have you been getting to the prison?"

"With Trace," I said. "But Tim wouldn't let us take Pass without telling you."

"Still loyal to our teenage pact." She smiled briefly. "Okay. I'll call Tim and explain why *I* have to do this. Liana can't hurt me anymore, but she could still hurt you."

On the bus the next day, I grabbed Trace's hands the minute he sat down, "Did you hear?"

"Yeah, my dad told me. Wow! This is just what you wanted."

"I don't know what I wanted. I had it all planned, what I was going to say to Liana, everything. Now it's out of my hands."

"I think it'll be okay. Tim was relieved."

"I'm scared to death," I said.

All week I tried to distract myself from the seriousness and perhaps hopelessness of what Sunrose and I were going to do. I spent a couple of afternoons with Avery, shopping for summer clothes, and one day, I stayed home from school and sat in the barn and talked to some of the wild horses that had been brought into the barn for first hands-on contact with humans. Later in the week, I debated my heart out over charter schools versus public schools. I won my debate, but I failed two algebra tests and got sent to the counselor's office for being late to class.

On the Friday of the approved visit to the prison, Sunrose and I left the ranch early, falling into safe conversations about the early blooms on the cactus and my debate victories. The larger debate, about the wisdom of what we were doing, we kept inside. I had not been afraid of going to see Liana for quite some time, but Sunny's restlessness began to wear on me. She drove achingly slowly and braked for every curve. She fumbled with the radio and finally took my hand and told me not to worry, everything would be all right. The sea glass rosary I had given her swung from the mirror in a sparkling dance.

At the prison, we were searched, Pass's collar taken off, examined and hooked back on, and our IDs collected. Then, we were led to the designated yard with Pass between us. A few prisoners wandered about on the patchy lawn, each group of six or so with a guard. Ten minutes went by, and no one appeared with Liana. The shepherd whined and looked up at us from time to time, as if to see what we required of him. Finally, the warden approached us. He began speaking in a mildly annoyed tone.

"Liana doesn't want to see the young lady out here. She said she likes the visitor's room, feels safer, but I took her to a window so she could see you...and the dog. She grabbed her throat and fell over. She's still unconscious. What have you done to my prisoner?"

"I need to talk to her," Sunny said, beginning to look stressed.

"I guess she'll have to wake up for you to do that," the man said.

"She saved Liana's life once," I said in Sunny's defense.

"Well, you may have to do it again," he said curtly. "Come on. Let's go see how she's doing. You can bring the dog. Prisoners don't normally die on me over their visitors."

He led us to the infirmary. Liana was sitting unsteadily on the edge of a bed. She shot one hand out as if to block us from view. "No! No! I'm not ready yet!" she gasped.

"Liana. It's okay. It's me. Kivuli."

"Africa?"

Liana let her hand fall at her side. I went forward slowly. I knew we couldn't touch, but I needed to reassure her. "Listen to me. We came to give you a gift, that's all. This dog is Paraíso's grandson. His name is True Passion. You can trust me, Liana."

Liana let herself look at me and then beyond at the German shepherd and the woman with her hand on the leash.

"Sunny?" she said in barely a whisper.

"I'm sorry I scared you. It's been a long time," Sunny said, but she didn't move from the spot. "Kivuli said I should come see you."

"Africa found you. She made sure you were all right. I didn't know where you'd gone. No one would tell me…'til Africa."

"I'm married now. I have a good life."

"No. No. You look like Sister Martha," Liana said, some confusion beginning to show. "She saved me. I don't know why."

"I did save you, Liana, but then I abandoned you. You and my convent and my Church, for some time. But I brought you a little reminder of our past."

True Passion went to the end of his leash and licked Liana's hand. "Paraíso? No, no, it's a trick!"

I told her to part the dog's coat on his left shoulder. Her fingers moved weakly, but she smiled. "Paraíso, I don't deserve to see you again," she said, forgetting that Dog's strip of merle was on the back of his head. "You look so wonderful, and I'm just a ragged old thing. Do you know what happened to Sunny? I was plenty mean to that girl, but I didn't want to be. I ended up loving her, didn't I? But I did an unforgiveable thing. I locked her up in that car so no one else could have her. She'll never forgive me, will she?"

Pass had his head in Liana's lap now. She stared into his amber eyes. "I know those eyes," she said. "What happened to that little girl, Dog? Can you take me to her? If I could just tell her how sorry I am. I would never kidnap her again. Okay, Dog, okay? Can she hear me?"

Sunny's face was tense, and she had a tight hold on Pass's leash, but she got a few words out. "I hear you, Liana. I don't know if I can forgive you yet, but I'm here."

"Hey, pretty lady, I just want the girl to know I'm sorry. I don't expect no forgiveness."

Pass put his head on the bed, pushing his nose under Liana's hand. Sunny flinched and the leash quivered in her hand.

"Good old Dog," Liana whispered. She put her hand against her heart.

I tried to help. I leaned toward the disoriented woman. "Liana, remember how you found that new part of Helen's painting? The thing no one had ever seen before?"

"The pile of treats. The other chances for the bad horse," she answered, seemingly clear-minded for a moment.

"Yes. That's why we brought the dog. That's why Sunny came herself. Look, she's not a little girl anymore."

Liana looked up from Pass's eyes into Sunny's. "Do I know you?"

"I called you Mommy once," she said. "But it was not easy."

Liana pressed her hand harder to her chest and began to shake. "Baby? My Baby all grown up. I raised you pretty good, di'n't I?"

"You molested me."

The damning words hung in the air. Pass pulled away from the bed and glanced up at Sunny.

"I taught my Baby a few things, like how to feel her own heart. I'm not sorry for that," Liana said, struggling now. "This girl, this Africa, she already knew how to feel when I met her. She held her hand through the bars."

"She doesn't know what you did," Sunny said.

"Jus' water under the bridge, Baby. What'r you going to do?" she said, a bit more of the flippant Liana returning.

Sunny took a step forward and bent down over the hard eyes. "I'll come visit you. We'll talk," she said.

"Who are you?" Liana asked, her eyes blank again.

"I am many souls, trying to be one. Can you wait for me?"

But without another word, Liana fell backwards onto the bed, and we were quickly ushered into the hallway. The shepherd lay down on the cold floor while Sunny and I leaned against the wall. In a few minutes, a doctor came out and spoke to us.

"I'm sorry to tell you Liana has had a massive heart attack. I'm afraid she's...gone. I'm surprised she could sit up and talk to you. Are you relatives?" he asked.

Sunny walked away and looked out a small, barred window in the gray wall. *And outside the bars no world.*

"I called her 'Mommy' once," Sunny repeated in a barely audible voice.

"And I called her 'Great-aunt'," I said.

Lies that would keep us tied to Liana forever.

"Are you going to make the arrangements?" he called out to Sunny, who had her back to him.

She barely slowed down. "No. We've done all we can."

"But—"

Sunny waved him off. "Call Father Zenwa in Ochala Junction. He'll help you."

Sunrose and I sat in the truck for a long time before starting home. Pass waited happily in the backseat, gazing out the window at the ravens circling over the empty yard and the razor-wired fences.

"I couldn't do it," Sunny said suddenly. "I couldn't forgive her."

"That's okay. It was hard enough," I said. "You could forgive Askay instead." I stared out at the prison walls, insurmountable and cold.

"I could, couldn't I? It might not do anything for me, but I think it would help you. You need that mistake to be forgiven, so yes, I forgive your great-grandfather. I know he loved me anyway. That cancels out a lot of mistakes. I'm just glad he never knew what Liana finally did."

"Me too."

Sunny had her hands on the steering wheel, but she didn't move to start the truck. "You don't think we killed her, do you?" she asked.

"Oh, no. They told me she hadn't been well lately. It was a good death," I said, then added quickly, "I mean, she got to say she was sorry. Not many people like her get to do that."

"Yes. A good death. Now, we must go on and have a good life." Sunny paused for a moment, then asked, "Did she answer all your questions?"

"No."

"Maybe I can answer them."

"I would rather have asked you from the beginning."

Sunny still didn't touch the ignition. The cold seeped into the cab. The questions about exactly what happened at the end would never be answered. That missing piece seemed to be keeping her frozen in place.

"But in her final moments…what did she see, Kivuli?"

"She saw you," I said. "And Paraíso."

Sunrose turned the key at last and we passed through the tall, metal gates. I was anxious for the warmth from the heater and didn't know why there was a catch in my throat. Soon, the prison was behind us. We didn't speak, just let the Nevada sundown dash its colors slowly across the sky. There wasn't a dark stroke among them.

When we returned to the ranch, Sunny said, "Kivuli, I don't think I can say the words 'Liana's dead' to anyone yet."

"Okay. What shall we say?"

When she pulled the truck up to the main house, she leaned over and whispered in my ear, "Just say we'll tell them in a few days. I need some time."

"I'll wait for you, Sunrose."

I went into the house and crashed on Askay's bed, the words "a good death" swirling in my mind. In the end, Liana died before grasping my hand, before tasting the sweet grass. Was seeing Sunny a small taste? Was touching Paraíso enough of a gift? I would never know. I pushed Trace's numbers on the phone, and he answered on the third ring.

"Where are you? It's getting late."

"We're at the ranch. We're all right."

"But what happened at the prison?"

"Sunny and I decided not to talk about it for a couple of days. We just want to think about how to tell it."

"All right. I can wait."

Sunny's mom was not as easy to side-step. When I finally came out of my room, Susan made me sit at the kitchen table. "Kivuli Farley, you tell me everything right this minute."

"Mrs. Rose, I promised Sunny I'd let her choose the best time, but I won't need to go back to the prison."

"That's something, at least," Susan said. "I'll warm your dinner."

While I took bites of Mrs. Rose's comforting chicken pot pie, I tried not to cry. In the end Liana had said all the right things, things I had wanted her to say for months, but could Sunrose or I trust them? The dying woman had been trapped between the memories of the little girl and the dog and the reality of the woman before her, the woman who held the leash.

Later, I did cry. I cried for the answers I would never have, for the shift in Liana's eyes every time she saw me waiting in the steel chair, and for the changes Liana made that would now do her no good. The abruptness of the end was wrenching too, the way Pass had licked Liana's hand, and the way she had said, "Who are you?" to the long-ago kidnapped child.

37

mothers and daughters

Tim drove up to Sentinel's on Saturday morning. He was there quite a while. I thought Sunrose must be telling him everything. Perhaps Tim would be the only one who heard her truest emotions about the way things ended. I didn't know what I would say. Just saying Liana's death was a "good death" did not seem like enough. After Tim left, Sunny called and asked me to come to her place.

I had not been inside their house more than a half dozen times, but I felt relaxed with Sunrose now and didn't mind the clutter and the trail of Catholic reminders. We sat together at one end of the living room sofa.

"Are you okay with everything?" Sunny asked.

"I'm getting there."

"Have you told anyone?"

"No. I promised."

"It's hard to know where to start, isn't it?"

"It seems like each person might need a different story," I said.

"I'm going to say she was struggling, she didn't know me, but she talked to Dog about finding the little girl she stole and telling her she was sorry. That should satisfy everyone."

"Does it satisfy you?" I asked.

Sunny began folding clean clothes that were piled on the other end of the sofa. She glanced out the window to a place in their yard where Julia was playing with Pass. "I believe there's only one thing that will ever satisfy me," she finally said.

"What's that?"

"God."

She put her hand on the top of a stack of Julia's frilly blouses and pink tights. "Liana never bought me clothes like these," she said. "When I finally went to school in the fourth grade, I must have looked ridiculous in brown khakis and boys' t-shirts."

I hesitated, but everything was out in the open now. "Do you think Liana knew who you were?"

"She knew me. She liked to deny it, to avoid what was real. I played that game often enough."

"I guess we should be glad…that it's over," I said, "but I feel… like something's missing. A conversation I never got to have, a tying together of all the things that were so…alive."

"Like what, dear?"

"Friendship. Remorse. Anticipation. Anger. Truth. Understanding. Trust. I don't know. Things that will never be resolved. Things that are final, that remain as they were, with no chance for anyone to change them or make a remedy." I took in a sudden breath. "Like the African sundown. Things that only exist for a moment, and then they're gone."

"What about those questions about your mother you thought Liana could help you with—though I can't imagine how."

Julia stuck her head in the front door. "Momma, I'm tired," she whined.

"Honey, I'm talking to Kivuli. I just need a few more minutes."

The child banged on the door with the flat of her hand. "You're telling secrets, I know."

"And I'm going to tell you later," Sunny assured her.

When we were alone again, I said, "I wanted Liana to explain how a person lives with her crime. If it makes a difference if she's paying for it—you know, going to jail or suffering because of it. I would have asked her if forgiveness changed anything, if love changed anything, and what the criminal could do if there was no one left to do the forgiving."

"Did you ever get any of those answers?"

"Some. But usually we got side-tracked. We talked about Avery, my gay friend, and a little about your mother. She didn't like the questions about *my* mother. And then, after I brought Helen's painting, she got more serious, said Hank's mom, Serena, had been right to want her out of Hank's life. I thought that was a big step for her, but all Liana's steps turned out to be too late, didn't they?"

"I don't know, Kivuli, but you did all you could. You should let this go now." She folded the last of Julia's cute outfits. "I told myself I had let this go a long time ago, but because of what happened to me, I've been way over-protective of Julia and obsessive about my faith. I want her to be Catholic, but if I had to choose, I'd want her to be safe. Mothers and daughters. How do we ever find the perfect ground?"

I watched her reach for a crumpled bed sheet and give up making a neat square of it.

"I think I can answer one of your questions, though," she went on. "For some people, the absolution of the Catholic Church is not enough."

"My mom depends on her absolution, I'm sure." I wondered why I was leaving Safina out of this conversation. Was it too complicated or too controversial?

Sunrose leaned toward the coffee table and picked up a statue of Mary cradling the baby Jesus. It was very life-like with its delicate features and warm colors. I had never seen anything like it.

"You and your mother will find what you need, Kivuli. You are a strong girl. I just hope you aren't wounded in the process. Think of your mother as wounded, wounded because she did something she couldn't amend. I'm not excusing it, but if you can forgive her a little,

I think that counts."

"I just worry that someday she will have to pay a big price, and my forgiveness will be too small," I said.

"That's when you will need God for yourself."

I hadn't gone very far down the path when Sunny called to me from the porch. "Tell my folks I'll be down soon."

I turned back and waved and then saw Thomas and Julia coming toward the Sentinel's house. Tom clung to his daughter's hand, steadying her on patches of ice. I hoped Sunrose would only say the kidnapper died. She had to say *something*. And then I heard a horse scream inside the barn. I froze. But I was too emotionally exhausted to face the problem. Whatever I could do for one of the wild horses would have to wait. And I had to consider the Roses, still on the dark side of what Sunny would tell.

When I opened the door to the ranch house, Hank met me with such a look on his face that I knew Sunny was too late.

"A prison official called," he said.

"Oh god."

"He wanted *me* to tell Sunny."

"He didn't know Sunny was right there in the room when Liana died?"

"I guess not, but—"

"No...I need to let Sunrose explain the rest," I told him.

Susan came into the mudroom and helped me out of my jacket, shaking her head. "Well, it's over," she said. "And I'm not sorry. I have no forgiveness in my heart." She hung my wool scarf over my coat and lined my boots up neatly with the others. Then, she straightened and seemed to speak into the room, as if not expecting an answer from anyone. "Do you think if I were Catholic, I could forgive?"

I felt numb, both from the cold and from the image of Liana

dying right in front of me. "I don't know, Mrs. Rose. I think it's just in a person's nature. I don't think you have to believe in God to forgive."

Hank put more wood on the fire, and the three of us sat down together in the kitchen. I felt like the Roses' child, being allowed to watch them struggle with their feelings over an old, and now a new, family terror.

"I saw Liana once—at the sentencing," Susan said. "I could barely stand to be in the same room with her, but I went for Hank. We were asked if we wanted to speak. Hank got up and said that she had done her worst, damaging his child, but what he would never forgive her for was hardening his heart. She couldn't look at him. Her eyes went everyplace, like a bird in a cage, but never landed on Hank. Finally, she looked at me, waited to see what I would say. But there were only screams in my mouth. All these years…I never got to speak my mind. I should have been there with you and Sunny at the prison."

"No, Mrs. Rose, you've been through enough. Liana did say once she wanted your forgiveness more than anyone else's. 'That would be some forgiving' were her exact words."

"Why didn't you tell me?"

"I wasn't sure I was going to tell anyone what I was doing, and then you always reacted so strongly to any talk of Liana or Sunny's missing eight years." I gasped with a sudden thought. "Oh my gosh! Mvua! Mvua must have a mother somewhere, a mother and a father! Their forgiveness of my mother would *mean* something."

"Your mother killed a woman named Mvua?" Susan asked. "How strange. Where was her family?"

"I don't know. I was so little. Younger than Julia. I wouldn't have known anything about Mvua's life. She was my art teacher, and I liked her. Later I learned that she…abused people. Just like Liana!"

"But Kivuli, you shouldn't stir all that up for your mother," Hank said. "She hasn't been accused, has she?"

"No. The evidence was never found."

"Your mother must live in fear," Susan said. "You must never look for the dead girl's mother, Kivuli. I tell you as a mother. It's the worst thing you could do."

Susan stood up from the table as a bundled figure came through the front door. "Oh, here's Sunny. We'll be all right now."

"I'm so sorry I shook everything up."

"I know," Susan said. "But it was bound to happen. After all, the prison called today with the news about Liana. If you had never come to America, feelings were going to be shaken."

I went to Askay's room and didn't hear Sunny's version of the events, but everyone at the dinner table was quiet that night. There didn't seem to be anything to say that could match the news about Liana's death and the things that were said inside the prison walls. Susan seemed about to cry at times, but she didn't. *A good Iroquois*, I supposed.

On Sunday, I called Trace. "Do you want me to tell you now or at school tomorrow?"

"I'll wait 'til tomorrow. I want to see your eyes."

We got to the debate room early after school the next day. Mr. Glen wasn't there yet, nor any of the other kids. We sat in a corner surrounded by books and audio-visuals and tapes of famous debates.

I knew we didn't have much time, so I made every word count. "Liana died in the prison infirmary."

"What?"

"Just minutes before, she had been petting Pass, calling him 'Dog', and asking him to find the child Sunny so she could tell her she was sorry! Can you believe it?"

"She said she was sorry right in front of Mrs. Sentinel?"

"She did. But she acted like she didn't know it was Sunny. Then, she called me 'Africa'."

"It makes sense to me," Trace said. "For so long, she's remembered Sunny as a young girl. The person she kidnapped never grew up in her mind. Mrs. Sentinel was just a lady accompanying you, a person she was meeting in her present life."

"We thought Liana was just playing a game, denying what was real. The forgiveness might have snapped her out of it, but it doesn't matter now. Sunny didn't forgive her. She couldn't."

"So now you think no one can forgive your mother?"

"I know exactly who can, but I'm not sure I have the energy to see it through."

Trace put his arms around me. Mr. Glen appeared at the edge of our embrace. "You guys okay?"

"Oh, yes, sir. Just having a debate between ourselves," Trace assured him. "We didn't know you were here."

"Who won?"

Trace smiled. "I don't think all the ballots are in yet."

"You kids can be so serious sometimes," Mr. Glen said, "but that's why I love you."

I looked over Trace's shoulder and waited until Mr. Glen's eyes caught mine. "We love you too," I said.

The rest of March, I clung to Trace like a life raft. The final confrontation with Liana had worn on my self-confidence. How could I begin another effort like finding Mvua's mother, or starting some of the wild horses that Dancing Horse had hinted I might, when I could fail at using the round pen way with the humans I cared about?

"What are you thinking about today, girlfriend?" Trace asked one morning on the bus.

"I'm wondering if I could actually *kill* someone who was hurting you or abusing an animal I loved."

"Whoa. Does that mean you love me?" He put his arm around me.

"I think I loved you the day we met."

"You love everybody."

"No, I don't. Like who?"

"Well, the Roses, Sunny, Dancing Horse, Mr. Glen—"

"Wait, Mr. Glen?"

"You look at each other like you had a secret between you."

I watched a rain shower pelt the window, blurring the sight of the luminous desert streaming by.

"We do," I admitted, "but it's not what you think." My mind wandered to that day in his classroom and many days since, when I caught him looking at me, how I felt when we passed in the hallway. There was a piece of kindling there waiting for a match. What would I do if he decided to break the rules completely?

"Anyway, you are too good a person to kill anyone," Trace went on.

"Does that mean you think my mom is a *bad* person? You have no idea what she went through—the bullying, my granpa not telling her the truth about her real father, seeing her best friend being slowly poisoned. Stuff like that adds up."

"It doesn't excuse murder."

"No. It's just that I want to understand it and whether or not I could do it—and whether or not I'd want forgiveness."

"I think you want to know if God could forgive such a thing," Trace said.

"If God could forgive such a thing, then there is a God."

"Sounds reasonable."

The bus had pulled up to the curb, and the driver was helping the smaller kids down the steps. He came back inside and called to Trace and me. "Are you two going to class, or are you going to solve the problems of the world first?"

38

wild horse

April caressed the land with color and hope—new growth pushing up from the half-frozen ground and luring humans outside. One Saturday, I walked up to the barn to brush Lazo. He was already shedding his winter coat. He would have to be blanketed for another month if the nights stayed cold. In a large pen at one end of the barn, four of the wild range horses paced nervously. Though the wranglers had worked with most of the horses in the round pen last fall after they were collected, many of them had been out all winter and were suspicious of this new environment. Hank's spring schedule called for four at a time to be handled in the barn with the ranch stock. "They need to get used to human routines and expectations," he said.

I noticed one dappled grey gelding that hung back from the others. His head was down, and there was a bite wound on his shoulder. I remembered the scream I had heard a couple of weeks ago. Could it have been this horse? I took Lazo's grooming bucket which had some salve in it and approached the pipe fence that corralled the grey and three others. The three veered away from me into one corner, leaving the grey by himself. I stuck my arm through the metal railing. I had nothing in my hand. I didn't want curious horses getting between me and the grey. A couple of mares snorted at me, but mostly they ignored me.

The grey must have been someone's saddle horse because he looked at me with more interest than the others. His head came up a little. I removed my arm and spoke to him. "I'm going to be your human for a while. Will you let me show you something?" The horse took one step toward me, away from the herd. I opened the gate and went in, bucket and all. The grey shied a bit, and the rest of the horses began pushing each other around.

I went to the center and stood perfectly still. When the grey turned his head back, I was between him and the other animals. I held out my hand again. This time I had the tub of Nolvasan. I took one step back, and the horse took one step forward, keeping an eye on his tormentors. I was anxious. I had to keep this space between the grey and the others. I had to show the grey he could trust me. I moved toward him. The mares lunged at me, and the grey flinched. I raised the bucket up in a threatening manner at the intruders, and they backed off. I let that happen a few times. Then I scooped out a handful of salve and moved slowly closer to the wounded animal. The other horses didn't try charging again. The grey waited.

I put the hand with the ointment behind my back and set the bucket down. I didn't want the grey to run away from the smell of the medicine. I found a couple of pieces of carrot in the bottom of the pail and offered one to the wild grey. He stretched out his neck. I stopped. He came up to me. Then he snatched the treat from my palm as I reached around and made one pass at the open wound with the salve. He jumped a little but didn't shy away. I knew the ointment didn't sting, and the horse was perhaps more interested in the possibility of more carrots. The grey and I stood looking at each other.

"I'll call you Grey Sky," I said in a low voice, thinking I would shorten that to Sky—a sharper sound with which to get his attention.

I picked up the grooming bucket. The barn door flew open, and some of the boys came in stomping their feet. The horses raced around the pen, the grey following at a safe distance. They huddled in one corner, but the grey didn't join them. As I left through the pipe gate, he turned his head toward me.

"That's the way, Grey Sky. That's the way."

"What'cha doin', girl?" one of the wranglers asked.

"Just making friends."

"Don't go thinkin' you're any kind of Serena now," another remarked.

I went back to the ranch house and called Dancing Horse. When he picked up, I didn't bother with *hi*, just said, "I want your help with one of the wild horses."

"Which one?"

"The dark dappled grey gelding."

"Good choice. I'll tell you why later."

"I've already touched him," I said. "I've put salve on that horse bite."

"I'll be damned."

"It wasn't easy. I had to deal with those other horses in the pen. I kept them away with the grooming bucket. I hope they aren't afraid of buckets now."

"Naw. I'm sure you did the right thing," Dancing Horse said. "The boys can put the grey in a big stall by himself. Can't have him getting hurt and being scared all the time. What do you call him?"

"Grey Sky."

"Okay, then. When do you want me?"

"I have debate team on Mondays and Thursdays. Any other day is fine."

"I'll come this Tuesday. Ask Hank or one of the boys to move him for you. Don't go in there again with all those horses."

"You're the boss."

"Since when?"

When Hank came in the house, I caught him before he removed his boots. "Mr. Rose, could you do something for me? Dancing Horse wants the grey gelding, you know, the dark dappled one from the wild herd, in a separate, double stall. Could you move him for me?"

"I could, but maybe I should ask whatever wrangler got close enough to doctor that wound."

"Well, that would be me."

"You're kidding."

"No. I put Helen's painting to the test…with a horse."

He asked me to bring him a cup of coffee so he wouldn't have to track his muddy boots into the kitchen. I fixed it the way he liked it with two teaspoons of sugar and a squirt of whipped cream. It pleased me to know Hank so well.

"What are you going to do with that grey?" he asked when I came back with the fresh coffee.

"I'm going to watch Dancing Horse," I said, "I'm hoping he might show me how to do a few things."

"Couldn't save Liana, so now you're going to save a wild horse?"

"Something like that."

"I imagine the horse could be a mite easier."

On the way home from school on Tuesday, I asked Trace to come with me. I had a surprise for him.

"I'm afraid to ask."

"I'm going to break one of the wild horses."

"Oh god, I'm going to lose you before I even *have* you!"

"Don't worry. Dancing Horse will be there to get me started."

I watched the greening desert flow by, the distant mountains turning purple through the diminishing snow, and I settled my mind so I could listen to the horse.

When we got to the ranch, Hank had cleared the barn of distractions, but Dancing Horse said, "No. The horse has to ignore distractions and focus on Kivuli. Then she can praise him for doing the right thing, and the horse can build on that."

The boys brought back a few horses, unpenned the chickens, and threw blankets over the rail. Hank busied himself filling water buckets and cleaning stalls.

"Oh my gosh, *I'm* distracted," I said.

"This is a lesson for you too," Dancing Horse said. "You are now on horse time."

He gave me a rope halter and sent me into the empty round pen with Sky.

"The shoulder looks better," I noticed.

"It does, but I'd like to give him a shot. That may have to wait because if I cause him pain right now, it may make your job more difficult. Go ahead and halter him. He's had that so it won't be new, but try to add some things you might want."

"Okay."

I climbed into the small ring. The horse kept swiveling his head to watch the men outside the rail. I knew how to do this. I slapped the halter against my thigh, but Grey Sky didn't look at me like Lazo did when I entered his space.

"Smart horse," Dancing Horse said.

I stomped toward the grey, and he flew away to the rail, looking for a way out.

"That's okay, that's okay. Keep him moving. Stay behind his flank," Henry said.

In less than two minutes, Sky turned his inside eye my way but kept running.

"Okay. Stop driving him now."

The instant I quit twirling the lead rope, the horse slid to a stop and swung his whole head toward me.

"Back up, back up!" Dancing Horse called out.

But I was already doing that. The horse took a few steps in my direction. I waited. Grey Sky looked at Dancing Horse once as if to say, *Who's training me here, you or her?* Then he came straight to me. I didn't try to put the halter on right away. I rubbed it all over him, careful to avoid the wound on his shoulder. When his nose touched the rope, I opened the noseband part and waited. He moved his nose this way and that, but I didn't chase his nose with the halter. I stayed still. The grey stuck his nose in the loop, and I said, "Good boy," and finished fitting it on him.

We did a few more things. Dancing Horse said for me to walk at the horse's shoulder and not let him go past my feet. "When you stop your feet, he should stop his feet." I knew this method, but the wild horse would need a little more precision. I had to keep pressure on the halter when he did the wrong thing and keep the lead loose when he did the right thing, more quickly than with a well-handled horse. Dancing Horse nodded his approval now and then.

Finally he said, "That's enough for today. You can take him back to his stall. Don't do anything different. Stop a couple of times on the way to be sure he stays with you."

After Sky was in his stall, savoring the sweet grass hay, Henry said, "It's a good thing he's likely had some favorable experience with humans." He patted my back. "And it's a good thing he's now met a girl with *feel*."

Trace, who had been standing quietly against the tack room wall, said, "I love this. A painting come alive."

Dancing Horse grinned. "A *horse* come alive," he said.

During the next two weeks, Hank turned Grey Sky out every morning into a pasture with the broke, dude string. After school, I was able to go out and catch the grey and take him to the outside round pen where three times a week Dancing Horse worked him left and right, trotting and cantering, stopping and starting, with and without a halter. Then he had me do the same things. This would take longer for me than for Dancing Horse, but he told me he wanted to be sure I was grounded in the basics before letting me get on him.

With Serena's way and his Native American way, Henry taught me to drive the horse in a circle and disengage his haunches into a nice halt. I learned to touch the horse all over his body with my hands, the ropes, and the saddle blanket. I would leave the woolen pad draped over Sky's head, and he would follow me, blinded. Some of these moves I had done with Lazo but never with a horse as sensitive and spooky as Grey Sky.

If I pushed the Indian to let me ride the horse, Henry would hold up his hand. "I am not going to send a broken child back to Africa. You must trust me."

39

living in the painting

As the days edged toward May, I was feeling despondent over the few weeks I had left in Nevada, until the surprise of Denari Robertson. One day, a lithesome black girl walked into the cafeteria, and I was not the only one to gasp. She looked like someone who had just come in from a movie set. I was with Trace, Avery, Donna, Manny, and Julia. Would this new-comer recognize me as black in that diverse group? Trace leaped to his feet and invited her over.

As she sat down at the end of the table, next to Julia, Trace announced with good humor, "Here we have a cross-section of our entire student body—too many tribes to name but equally loved, and our star, the Tanzanian, Kivuli Safina Farley."

The new girl did not miss a beat. "I am Denari Robertson," she said. "and I am extremely pleased to meet you all in this Nevada outpost I was sure would not possibly interest me." Then, she looked at me, "A Tanzanian? I can't believe it! There were hundreds of blacks in my school in L.A. but not one from Africa. We called ourselves African-Americans, but I don't think that's accurate. Maybe if we have one parent born in Africa or something. But still, who are the true Africans? Not us. We're Americans who just happen to be black."

"We could use you on the debate team," Trace said.

My friends called out their names, and Donna asked what had brought her to Ochala Junction.

"My folks bought an outfitting business, and they know *nothing* about it! I think my dad's ridden a horse once in his life—and it ran away with him!"

"Oh dear," Avery said.

"He thought he'd just hire people when we got here. He figured there'd be lots of cowboys and Indians who needed jobs. Oops, that didn't sound right." Denari clapped her hand to her mouth.

Trace pulled his arms back as if aiming an arrow into her heart, but he was smiling.

"The family I'm staying with owns a guest ranch. Maybe they could help your folks get started," I offered.

"Are they black?" the girl asked.

"No. Most of them are Native Americans, but the place has been owned for generations by a white family, the Roses."

"They're my grandparents!" Julia added.

Denari put a hand to her chest. "You guys are just taking my breath away. I'm too excited to eat!"

Donna slid her tray under the girl's nose. "Oh, you've got to try the soft tacos. They're great! Made with venison."

"That would be a first for me," she said with a suspicious glance at Donna's tray.

Manny, who looked to be already in love, asked Denari what grade she was in."

"Tenth," she replied.

"Perfect," he said. Her age, her mischievous eyes, her slim waist, her expressive smile and friendly manner were perfect for Manny, I imagined.

She turned back to me. "But why are you on that ranch?"

"My Maasai great-grandfather lived and worked there for much of his life, more than forty years, at least. I came here to learn more about him and the people he loved."

"How wonderful," Denari said. "How long will you be here?"

"I'm afraid I'm leaving in June," I said.

"Oh no! I may never meet another native African in my life!"

Denari took a bite of Donna's taco. Donna and Avery said they wanted to get to class early and that they would catch up to her later. Manny was eating his lunch as slowly as possible.

"I know another African right in this town. The priest at St. Mary's, Father Zenwa," I told her.

"Are you Catholic?" she asked.

"No. But my mom and her girlfriend, who lives with us, are Catholic, as well as my grandfather and many of my schoolmates. I'm still thinking about it," I admitted.

"That's a lot of information in a short sentence!"

"I'm not known for reticence."

"My mom was a nun," Julia said, not to be left out of the revelations.

The bell rang and jarred them back to reality. Trace told Denari how to find the debate room and grabbed my books to walk me to World History.

"I have the debate coach for my next class. I'll see if he has a spot on the squad," I said. "I'll get your phone number later. I'm sure the Roses will want to meet your folks."

Manuel took Denari's books and went with her, looking to me like one of Lark's puppies.

On Friday, Dancing Horse was waiting by the round pen when I got home from school. Grey Sky was already in the ring, and there was a saddle on the rail. I raced inside to change my clothes and gulp down a glass of milk. Susan gave me a hug.

"Please be careful on that horse," she said. "And ask Henry to supper when you get a chance."

I ducked under the rail. Grey Sky stood in the middle of the pen. He was breathing heavily.

"I moved him around a little bit for you," Henry said. "I wanted to take some edge off of him, but I think he's ready for you. You ready for him?"

"More than ready. Do you remember what you promised?"

"What was that?"

"You'd tell me why it was a good thing I chose this horse to ride."

"I remember. So ride," he said.

Dancing Horse had already haltered the horse. I kept the lead over my arm, swung the saddle up on his back, and cinched it up without worrying him. Sky seemed to know this part someplace in his mind and trotted out to the perimeter of the pen after I unhooked the halter rope and asked him to go away from me. He didn't buck. I stepped toward his shoulder, and he reversed direction. When I stopped driving him, he turned his head toward me. I backed up two steps, and he came in.

I tightened the girth, attached the lead rope again and placed my hand on it where it would be when I was in the saddle. Grey Sky bent his neck following the pressure. When he dropped his neck softly at the poll, I released the lead. Then I brought my hand out a ways from the horse's neck and put pressure again. He moved his haunches away, crossing his inside leg under his outside leg. I asked him to do this in both directions a few times and then stepped into the stirrup with my left foot. Sky waited. Dancing Horse didn't say a word.

I ran my hands over his rump and stroked his neck, still standing in the left stirrup. I moved the lead rope into the position I had taught him was the signal to keep his feet still and bend his neck toward his shoulder, which now had my knee behind it, in his line of sight. Then I lifted my right leg in a gentle arc and put it down on his right side, slipping my toe into the stirrup. I released his head and looped the rope over his head to the right side. When I took up the slack in the rope, I put too much pressure on it, and he started to move his feet.

"That's okay," Henry called. "Let him think you meant that. Let him move his haunches. The instant he stops his feet, release that rope! Then go back to the other side. Get some success there with what he knows before you try the right side again. You're doing great."

All the time Dancing Horse was talking, I was letting Sky move his haunches, encouraging him with the pressure on the rope and a little bit of leg on the right side. I felt the horse begin to think he might be tired of that and try something else. I took my leg off of him. He stopped moving, and I threw my hand forward to loosen the rope. "Good boy," I said and flipped the rope to the other side.

Henry had taught me how to use my legs, first left and then right, against his sides at the girth to ask for the walk. Soon, I was going around the small arena, stopping and turning, bending Sky's neck and moving his haunches, and then going forward again. Dancing Horse backed away from the rail and let me practice those moves he had taught the horse how to do from the ground and now I was asking the horse to do from his back.

"Henry?"

"It's your moment, girl. Enjoy it."

We moved around the arena as one. I rewarded Sky with full stops, strokes on his silky neck, and soft words. It didn't quite seem like enough to me, but Henry said not to worry, the horse would build on those small moments and look for them. When the grey went off on his own, I asked him to do that thing longer than he might want or maybe with a bit more energy. When he gave to me, hesitated, softened, stopped his feet, I took my legs away and dropped the rope. Pretty soon I could quit driving with my legs and seat, and he would stick his feet to the ground like a gymnast.

"This is amazing, Henry," I called out once.

"Timing, my girl," he said. "Timing and feel. You can let him off any time now."

An hour had passed. Shadows had begun to cross the sandy floor, and a crisp breeze had sprung up from the west. I dismounted and headed for the gate. I asked Sky to wait so I could go through first. Henry met me with a big grin on his face.

"I forgot I was supposed to ask you for dinner!" I said.

"Sounds good, champ."

"Now tell me about this horse," I insisted.

"Let's go to the house. I need to ask Hank something first."

One of the wranglers grabbed Sky's lead from me.

"I should take care of him, Henry."

"We'll make an exception tonight. I can't stay too long. I'm sure the horse will be just as happy to have his dinner and let the boys handle him."

When we pulled our chairs up to the oak table where Hank was already seated, Susan appeared with a giant bowl of fried chicken. Everyone knew it was Henry's favorite. He grabbed a thigh and started in.

Susan touched my shoulder. "I don't know everything about what you were doing out there, but when I glanced through the window now and then, you seemed right at home on that horse."

"Another Serena in the making," Dancing Horse said. Then he asked Hank if he had any records about Grey Boy and his line.

My heart skipped a beat. *Who is Grey Boy?*

"I might have," Hank said. "My dad was pretty good about keeping track of that kind of stuff. I'll have to look through his papers. Why?"

Dancing Horse winked at me. "When I was helping the boys round up those renegade horses last fall, I noticed a dappled grey loping with a big easy stride. Kind of reminded me of Julian's Grey Boy. I know your dad bred him to some excellent mares—some his, some other ranchers'. And many of those were re-bred and produced fine stock. Didn't Sunny have one of those greys after she came back from California?"

"Yes, she did," Hank said. "I'd kind of forgotten about him because Sunny was more interested in the Church then."

"When Kivuli chose that grey out of the wild bunch, I got to thinking how great it would be if he came from Grey Boy's line."

"That would mean someone might claim him as a run-away," Hank said.

My heart sank. Then I brightened. "I've read about Serena and that grey horse, a grey horse that belonged to her husband, Julian. Askay says a lot about the horse! I didn't know it could be so important to me!"

"After dinner we'll read some of those entries together," Hank promised.

"I can't be staying, but if you'll get me those records, I'll do a little research this week," Dancing Horse said.

Hank said he knew right where they were if Henry could stay a minute.

A while after Henry left with the files, Hank and I sat on the couch with Askay's words in front of us. We skimmed through the tattered pages, stopping when we saw Serena's name or anything to do with horses. There were a lot of entries like that, but one caught my eye. Hank read the passage out loud.

julian break hand cannot ride I see him leaning on rail serena on big horse cantering she part of horse like part of Julian going this way and that with balance and joy he trust only serena with grey only serena with his heart

I turned a few more thin sheets.

"Here's another," Hank pointed out.

mr Julian still in pain but stand watching serena on big grey choose her joy in horse and his joy in her over pain horse dancing in a new way so beautiful like a painting

"Hank, this is your mom and dad! This memoir must be so dear to you. I could never take it away from you."

Hank put it down for a moment. He shook his head. "I had most of these pages for many years but kept telling myself I'd read them later. I'd glance at a few now and then, but I never saw the words that he wanted to save me from whatever Liana was planning to do."

"Sometimes I'm sorry I found them."

"Somebody would have found them, sooner or later," he said. "But you gave your great-grandfather a way to tell me…at last."

I put my head on Hank's shoulder. That was the best thing he could have said to me in that moment.

"You'd better get to bed now, Kivuli," Susan called from the kitchen.

When Dancing Horse came back for the lesson on Tuesday, I already had Grey Sky loose in the round pen with his tack nearby. Henry motioned to me to come up and sit with him in the viewing box. He had a small file from the large stack of files he had taken with him on Friday.

"I didn't find anything specific, but what I did find you may not like," he said.

"Just tell me."

"I narrowed things down to breeders and folks within a hundred miles of this ranch, thinking the horse could not have run here from Colorado, say, or Florida."

"Right."

"There were a lot of nice horses with Grey Boy's pedigree, names and dates and photos of foals and registration papers, but after Julian died, no more records were kept. Your Grey Sky would have to be from a more recent breeding. The thing to do would be to call some of these local people and ask if they'd lost a horse from that particular blood line."

"Are you going to do it?"

"No. The horse is just fine where he is. But we'll never know if he's from Julian's Grey Boy."

"Maybe they'd sell him to Mr. Rose," I said, "if there was such a horse."

"You going to take that chance?"

"No."

"Well, go get ready to ride then," he said.

I trotted and cantered that day. Henry was mostly quiet, just adding little things for me to do to keep Sky's attention and release the pressure whenever I could. I had never felt this unity with any of my Granpa Farley's horses.

"I'll see you Friday, Kivuli-from-Africa," Dancing Horse called out to me as he took the file from the bench and went to the ranch house.

Then, Denari Robertson called. I was in the barn, cleaning my saddle and bridle. The headstall was like new because, though Sky had worn it a few times, I still rode with the halter and lead rope. "Just a minute," I told the girl. "I have to wipe some Neatsfoot Oil off of my hands."

When I picked up the phone again, Denari said, "What's Neatsfoot Oil?"

"Oh my gosh, you guys better get over here and stay at least a month!"

"That's kind of why I called, besides wondering if you could help me with English. I cannot diagram a sentence to save my life!"

"I'm afraid ranching life is kind of like diagraming sentences," I said. "Each part in its place properly connected to the main part."

"What?"

I groaned. "Oh, lord. Listen, Denari, I haven't told the Roses about you guys yet. Things get a little hectic around here in the spring, and we have some range horses that need a lot of attention, but I promise I'll call you back tonight. I think Mr. Rose is hiring now for the summer season, so he'll have a lead on some expert wranglers."

"Oh, great. My folks just don't know where to begin. The ranch came with a dozen horses, but we don't know anything about them. There are nameplates on the saddles, but we don't know the horses' names! Frankly, we don't know how to put the saddles on anyway."

"Denari? Why did your folks want to do this?"

"We had to get out of L.A., and the place was cheap. My dad said, 'How hard can it be'?"

"Would they take my advice?"

"Like what?"

"Like come and work for Mr. Rose this summer, maybe bring all those horses and get help sorting them out with tack, abilities, safety issues, health issues, age issues, shots, worming—"

"Kivuli! You are scaring me!"

"It's a tough life, but I'm sure you can learn it. Let me call you back. I'm late for dinner."

"Okay. Thanks, Kivuli."

In Askay's room, I cleaned up for supper and tried to decide how to tell Hank and Susan about the Robertsons. There was a high probability the Roses didn't need any more projects just then and would think I was off on another mission.

I ate three bites of mashed potatoes and gravy, one of my favorite American foods, and began with, "I might have a problem."

Susan smiled. "What else is new?"

"Well, it might be more of a problem for you," I said. "I have a new friend at school. She's an African-American girl from L.A. That part's good. What's potentially not good is her folks bought an outfit around here someplace, and they have no idea what they're doing. They don't know anything about horses or riding or fencing or feeding or irrigation or—"

Hank held up his hand. "Are they the ones who bought the Sawyer place?"

"I have no idea."

"Old Grant Sawyer told me he was selling to a black couple, wanted to know if I thought that was okay. I told him anybody who could fix that property up and make a suitable guest ranch out of it was okay in my book. What's your friend's name?"

"Denari Robertson."

"I think that was the couple's last name," Hank said.

"Can you help them?"

"I'd like to help them, but I can't run two ranches. That place is about five miles from here, which isn't too bad, but the days just aren't long enough to be traipsing back and forth."

I thought of my father running two coffee plantations, constantly on the road between Arusha and Moshi. Sometimes he was too tired to speak when he came home. It was too much to ask of Hank.

"Maybe they could work for you in exchange for you helping them with their horses," I said.

"Grant left horses there?"

"Twelve."

"Oh, lord."

We ate in silence for a while. I wondered what I could do to help the Robertsons with the less than two months I had left.

"You didn't make any promises, did you?" Susan asked, as she started clearing the table.

"No. I did say I'd call Denari back tonight."

"Tell her I'll stop by to see her folks this week, check out the horses, and the situation."

When I got Denari on the phone, the first thing I asked was if they were feeding the horses properly.

"Someone from the reservation is taking care of them, but I don't know how reliable he is. He drinks."

"Denari, I could help with the horses, but I think you need more than me or a drunken Indian. Tell your folks to please listen to Mr. Rose. He'll come see them this week."

I crawled under the covers in Askay's bed. I felt clear at last of the anxiety over Liana and was beginning to see a way out for my mother. I slept, free of dreams.

40

Catholic expectations

Then, Sunrose went away. The afternoon before my next lesson with Dancing Horse, she came down to the round pen when I was riding Grey Sky. I was practicing, sharpening a few moves, to please Henry. Sunny climbed up into the spectator box and took the bench closest to the rail. She didn't have any make-up on, and she sat very straight in a plain brown dress. Her hair was pulled back and held together by a piece of lace. The sea-glass rosary on her chest sparkled in the rays of the dying sun.

I was reminded oddly of Julia's plain Indian doll but let that go and went to work. I disengaged Sky's haunches left and right, walked in larger and larger circles, asking him to move out with my inside leg. Then, I did the same thing with a light pressure on the reins, releasing the pressure whenever he arched his neck and moved forward. I did most of the maneuvering with my legs and the turn of my head. Sky willingly followed these aids, and when I was satisfied, I dropped the reins and let the horse stand quietly for a moment. That was when I noticed the suitcase on the ground outside the arena. What was going on?

Grey Sky fussed with the bit, so I gave him something else to do. Soon, I had him loping his big easy gait around the edge of the ring. I hooked the reins on the saddle horn and put my arms straight out in the air, feeling the horse's strides with my seat bones. I glanced up, but Sunny didn't smile. I gathered the reins and halted by the grandstand.

"That horse reminds me of a horse I used to own," Sunrose said.

That was the last thing she ever said to me.

I reversed direction and loped the other way. Sky stumbled in a deep spot in the footing. I checked his pace and then stopped to make sure he hadn't strained a ligament. When I looked up again, Sunny was gone. I cooled the horse down and led him to the barn. Thomas was blanketing Julia's pony. He seemed to be taking extra time with the buckles, so I put Grey Sky in his stall and went over to him. His face was wet, his eyes swollen, but all he said was, "I'm sorry, Kivuli."

When I got to the house, I hesitated. I could hear raised voices. It seemed Hank and Susan were not talking to each other but to someone else. I opened the door and crossed the entry. The Roses had their phone on speaker: the other voice was Father Zenwa's.

"You can't let her do this…please," Susan said.

"I tried to dissuade her. But a religious calling is a powerful thing. She has been telling me for some time that she wished to return to the convent, that she was very distressed," the priest said.

"But I thought she was finally over Liana," I interrupted.

"She told me recently something was missing in her life, something that had been strong was fading, and she only discovered what it was when she went to the prison," Hank said. He ran his hands through his hair and left them there as if trying to push away a frightful vision.

"And what is that?" Zenwa asked.

"Her faith in God," Hank said. "Isn't that something you should know?"

I sat down at the kitchen table. The Roses leaned on the walls, the chairs, the sink, pressed their hands against the table, held each other. They could not sit down.

"It feels like that day ages ago," Susan said.

"The day she left for St. Mary's?" the priest asked.

"No. The day she was kidnapped." Her normally tan face was drained of color and her eyes were wet, but no tears fell.

"In a little while, you'll see her. She isn't gone," Zenwa said softly

Hank slammed his hand on the table. "But what will this do to Tom, and Julia?"

"She said she has struggled to be a wife and a mother. She wants something better for them," Zenwa answered—cautiously, I thought.

"That's crazy. That's just plain crazy. She loves them," Hank said.

"Yes, she does," the priest said, "but there's someone she loves more. Please don't repeat this to anyone. I'll come out to see you soon."

Hank hung up and shook his head as if trying to wake up from a bad dream.

"Oh, what have I done?" I said.

Hank took my shoulders. "This is not your fault. Sunny told me before you ever came she wanted to go back to the convent. I had no idea she was really going to do it. But a few days ago, she said something odd to me. She said whatever she decided to do, that you would understand."

"But I *don't* understand."

Hank went on. "Sunny said, 'That girl is searching for answers. She'll be happy I have found mine.' I didn't push her to explain."

"But how will Thomas get over this? How will he understand it?" I asked. And then, I realized that my father had lost my mother in a lot of ways to Safina, and he hadn't fallen apart. He seemed glad Suzanna could have what she needed. But Thomas was not Askari. Tom was Catholic and had Catholic expectations about his life. And Julia! Her independent spirit could not be prepared for this. And I had promised Julia everyone would take care of her mother and keep her safe.

Susan lifted her hands in the air, and then let them fell limply at her sides. "Kivuli, we don't blame you. Sunrose has never been the 'Sunny' that we loved before she was kidnapped. We could never have her. God may as well," she said.

"I will stab you when you least expect."

The last weekend in April, Hank and Thomas and a couple of the boys drove over to the Robertsons to see what they could do. They came back with seven horses and one less wrangler, an experienced hand named Winston. Hank spoke to the small crowd that had gathered to find out what was going on.

"Winston stayed to gentle three geldings so Denari and her folks can be safe on them. We had to euthanize a couple of cranky old mares who probably had ovarian tumors, judging by their behavior. The Robertsons hired Jocko D. from the reservation to feed and do barn chores. They'll give him room and board if he'll cut back on the drinking, which I guess they had heard about before the boy showed up."

Everybody laughed, most with sympathy for the Indian youth who had worked and been fired from almost every ranch around, according to Susan, who stood with me by a pen that held the Robertson's horses. No one moved, as if wondering what else Hank might say about helping the new family or about the absence of his daughter.

"We can handle this. I know you think I am overwhelmed by... things, but the ranch is still here. The stock needs feeding. The guests need safe rides. The garden needs tending. We have jobs, so let's get to it."

His handsome face was shadowed by his hat, but I could see the determined set of his mouth and uncompromising gleam in his eyes. In that moment, I loved him fiercely. He had sounded so much like my father, steady and unbreakable in the face of loss.

Sunday night, Susan set Hank's plate of beef stew and cornbread before him and said, "You are a saint, Henry Rose."

41

the poem

One afternoon, in the early part of May, I was studying for an algebra test when Hank knocked on my bedroom door. He had a ragged piece of paper in his hand. On it were faint words, fainter than Askay's trembling script. He didn't give it to me immediately but instead handed me a creased photograph of two people in wedding clothes.

"Do you know who this is?" he asked.

"Not for sure."

"Julian and Serena. The day they were married in this house."

"Oh, wow! They are gorgeous!"

"They were so in love," he told me, "but before they met, they both had troubling relationships. I think you've heard something about that. I know I promised to show you this a while back. We can talk about it or not. I'm not sure I have it all figured out, but maybe it was meant to mean different things to different people. I've always thought my mom would only want someone who appreciated it to read it."

I took the page from his hand. It was Serena Rose's poem. Hank left me with it. I looked at it, already choking up.

> *I have danced in the red snow*
> *where the spring has frozen*
> *where she finds me open*
> *I do not flee*
> *with my fresh wounds*

*I feel her hunger
chance that dangerous ground
put my paws in her traps —
those lovely promises
that glint in her eye
at how I languish*

*I am the bait
that melts the ice
in her hunter's sights
but her arrows fly —
come sigh kiss cry*

*And I go down to that little death
falling
falling
no dance left
her fingers locked on my spine
her strong jaw
gnawing on bone*

*That trace of crimson
floating the white tide?
it's only my heart
unconsumed*

    I was holding the words written for another woman in another time, an admission of a fearsome kind of love that could have demolished Serena if she had not ventured onto the ranch of the blue sky. I had a startling thought: *this was the kind of love Sunny wanted from God.*

I whispered the words, "Come…sigh…kiss…cry," and then an admonition for Sunrose—marry your god, and springs will freeze and you will know the most dangerous ground of all."

I folded the poem carefully and placed it in Askay's journal. I called Father Zenwa. "Hi. It's Kivuli. I need to show you something."

"I'm free on Friday. I could come to the ranch. After school?"

"Oh, would you? I have a riding lesson with Dancing Horse. You could watch. He usually doesn't like observers, but he's partial to you."

"I'd like that," the priest replied.

The next day, at school, I was severely distracted. I was haunted by the poem. There was no one with whom I could share it. It was too personal—and fierce. But when I saw Avery on the gym field, I ran over and tucked the poem in the pocket of her polo shirt. "Let's talk on the bus. Maybe Donna can sit with Trace."

"What'll we tell them?"

"I need some advice—you know, girl stuff."

"Are you going to explain what this is about?"

"After you read it," I promised.

In Spanish, Manny passed me a note of his own: *"Go look at the roses!"* I was always running so late to my first class that I had barely looked at them since the snow melted, and now those roses would bloom long after I returned to Africa. Manuel hovered with such adoration around Denari, I began to fear the roses would be cut surreptitiously for the love of his life.

Where did I fit in all these passions swirling around? I loved Trace, but I didn't wish to "go down to that little death" or have "his fingers locked on my spine." I felt a shiver of pleasure when I was near Mr. Glen, but I certainly didn't want to "chance any dangerous ground" with him! Would I ever know anything as wild and beautiful as Serena's first love? Could I handle the pain as well as the thrill?

My last two classes dragged, and then Trace and I were walking across the field to Mr. Glen's debate club. Denari greeted us at the door.

"Hey, how's it going with those horses at your place?" I asked.

"I think we're getting the hang of it. Mr. Rose's wrangler, Winston, is very patient with us. If that Indian boy could only do the chores more responsibly—whoops! I'm sorry, Trace!"

"Well, we aren't all geniuses!"

"So, Denari, do you want to come home with me Friday and see me ride the horse I broke…well, almost broke. I had a lot of *Indian* help."

"Oh, gosh, I'd love to! Can my parents come too?"

"Lots of room in the bleachers," I said.

"Okay, kids, grab a debate prompt! One on one today," Mr. Glen told us as he put a basket on his desk filled with "issues" to titillate us. "I see we have an uneven number. Kivuli, you can be with me."

Oh, God.

Later, on the bus, Avery told Donna to please sit with Trace, that she had something important to talk to me about, and led me to the last seat. The bus had barely begun to move when she retrieved the poem from her purse and spread it out on her lap. "Who wrote this?" she said with fervor.

"Tell me what you think first."

"I think this the saddest poem I've ever read. This is about a love that was never fulfilled. The writer was willing to be torn apart for the love of the other person, his or her bones to be gnawed on, for Heaven's sake. Metaphorically, of course, but still…"

"Do you like it?"

"I adore it!"

"But have you ever felt that way? Just so totally…desirous…of a love that could hurt you...kill you even?"

"No. I don't get involved with people who are dangerous, who can rip that emotion out of me and then not...follow through."

"What are you talking about?" I began to feel uneasy about letting Avery read this poem.

"Kivuli! The last line! The writer has gone through hell to be with the lover, gets torn up and is bleeding, but the heart is left "unconsumed."

"I don't get it."

"They never made love! One of them refused. Who was it? Who wrote this?"

"Oh, my God, Avery... Serena Rose. She wrote it to a woman named Carla before she met Hanks's father."

Tears were rolling down Avery's cheeks. "But what did Hank know about this?"

"As much as he could imagine, I guess. He buried Carla in the family graveyard...because he believed that's what his mother would want."

Avery carefully folded the page up and put it in my hand. "Thank you, Kivuli. Thank you for letting me see this. I'll keep it to myself... but are there more of these? More of Serena's poems?"

"I'll ask. I'm curious myself."

The bus stopped at Avery's corner, and she and Donna got off. Trace was already gone.

When Friday arrived, I was nervous. I saw Father Z pull up to the outdoor round pen and then the three Robertsons. Tim and Stuart had come with Trace. The Roses were there sitting with Thomas and Julia. I could feel all the ghosts of the past: Helen and Henry, Julian and Serena, Tyrone, and Askay. I supposed Carla too. Dancing Horse stood by the gate holding Sky.

I started on the ground with driving the horse away from me, left and then right, and drawing him back to the center. Pretty soon, Sky wasn't noticing the visitors and had eyes only for me. After I saddled him, I put my foot in the stirrup. He started to walk off. I stepped down and backed him to the exact spot where he had left me and put my foot up again. He lifted one hoof. I put my foot on the ground. The next time I stepped into the stirrup, he didn't move a muscle.

"Good boy," I said, and I sat still in the saddle to make sure he didn't anticipate my cue for the walk.

The viewers in the above us seemed a little bored. They talked among themselves and hardly glanced my way. Didn't they know that just a few weeks ago Sky had been been a half-wild range horse? I circled, reversed, and halted. I slid to a stop from the trot and from the canter. Sky went forward from my legs and came back from my seat. I barely touched the reins. Finally, I tried asking for the canter from a halt. The horse trotted out enthusiastically, and I stopped him. I took some feel on the reins, placed my inside leg at the girth and my outside leg back slightly and gave him a firm nudge. He lifted into the canter like, "Oh, *that's* what you meant!"

I loosened the reins and walked along the rail of the pen. When I reached Dancing Horse, he said, "Pull the bridle off."

Suddenly, it got very quiet. I didn't hesitate. Henry would never ask me to do something I couldn't do. I leaned forward and slipped the leather headstall and the loop of parachute cord reins over Sky's ears and handed them to Dancing Horse.

"Just do what you've been doing," he said.

I walked a few steps and then asked for the canter before Sky got to thinking something was different. I tried to concentrate on the horse and still hear what people were saying.

Mr. Robertson said, "I don't believe this!"

"My mother taught the guests to ride this way, the ones who were interested," Hank told him.

"You'd better send this girl to me," he responded.

"Sadly, she's only here for another month or so."

"Don't you just make the horse do what you want?" Robertson asked.

"Actually, you need the horse to think it's his idea to do what you want," Hank answered.

In the ring, Grey Sky didn't complete the turn I asked for, so I put my arm out to one side to block his motion. He went the other way, and I gave him a stop as a reward.

"That's where the learning curve begins," Hank commented.

"Where?" Denari's father again.

"If you didn't see it, you're farther back down the learning curve than the horse," Hank said.

Mrs. Robertson clutched her husband's arm. "Honey, I think we came to the right place."

"That's enough now, Kivuli," Dancing Horse said. "I'll put him away so you can visit with your friends."

"You're an angel," I whispered.

"Just an old Indian, feeling the ghost of Serena Skye Rose," he said.

"Serena's maiden name was *Sky*?" I gasped.

"Yep...with an 'e'."

Grey Sky and Henry went off to the barn. The Roses took everyone else with them to the ranch house. I was left with Father Zenwa.

"That was brilliant," the priest said, after I climbed into the grandstand and sat down with him.

"I've learned a few things since I saw you last."

"Not just about horses, I suspect."

"No. How 'bout 'death is the end of all discussions'."

"Oh my. Where did that come from?"

I was tired, but when else could we have this discussion? "Did you know Liana?"

"Only through Sunny," he said. "Maybe a little through you. Are you sad she died?"

I shivered in the late afternoon air or maybe from the ghosts passing by on their way to a better place. "I would have been sad if she'd not said she was sorry for what she did or if Sunny hadn't gone to see her, whether she forgave Liana or not. Just being there was a kind of forgiveness if she couldn't say the words. But here's my question. Sunny stood there with her god like a fortress. Liana looked at her with no god in her heart. She didn't see Sunny. She spoke to the child she had molested and the dog she had not been very good to. It seems to me the connection got broken before either woman could make it real. Now Liana is dead, and Sunrose might as well be."

"How do you get your homework done with all this debate going on in your head?" the priest asked.

"Well, I'm going home soon, and when I get off that plane, I want to have the most points, metaphorically speaking."

"And what do you want winning the debate to get you?"

"Forgiveness for my mother and Safina, forgiveness as true as if Mvua had come back from the grave."

"Oh, child, you are standing at the edge of a large sea. What you desire could drown you or buoy you up. But here's something to think about. Can those women be forgiven if they are not sorry?"

"I want to believe they can. Being sorry could be a step toward forgiveness."

"Yes, I think so too. Maybe the most important thing is that Liana said she was sorry, if it was only to her vision of the child Sunny and the dog."

"Oh, that's it! It's the regret that counts! The Church can't save you or forgive you or absolve you if you're not truly sorry for what you have done!"

The priest nodded. "That's the truest thing you've said to me."

I wanted to say the words again so I could never doubt them, so that this wonderful priest would see inside my heart. "A person doesn't have to be Catholic or say a rosary or do penance or believe in God. She only has to hate what she's done and not do it again!"

"I hope so, my dear. Otherwise the world would be an intolerable place. It isn't just God who holds us to a high standard, it's our own goodness, the standards of our own souls."

The light in the western sky wavered and resisted its descending. Horses loped across the pasture to their piles of hay. I reached into the pocket of my jeans and pulled out my last piece of resistance.

"You said you wanted to show me something," Father Zenwa said.

I handed him Serena's poem and watched his face while he read. "Do you understand this?" he asked when he finished.

"Yes. I do. But not because I get an A in Honors English."

"Hmm. And why did you want me to see it?"

"I think Sunny has fallen into a trap," I answered. I looked out to the darkening mountains. I could barely see beyond the barn.

"How so?"

"There is no god," I said.

"Oh my dear child, yes, there is. Who wrote this?"

"Serena Rose."

"Did she live a good life?"

"She saved a lot of horses and people. She was widely loved. Then, she was struck by lightning."

He gripped the cross that hung around his neck. "I don't think you are going to talk a priest out of believing in God."

"I'm not trying to. I love you."

"Ah! A sight or a sound that has no other explanation!"

42

the legacy of Helen Rose

Late the next morning, Faith Collins picked me up in her Mustang for a trip to the County Library in Elko. I asked her what color the restored older car was as I got into the front seat.

"Champagne," she said.

"I love it!"

"It's one of my favorite colors," Faith said. "Weird, huh? It doesn't seem like a real color."

"I've seen that color in the sky. I like it too."

I hadn't told the Roses where Miss Collins and I were going. I wanted to find out why Helen's paintings were in the library and who was responsible for them. The spring rains had greened the desert beyond compare. Washes and gullies were full, and in some places there was standing water in low swales in the land. I wished for the talent to paint what filled my eyes, something beyond the colors and shapes, something of the endurance and permanence of its heart.

We entered the city, and Miss Collins drove directly to the public library. She told me she had been there many times to study some of the rare art books they allowed teachers and scholars to use, that she had seen Helen's paintings in the section titled "World Cultures." We walked through several rooms, and I tried not to be distracted by the rows and rows of books I would never have time to read. We turned a corner and saw the sign "World Cultures." On the walls above the stacks, in one corner with African art and artifacts, were the watercolors of Helen Rose.

I felt like weeping. The paintings revealed villages, grasslands, and vast savannahs. Some showed animal life; others pictured street markets and children herding goats along the roadside. Miss Collins and I lingered at every one. We didn't speak. But Faith moved a little ahead and suddenly motioned for me to come to where she was standing.

"Didn't you say your great-grandfather lived on the rim of the Ngorongoro Crater?"

"Yes."

"Look." Miss Collins pointed to a detailed and colorful watercolor.

Among paints the red of the crater earth, yellow of the wheat and corn fields, gray-green of the acacia trees, and burnished tones of human skin, was the figure of a wiry farmer, his purple- and gold-robed wife and two children playing in the dust—a tiny girl, maybe two years old and an older boy holding out his arms for his sister. *Iyeala and Tanal.* It had to be. The children Askay had left behind. I had to sit down in one of the large chairs by the exhibit.

"Miss Collins," I whispered again. "That little girl was my Grandmother Iyeala."

"Oh, I thought there might be a connection to your story. What shall we do?"

"Can we find out who owns them?"

"Let's do that. Come on."

We went to the main desk and questioned a young woman about the paintings.

"Oh, I'm new here," she said. She removed her lavender-framed glasses and squinted at us. Then she put them back on hastily and asked, "Which paintings?"

I spoke up. "The ones in the Africa exhibit."

"I haven't seen those yet, but I believe there's a pamphlet that should help you." She searched through the file cabinet behind her. "Here you are," she said, and handed me a thick booklet with a collage of the art of world cultures on the cover. "Is this for a school project?" she asked.

"No. A family project. I'm the great-granddaughter and granddaughter of people portrayed in one of the paintings."

The librarian stared at me. "How do you know that?"

"It's a very long story, but there is no doubt about who is in this particular painting. I need to return it to the rightful owner."

"That may not be possible," the librarian said.

"Nothing is impossible," I said.

Faith and I took the brochure to a table close by. Helen's paintings were inside, catalogued and described. In the last paragraph was a startling statement: *"These watercolors were donated by Helen and Henry Rose in 1949. The works were painted in the East African country of Tanganyika (now Tanzania) and are the only works by an American artist of this part of Africa recognized by the Library of Congress."*

The librarian was suddenly standing over us. "I found something in the file titled "Contracts" that might help you. I can make a copy if you like."

"Thank you so much," I said. I turned to the section on *East African Art*. "Miss Collins, listen!" I read a few lines out loud. "'The County Library does not own the paintings by Helen Rose. They were given to us for display only and are ultimately the property of the Rose family, the living relatives of Henry and Helen Rose of Ochala Junction, Nevada. There is a contract to this effect on file at the county courthouse'."

"Oh, Kivuli, this is wonderful. We could retrieve the paintings for Mr. and Mrs. Rose!"

"I don't think you and I could do it," I said. "Probably only Hank, or maybe Sunny, could actually ask for them. I only want the one of Askay and his children. I mean, I want Hank and Susan to have it. It belongs in Askay's room at the ranch. It makes what he gave up for them real."

Miss Collins closed the file. "The Roses might be worried. We've been gone a while."

"But how can I leave without that painting?"

"Let me try something," she said.

The two of us waited in a line that had formed. The new clerk seemed nervous trying to direct visitors and check out books, but Miss Collins did not let that deter her, and she got right to the point when we reached the desk.

"This file says the library has a contract with the Rose family and that they are, in fact, the owners of the paintings. We are personal friends of the Roses, and we would like to take one of the paintings to Helen's grandson, Hank Rose. Tonight."

"This is highly unusual," she said.

"Probably," Faith said, "but this file says the paintings belong to the Rose family."

"Then someone from the Rose family will have to take them back. There's nothing else I can do. I'm sorry."

I couldn't stand this difficulty, and it wasn't the young clerk's fault. "Faith, let me tell Susan. They aren't going to just let us walk out of here with a painting, especially not one that's been here, oh my gosh, over sixty years! Mrs. Rose will know what to do."

"I think you're right."

The librarian gave us the phone number of the manager of the library. I turned to Faith. "Let's go back and look at the painting again. I may be gone before it can ever be recovered."

The corner with the watercolor was dimly lit, but the scene leaped out at me before I was half way across the room. I stood before it again. How could Askey have left those children? He must have been desperately poor. He must have planned to make a lot of money and return one day. I thought of all the years the painting had hung in the library, quietly shining over Americans coming and going, studying the art, remembering Helen Rose, but never knowing that the African she painted was living in their midst.

On the way to the Crossroads with Susan on Monday, Julia said matter-of-factly, "Momma went to be with God." She was looking out the window and didn't seem to be addressing anyone in particular.

Susan glanced in the rear view mirror in surprise. "Honey, your mother is not dead."

"She isn't?"

"No."

"But that's what Daddy said."

"Julia, your mother wanted to be a nun again. She's very much alive, and she loves you."

"Oh. But doesn't that mean she's married to Jesus? She can't be my momma anymore?"

"I think it's just a heavenly union, not like the marriage to your father," Susan continued explaining to Julia.

I wondered if that were true: was Sunny still married to Thomas?

"Well, I'm glad she's not dead, but I don't think I'll see her ever again," Julia announced, and then she began to color in her coloring book.

With Julia distracted, I jumped at the chance to ask Susan about Helen's paintings. "Mrs. Rose, do you and Mr. Rose know where all his grandmother's artwork is?"

"I suppose," she said. "Helen could have sold some or given some away. Why?"

"I found a few of her watercolors that I don't think Hank knows about. There's one, especially, that I'd like to get back for him before I leave."

"You found paintings we don't know about?"

"At the County Library, in Elko. Miss Collins took me there Saturday. She'd seen them. She thought I should too."

"Oh, my, Kivuli, what other surprises could there be in this life!"

"I think this qualifies as a good surprise," I said.

Susan maneuvered the truck around a pot hole carved by winter ice, causing Julia to send a long yellow crayon mark outside the line of the sun in her coloring book.

"Gramma!"

"Put your things in your backpack now, Julia," Susan told her. "We're almost to the Crossroads." She glanced at me. "Tell me what you found."

"We found a series of African landscapes. They were donated to the library, for display only, in 1949."

"We had no idea!" Susan said with some amazement, "What else do you know?"

"I know you can get them back. There's a contract in the county courthouse signed by Helen. A family member has to request them. Could you do it, and we can surprise Mr. Rose together? He may want them all back, but I want to give Hank just one."

"Which one?"

"The one Helen painted of Askay with his wife and children on the rim of the Ngorongoro Crater."

"Oh, my goodness," she said. She began to slow down for the bus stop. "Do you want it to show Hank how much Askay gave up for the Roses?"

I hesitated because I thought that was partly true, but I answered, "I hope it would be to show Hank how much my great-grandfather loved Helen and Henry and their children, that he stayed in America for them." I gathered my books and put my hand on the door handle.

"I'll do it, sweetheart. It will be a great gift," Susan said.

When Trace got on the bus a few stops later, I asked him if he wanted to go riding after school. "Just a short ride. I need to take Sky out of the round pen, and I don't want to go too far from the ranch."

"You're not going to debate club today?"

"Denari told me on the phone earlier that Mr. Glen was going to cancel today."

"I'd rather ride with you anyway," Trace said. "What about Dancing Horse?"

"He never comes on Monday, but he said I was ready for the world outside the round pen."

What I was not ready for was the realization that I missed that damned Liana. And I missed Sunrose too, with her house full of trinkets and her heart full of God.

43

the right grey horse

Julia sat with us on the way home from school. She didn't seem overwrought by her mother's disappearance. She chattered on about her soccer team and winning her 2nd Grade spelling bee. Either she was pretty good at covering up her feelings, or she didn't care that Sunny had disappeared. When we got to the Crossroads, she skipped across to Susan's car with an A paper from her geography class—the mini descriptions of the places on the map I had helped her with during Christmas break.

"This cannot be real," Trace said, when Julia began singing a song she had learned in music appreciation. "I want to cry for her," he whispered in my ear.

I told Susan that Trace had permission to come home with me to ride that afternoon.

"That's fine, but Kivuli, you need to prepare yourself for something you're not going to like," she said.

"Did someone die? Pass? Lazo?"

"Oh, no, dear, but Hank got a call from a rancher about the range horses. He said his "then girlfriend" had lost a dappled grey gelding almost two years ago and asked if he could come see what we had."

"No! No! No!"

"Honey, these are not our horses. Some folks may have forgotten about one or two of theirs that fell in with the wild ones, but apparently this particular horse was his 'now wife's' favorite, and she's been heartbroken."

"Well, they didn't look very hard! Sky's been here for months."

"Hank didn't aggressively advertise that we had that bunch, but word gets around. I'm sorry, Kivuli, but losing things is part of life."

"I lost my mother," Julia interjected.

"Maybe it won't be the right grey horse," I said.

Trace grabbed my hand. "It'll be okay."

"But who's going to take me to see the puppies now?" Julia lamented.

When we turned down the ranch drive, we noticed a luxurious matching truck and horse trailer parked by the barn. I threw my books on the porch and headed for the arena, where a group of wranglers had gathered. I opened the gate, and there was Grey Sky all tacked up with a huge shank bit in his mouth, twirling around a portly, red-faced man who was trying to mount him. I could hardly think straight, but I had the bridle off the horse in two seconds. Sky saw me and kept his feet still.

"What the—"

"Excuse me, sir, but this horse doesn't need all that bit!"

"And how would you know?" he snapped. He picked up his tack from the ground where I had dropped it.

"Step back and I'll show you. I mean, step out of the arena… please."

The man was too surprised not to do what I asked, and I quickly shortened the stirrups and mounted. I placed my legs and asked Sky to spin on his haunches, first fast, then slow, then fast, in each direction. Then, I cantered off to the rail and tracked to the left, the horse's best way. I was glad I had worn jeans to school that day. My flat shoes were not the safest thing for riding, but when you follow your instincts, you don't always have the right equipment. I didn't want to push Sky and perhaps cause him to make a mistake, so I slowed to a jog and did a few figure eights and then stopped and backed the horse up the full diameter of the round pen.

The stranger did not take his eyes off me the whole time. I dismounted and Sky followed me to the gate. I haltered the horse and asked him to go through the opening ahead of me in controlled steps on a loose lead. As soon I got to where Hank and the man were waiting, the stranger said, "I think I owe you a training fee, young lady. How much do you want?"

I had had a little time to think, so I answered with as reasonable a voice as I could. "I'm going home in a month. All I ask is that you let the horse stay until I'm gone. Leaving is going to be hard enough without having to say goodbye to him right this minute."

"I don't know," the man said. "It's my wife's horse."

"Maybe your wife would like to learn to ride him without that punishing bit," I suggested.

He smirked. "How old are you anyway?"

"Fifteen, next month."

"Oh, Teresa would never take lessons from a child."

"I don't mean lessons with *me*," I said. "I mean lessons with Henry Dancing Horse, the man who taught me."

"I don't think she'd take lessons from an Indian either."

"Well, that is her loss."

Hank turned to the stranger. "Mr. Larkin, one month is only going to make this horse better for your wife. Can you not break this child's heart today?"

"Let me call Teresa. It's her decision," Larkin said.

"Oh, and I'd like to see the horse's papers and his pedigree back about thirty years, if you don't mind," I added.

"Of course," he said smugly, and went off punching numbers in his cell phone.

Hank handed Grey Sky to one of the boys, and he and I went to the grandstand to wait with Trace and Julia. This was the first time Julia didn't have to "go right home" since her mother was not waiting for her. The seven-year-old might be feeling her first taste of freedom.

"Grandpa, can't you buy Grey Sky for Kiki?" Julia asked.

Hank stroked his granddaughter's hair. "I don't think the man wants to sell him. His wife has been missing him for a while."

"Julia, it's okay," I said. "I'm going home. The woman might as well have him back." I turned to Trace. "I guess we won't get to do that trail ride today."

"We still have a month. It'll happen."

Mr. Larkin came back and climbed up to us. He was smiling. "My wife says not to take the horse away from a girl that can ride like that, says she knows Dancing Horse and will call him about lessons," he said with an odd expression. "I had no idea she knew any Indians."

I had to hide my momentary disappointment. How long had Dancing Horse known Grey Sky could have been Teresa's? Had she told him about the disappearance of her grey horse, her favorite horse? Did Henry know someone was coming to take Sky away?

Larkin offered me some papers. "Here," he said. "I found these in the truck."

His name was Storm, right there on the papers. There were sires and dams listed pretty far back. They had names like Grey Star, Shades of Grey, Grey's Away, Grey Heart, and then I saw another name, and my breath caught in my throat—*Grey Boy*.

"Hank! Look! Here's Grey Boy, right here!"

"I see that," Hank said and leaned over to look at the other files in Larkin's hands. "So, Mr. Larkin, do you know about any of these other horses?"

"Storm's father, Grey Heart, went to California. He's a reining champion, probably retired. I think he's about twenty now. I have a picture of him somewhere."

"I call him Grey Sky," I said.

"Well, that's about what a storm is," Larkin said. "If you want, Mr. Rose, I can make up a lease agreement, no charge of course. I should pay *you*. I knew I didn't dare get on that horse after this girl here's demonstration. Why didn't you tell me about her?"

"I thought I'd see how you did with the horse. If I could see you might damage him, I was thinking of ways to keep him from you," Hank replied.

The man grimaced as if this was downright deceitful but then gave a resigned shrug.

"Where's home for you, young lady? Why are you leaving next month?" Larkin asked.

"My home is in Africa. Dar es Salaam, Tanzania."

"Heavens! I never would have guessed that!"

"Life is full of surprises," Hank said.

"A wonderful surprise for Teresa, for sure," he said. He gathered his papers and the tack and went down the stairs.

As Larkin left, I watched until he and his rig passed under the archway. Another pick-up came through at the same time.

"Mr. Rose, Henry is here," I told him.

"I figured. Let's go in."

Dancing Horse got out of his truck, but he didn't look at me as we made our way to the ranch house. When we got inside and sat down at the kitchen table, he handed me a large brown bag.

"You can look later. Let's talk," he said.

"Just tell me what happened."

"I'm so sorry, Kivuli. Teresa called me last week. She said maybe they'd found her horse. She was so excited. But I told her to be sure she could give Storm as good a home as the people who'd been caring for him. I didn't tell her I'd already figured out where he was. I was caught in the middle."

"Who is she?"

"She's a close Harvard friend of my daughter, Rachel. Larkin doesn't know any of this. He came along right about the time the horse disappeared. I told Teresa I'd keep my eye out for Storm, but many months went by, and when I saw him in that herd, I didn't want to believe it. I kept quiet. Teresa and Larkin went off on their wedding trip, and the horse needed care. Then, you chose him, Kivuli. What could I do? I thought he'd be the perfect one for you to learn about Serena's way, because he wasn't entirely wild. Still could be a challenge though. Didn't want to take that away from you. I made Teresa promise to let me help her when she got him back. Larkin will just have to deal with it," Henry finished, half out of breath. "Open your present."

Inside the wrinkled bag was a horse hair bridle of many colors—reds and golds and greys—like the Nevada sunsets with traces of storms.

"I made it for you," Henry said, "from the tail hairs of all the wild horses I could get near and some from Lazo."

"I love it! But it's too beautiful to use."

"No. I want you to go home and put it on one of those African horses. Send me a picture."

"I'll do that, Henry. I'll be glad to do that."

"Are we good then?"

"We're always good."

"Henry? Stay for dinner?" Susan called from the kitchen.

"Thanks, Susan, but my wife is fixing some big Indian stew."

"Take some fry bread anyway. She won't have to make that," Susan offered.

"Okay. She'll appreciate that."

"Henry," I said, catching him before he put his hand on the front door, "can you do that lady's lessons while I'm at school. I don't want to watch."

"I'm not doing any lessons with her until you are on that plane over the Atlantic," he promised.

I gave a sigh of relief. "But doesn't she want to see him?"

"I told her she's been without him for two years, she can wait another month."

He stood by the door and waited to see if I had any more questions. He had come all that way on a day he didn't usually drive to the ranch, so I tried to think of something else to make him feel the trip was worth it.

"Do you like her?"

"Sure…but not like I like you, Kivuli-from-Africa," he said. And then he opened the door.

I raced back into the kitchen where I hoped Susan would be alone. Hank and Trace had gone up to the barn to help Thomas with evening chores, Julia tagging along behind.

"Tell me. Tell me!" I cried impatiently.

"You'll be happy. I've made arrangements with the library director. I have to show Hank's birth certificate and his passport to be able to claim one of the paintings. If we want more, Hank will have to go himself. There may not be time before you leave, but I will do it."

I relaxed. "That's good enough for me."

44

a trick in the nick of time

On Wednesday, we got out of school early because of graduation practice, and Trace took us home in his red truck for the first time. Julia wanted to be left at Trace's to play with the puppies, and all the adults had agreed that would be all right. Tim or Stuart would bring her back to the ranch later. Hank had already tacked up Grey Sky for me, Lazo for Trace, and the most trustworthy dude horse for himself, in case Trace or I needed to trade. *What if we both needed to trade?* I wondered.

We started off east, Pass loping along happily beside us, and Hank explained we were going to be the first "guests" to see a new campsite closer to the ranch for future overnights. The boys had already built a shelter with a wide porch on a shelf of land about half way up the ravine and not directly in the gulch. The shelf lengthened out into a kind of mesa if higher ground were ever needed. We didn't imagine that would be today. The sun beat down on our backs, and there wasn't a cloud in the sky.

We splashed through rivulets of water left over from the spring rains, and once a bobcat ran along beside us and then crossed the sandy track in front of us. A couple of times, Sky broke into a trot without being asked, and I had to bring his head around and push his haunches over until he stopped his feet. He got the idea pretty quickly.

"We're just going to walk," Hank said. "The grey is new to this free range life with a rider on his back."

"Okay by me," Trace said. Lazo was dancing under the Native boy's seat. "I'm not entering any Indian Relays soon."

A slight breeze ruffled the horses' manes, and there was electricity in the air as we approached the foothills. I didn't want to believe it, but I thought I heard thunder far up in the mountains. A creek tumbled out of the canyon as it narrowed, but there was that raised platform and a hitching rail close by.

"We might be glad that roof is already on," Hank said.

Columbine and larkspur shot up from the stream banks, and here and there, water had flowed out of its bed and nurtured patches of green grass. Against one canyon wall, wild hollyhocks spread themselves in six-foot undulations of pink over the rocky soil. We watered the horses and tied them close by. A few drops of rain pelted our cheeks as we climbed up on the platform that would later be the porch of a more secure cabin.

We huddled together against the temporary posts and spread our rain slickers over us. Pass explored what might have been a fox den on the other side of the stream. Trace rubbed an already sore knee. Hank said he'd lengthen his stirrups, that sometimes that helped when you were not used to riding.

"I like it out here," I said. "I feel so safe, like the rain will dampen down the passion of the ghosts in our lives."

"What ghosts?" Trace asked.

"The ghosts of the Africans who came with me—my Aunt Kivuli, my Grandmother Iyeala and her brother Tanal, the soldier my mother killed, Mvua—people like that."

"Yeah. Some ghosts can find you wherever you are. Mine come when I hear a train," Trace said.

"I remember reading about that," Hank said. "I'm sorry, son."

"It's something you don't get over. Until you can find a place to put such a loss, you just deny it, don't talk about it."

"Like Julia," I said.

Trace pulled his jacket more tightly around him. "Right," he responded. "At first, I thought she was acting in a callous way. But then I remembered I was exactly like that, just acted like it was no big deal I'd never see my parents again. I didn't know how to feel. Someone should keep reminding Julia her mother's alive."

"I think Thomas is doing the right thing, just letting Julia be whatever she wants right now, not treating her like a child who's expected to have a tantrum or fall apart," Hank said. "I don't know who's going to be there for Tom. He's asked me to give him six of the wild horses to break."

"That's what I'd do if I needed to distract myself," I said. "I remember galloping wildly around the plantation when those detectives were hanging about. I came quite close to knocking a few of them down. My father had to *bench* me, as he called it. I didn't know what that meant. He said something like 'taking players out of the game because they are injured or dangerous to others.' I assured him I was not injured, and he said 'but you're dangerous.' I guess that's been the story of my life since then."

"I knew you were dangerous the first day I got on the bus!" Trace said.

Just then a sound like thunder boomed again, much closer, and rain began to fall in earnest.

"Oh, god!" Hank cried. "Let's go, kids!"

Trace was on his feet, but I didn't fully understand, just followed the guys to the horses. Pass was even farther out now on the other side of the creek.

"Leave the halters on! Kivuli, I'll take Sky! You ride Lazo! Trace, you take my horse! We're going to have to run!" Hank was shouting above the now pounding rain.

The creek was rising as we rode down the ravine. The trail was so rocky we could only trot at first, but as soon as the canyon widened, Hank yelled, "Go!"

We ran. The horses struggled to find their footing. The flash flood gathered momentum and filled the arroyo behind us with a sound like a freight train. Then, I understood. The rain had turned the placid stream into a river, and it was surging to overwhelm us. I searched for Pass. He was running but directly in the still dry channel. He would never hear us calling in time.

"Bear left! Bear left!" Hank yelled.

The ground rose up slightly toward the sandy mesa, and the horses lunged for higher ground. I saw Pass hesitate, and I drew the sharpest image I could in my mind of the dog tracking left in front of us and racing up the slope. He turned. The torrent spilled out of the canyon and widened across the plain of the desert. It lapped against the flying hooves. We didn't look back but kept our mounts on the uphill side, aiming higher and higher. Soon we were at the top of the incline, and Hank signaled for us to halt.

The horses sides heaved, and they dropped their heads, searching for air. The three of us dismounted and stared at the country from which we had just escaped. Water stretched across our tracks, but it was shallow now and not rushing, quiet like a lake or a mirage.

"You guys…did great," Hank said, gasping for air. "Oh God, where's Pass?"

"Right here beside me," I said.

"He couldn't have heard you. How did you—"

"I didn't use my voice," I said.

Hank's gasps turned into sobs. And then, in the distance we saw a group of wranglers riding our way. The flood seemed to be receding and soaking into the desert. Hawks swooped down on drowned creatures. Seeds that had lain dormant for seasons would sprout through the damp sand and carpet the ground with grass and tiny wildflowers in a week.

"Hasn't been a flash flood like that in years," Hank told them, "but conditions were just right."

"So much for loving the sound of the rain on the roof," I said.

Hank pointed to the washed out road on the opposite side of the channel. A herd of mule deer skirted the dark earth. Some of the females stared back at the forested grove where newborns could have been trapped or swept away.

"Life and death in the same waters," Hank said. "But the mothers will go back. They usually leave the little ones on high ground. If the fawns stayed where they were told, they'll be all right."

We picked our way around watery places that could be sink holes and still trip the horses up. Finally we reached the drier part of the road that led back to the ranch. The wranglers met us about a mile out.

"We got worried about you guys being up in that canyon," one of the boys said.

"We had quite a ride," Hank said.

"You want us to go look for dead game?" someone asked.

"Nah. Let the wolves and coyotes have them. Ravens and eagles need their share too."

When we got to the barn, we spent some extra time grooming the horses and oiling their saddles. Susan brought us fat sandwiches and hot chocolate.

"Mrs. Rose, this is just what we need. We are too tired to think," Trace said.

"What happened?"

"I saw my first flash flood," I said, "and almost my last!"

"That bad, huh?"

"Mr. Rose got us out of there just in time," Trace added.

"How did Pass escape?" Susan asked.

Everyone looked at me including some wranglers that had gathered around us.

Hank said, in a shaky voice, "Kivuli disobeyed me...and saved his life."

We sat on hay bales while some of the boys cooled out our horses and groomed and watered them.

I sipped my drink, but I hadn't taken more than one bite of my sandwich.

"Are you okay, sweetie?" Susan asked.

"Yes. I was just thinking about my mother crossing a flooded river in Africa. The horse had to swim for all he was worth. She'd stolen the gelding from my Granpa Farley's string at the military base and only had a few food supplies and a questionable map. She was my age, maybe a bit younger. I have much more respect for her after seeing that raging water."

"The beginning of a relationship," Susan whispered to me.

I looked at the faces around me: Hank, Susan, and Trace enjoying their chicken salad sandwiches, Sky and Lazo and the dude horse, whose name I still didn't know, hanging their heads over their stall doors, and True Passion, lying beside me and still breathing hard, and the wranglers beginning evening chores. I felt complete. I felt like an American.

45

june

When I looked at Faith Collins, I thought of us standing together in front of the painting of my ancestors on the rim of the Ngorongoro Crater. She was giving us our final assignment and the weekend to complete it.

"I'd like you to do an impression of a painting or sculpture that appeals to your emotions. Don't copy anything," Miss Collins said. "Just paint what you feel when you look at the artwork. Then, I'd like you to give a short history of the painting, the artist, and the reasons you chose it, if this information is available to you."

My first choice would be the painting in the County Library, but I couldn't get it without spoiling Hank's surprise. Miss Collins gave me a knowing smile. So I went home that day and took Helen's sunset watercolor off my wall in Askay's bedroom, thinking of Sunrose. The yellows, and umbers, and madders of the painting, the warmth of hope of light, could have blessed the recovered child, but the adult Sunrose had not taken it with her to the convent or to her married life, or to her now indelible, cloistered silence.

Helen's painting would go to Africa, where it could stand in the swiftly descending darkness of my own sundown. It was everything Nevada had given me, everything the Roses had given me, Sunny's sorrow in the fading light, Dancing Horse's strength in the line of the mountains, and Sky's dappled grey in the storming clouds.

When I told Hank why I had chosen the sunset painting, he said, "That's what I would have chosen for you," not knowing that I had chosen one for him that he had never seen.

My version of Helen's watercolor, however else it resembled or not the Nevada truth, would have the effect of the light struggling with the dark: the story of my life in America. I signed my full name and then wrote the history of each rendition.

Ten days before I was to step on the plane for my homeward journey, I took the paintings to class. I placed Helen's watercolor next to mine on the easel Miss Collins had provided and put my hand on the edge of the older one.

"A sunset like this," I began, "is something I will never see when I get home to Africa. On the equator, the sun sets before you can mix these paints. It's light, and then it's dark. But I love the symbolism of this American painting, the light lingering in the sky, not rushing into the darkness. It was done by Helen Rose, and she knows what I'm talking about. About seventy years ago, she and her husband, Henry, came to Tanzania. They were traveling on the rim of the Ngorongoro Crater, and they saw a lean, strong Maasai herdsman tending his goats on a grassy hill. He spoke no English and they no Maasai dialect, but something connected between them. Their guide translated. Would he come to America and work for them on a big horse and cattle ranch? *Oh, yes! He could cook.* Could he take care of children? *He had two children of his own.* Would he be willing to leave them and go across the ocean with the white people? *Yes, please, he'll go to America.*

"He left his family and adopted the American family. He saw the Nevada sunsets, and he never went back. That's the sunset Helen painted. She and her husband loved the African, and their son, Julian, loved him, and his son, Hank, buried him on the Rancho del Cielo Azul in 1988. His name was Askay, and he was my great-grandfather. In my painting I have tried to show what *I* have seen in your American sunsets, perhaps a little stormier, a little more dangerous. I'm leaving my painting for the Roses. They've given me Helen's, so I can watch the Nevada sunset from my home on the equator whenever I'm not ready for the dark."

"Now, I believe all of us will think of you, Kivuli, when we watch our sunsets," Miss Collins said. "Who would like to go next?"

No one volunteered.

When I got home that day, I hung my painting in the place where Helen's had been and started to pack hers in my suitcase. The frame seemed loose, as if someone had removed the canvas and then reframed it. I ran my hands over the paper backing. It was thin and worn but not as much as might be expected with a procedure from Helen's time. In one corner, I felt a ridge underneath like something was lodged there.

My heart began to pound. I reached for a pair of scissors and then hesitated, but only for a moment. The picture was mine. Why shouldn't I know what was hidden there? I cut a slit just big enough to reach the object and pulled out a folded piece of paper, opening it slowly, my hands trembling.

There, in Liana's handwriting were the words: *I will stab you when you least expect.*

The room spun. I sat down in my great-grandfather's chair and held the note that determined the fate of the little girl he would never know. Askay must have imagined someone would find the note someday, and the trouble, whatever it was, would be over. In that, he was right. I tucked the paper back in the small hole I had made. I would seal it better when I got home.

I could will the painting to my children. They might fly someday to America to find Trace or Julia or Avery or a dappled grey horse from the line of Julian's Grey Boy. I supposed by then the animals and people I loved would be someplace out of reach: Dancing Horse off doing half-passes in some heaven, the Roses in the ground up by the cabin, Tom Sentinel in a Catholic rest home, still hoping for a glimpse of his Sunny, Father Zenwa in his Catholic paradise, and True Passion buried up by the barn, close to the grey horse struck by lightning decades ago at Heaven's Door.

I went out to Askay's garden, although it didn't really feel like goodbye. Susan was picking tomatoes and looked up. "Oh Kivuli! Reena Stone called earlier! You should call her back before it gets too late. I think she's in New York."

I dialed the number, and Reena answered. "Hey, sweetheart, I'm going to Africa soon! Let's have our ride there."

"Oh, Mrs. Stone, oh, yes! Do you know where to find me?"

"I have an address in Dar es Salaam near the waterfront."

"Yes, that's it. We can ride out of the Military Post, where Granpa Farley can still procure mounts, or just a mile from the house at Ocean Acres, where Suzanna and Safina stable their horses."

"You choose," Reena said. "You sound good. Did you find your answers?"

"Some of them," I answered. "There are always more questions, right?"

"I'd say so. I guess we'll have a lot to talk about."

"You will not believe it!"

After I hung up, Susan said, "That is one fine lady. You should listen to her."

"I think maybe I'm going to do more listening from now on."

On June 12th, I turned my books in and said goodbye to my teachers. When I got to Mr. Glen's room, I waited until last student left. He was shuffling papers into his briefcase. I saw the sea-glass rosary in one corner. He looked up.

I spoke before I lost my nerve. "This is definitely my hardest goodbye, Mr. Glen. I don't know why."

He closed the briefcase and moved closer to me, but he didn't touch me.

"I think we understand each other, Kivuli. Maybe we have learned something from each other about what's important in life, things we can always hold in here." He put his hand over his heart.

So I said. "Maybe someday you can come to Tanzania and walk on the beach at Dar es Salaam."

"Will you walk with me?"

I imagined that briefly. I didn't think it would ever happen, but why not give him the biggest gift I could.

"We can pick up sea glass for a rosary and watch the ships coming in from all over the world and talk about the African history that's in your lesson plans now," I said. "Maybe about where our lives are going and what fulfills us."

He smiled, and his blue eyes did not waver when he said, "I do love you, Kivuli Farley."

I walked to the bus and did not look back. Julia and I sat together. Trace had gone home earlier, saying he would call me later. Thoughtful boy, letting me have the last word with Mr. Glen. Julia sat very still. She was not coloring or jabbering as usual.

"Hey, what's going on, girl?"

"It's just that I always went right home and there was my mother, always, as long as I can remember. She was waiting for me."

"I'm so sorry, Julia. Maybe you can be especially nice to your father. He misses her too."

"He's got those wild horses now."

"Well, maybe you'll just have to be a little wild horse then," I said and leaned against her all the way to the Crossroads.

Father Zenwa was in the living room when Julia and I got home. Julia had been staying with the Roses after school since Thomas was busy until dark with the horses in his charge.

"My two favorite girls!" the priest cried.

"How's my mother?" Julia burst out.

"Well, funny you should ask, little one. I have a letter from her just for you."

"Really?"

"Really," Zenwa said, and he handed her a blue envelope with a pink ribbon tied around it—Julia's favorite colors, I remembered.

Sunny's daughter bounded off to show her Gramma Susan, and I was left alone with the priest.

"Is Sunrose okay?" I asked.

"I'm not allowed to say much. Sunny has taken a vow of silence for a short time, but she seems at peace. I asked if she had a message for everyone, and she wrote one word on a slip of paper—'Forgive me.' I hope she gets that forgiveness so she can live in joy and celebrate her vows."

"I don't understand it. She thought I would, but I don't. Tell me what to do."

The priest took my face in his hands. "Live in joy, and celebrate your dreams. You will make mistakes, but there will always be hearts that will take you in. God will too."

Then, he put one hand on my head. "I bless you, Kivuli Safina Farley, in the name of the Father, the Son, and the Holy Spirit. Amen."

"Amen," I said.

"I'm not going to say goodbye," he said.

I didn't say it either and hugged him instead.

46

pressure/release

Sundown seemed a long way off, so I changed my clothes and went out to ride Grey Sky. As I led the horse into the round pen, I saw Hank up in the viewing stand, as though he had been waiting for me. I put the gelding through his ground exercises, mounted, and moved out to the rail. The horse seemed settled, so I worked on the skill that caused me the most trouble—flying changes. I focused on giving aids as clearly as possible, and soon I was riding at the canter in figure eights, doing flying changes of lead through the center. After the fourth time, I halted and gave him the reins. He dropped his head slightly as if waiting for what I might ask next. I hopped off and removed all the tack. Still he waited.

"Go roll and play, silly," I said and waved him away.

I went up and sat down next to Hank. We watched Grey Sky just being a horse. Pretty soon he would just be Storm and probably would never be asked to do a flying change again.

"I've been riding him, you know," Hank said, "to see how he'll take to folks other than you. How'd you get those changes to the right so easily? I always notice he's a little resistant on that side and gives me trouble."

"I've been working on that. I keep some pressure on that side, hold my legs steady on the right lead cue, even if he goes clear around the circle on the wrong lead. The minute he changes to the right lead, I throw the reins away and get off. The correct changes started happening sooner and sooner as I passed the center. The first time he changed right in the center, I quit for the day and turned him out in the big pasture."

Hank looked at me thoughtfully. "That's just what Serena did with a particularly dangerous, resistant human."

"I won't be here long enough to find out everything Serena did, I guess," I said, but I suspected I already knew this story.

"I should leave you with this because it ties so many things together. I'll spare you the ugliness, but my mom took many small steps with this person, like you did with Sky, and when there was finally a big change, something no one believed was possible, Serena gave the woman one of Helen's paintings.

"The bronc in the round pen," I said. "Ty told me about Miranda that day we rode out to the graveyard."

"Yes. I told Ty he could tell you, but I didn't know he had."

"The painting made her think about someone besides herself and gave her hope about herself at the same time."

"It did."

"What happened to her?"

"She got cancer. Near the end, Serena asked her where she wanted to be buried, and the woman said Towering Peak."

"But why there?"

The sky was darkening above the orange and crimson glow of the sunset. There was no breeze.

"That's the first place Serena put pressure on the woman, and then was able to release, to give her a way to change," Hank told her.

"I put a ton of pressure on Liana, but I never knew when to release."

"There's some new thinking on this method that says we should offer the release *first*, and then the pressure. I think that's what you did by just showing up in the visitor's room," he said. "I wouldn't have done it. Not sure I wanted you to do such a thing, but you know what? You took a chance with another mad woman to help my daughter see a different part of herself, maybe a part she's been searching for for a long time."

"But now, she's gone. I hate that she left, not telling anyone, not saying goodbye to Julia."

"Maybe she was never really here. Kidnapped but never found."

That was the sadness no one would ever get over.

"Maybe God will find her…on a road somewhere?" I offered.

"Not sure what I believe. Someday I'll ride up into Heaven's Door and see if there's a sight or a sound that has no other explanation."

"You remembered that story?"

"Yes, and I've passed it on a few times. See what you started?"

We remained there while our heavenly piece of Nevada slowly let go its claim to light. But the darkness had never felt so comfortable to me.

"Let's go put your horse away and have some supper," Hank said.

I caught his arm before he could stand up. "There's one more thing. I hope it was all right to show my friend, Avery, Serena's poem."

"Well, Carla isn't exactly a secret. And those relationships are rather more accepted these days. How did Avery react?"

"She cried. She had seen something in the words that I hadn't. She wants to know if there are more poems like that—about Carla."

"I believe there are. Tell the girl to come see me. We can read them together."

"She'll be so pleased."

The afternoon before graduation, Manny and Denari came to the ranch to ride with Dancing Horse. Manuel caught on quickly to the idea of partnering with the horse, paying attention to the horse's mind and feet, and making a game out of figuring ways to engage the horse in what he wanted it to do. Denari, on the other hand, was as scared as a newborn kitten, grabbing the saddle horn with both hands and holding on for dear life.

"What do you think is going to happen?" Henry asked her. "The horse hasn't moved his feet yet."

"What'll I do when he does?" she asked in a shaky voice.

"He isn't going to move until you tell him to. We might be out here all night at this rate."

"You mean I have to *direct* him?"

"That you do, my girl," he said. "Kivuli, run get me a lunge line, will you?"

"Sure."

I wondered where Denari had been all her life. How could she have been raised in California and not know a few basics about riding horses? I knew a lot from Hank's California equestrian magazines, and I had only been in America for one year. I returned with the long, nylon line. Henry looped it through the bit ring on the left, ran it over the horse's poll, and clipped it to the right bit ring. That way he could keep the horse shaped up better for Denari. She still clutched the horn.

"Aren't I supposed to hold the reins?" she asked.

"Someday," he replied. "Just imagine with that death grip on the horn, how your hands on the reins would feel to the horse. You just worry about your balance. You'll take your hands off that horn long before you put them on the reins."

And so it went. Dancing Horse only walked the horse until Denari could release one hand at a time and relax it on her thigh. Pretty soon, he got her heels down, her seat bones secure, and her back a bit straighter than a panicked crouch.

"This is fun," she said.

"Can you take both hands off now?" Henry prodded.

"But what'll I hold on with?"

"Anything but your hands," he ordered. "Soon as you can ride him with both arms stretched out straight at the walk, trot, and canter, then I might consider giving you the reins."

I remembered my Granpa Farley doing something like that with me. *Granpa Farley!* He would be so proud of what I had learned from Dancing Horse. Maybe now my mother and Safina would let me ride their hot Thoroughbreds.

Manny was loping out in the large arena on a loose rein. His seat was glued to the saddle. I hoped he would get good enough to help the Robertsons in their unfamiliar adventure. I gave him a thumb's up and then shielded my eyes against the lazy sundown in a clear, blue sky.

47

what love has done

At graduation the next day, Trace and I sat with Avery's father. Avery and Donna waved to us as they walked down the aisle and took their seats with the other seniors—all twenty-eight of them. I noticed the girls were wearing the African bracelets I'd given them. I had already packed the things they had given me: turquoise pendants, a basket woven with other desert stones and eagle feathers, a carved soapstone horse from Marci, and the picture of Askay and Hernando from Manny. With those gifts, I had placed Henry's horsehair bridle, the Roses' present of Helen's sunset watercolor, a photograph Thomas had taken just for me of raptors soaring high on the thermals of Heaven's Door, and the little piece of mahogany from the mountain tent camp ride.

I knew when I opened my bags in my room in Dar es Salaam, I would cry.

Later that night, Thomas came into the barn where I had gone to see the just-weaned puppies that were to be Julia's and Sunrose's. I was startled to find three of the handsome creatures. Tom picked up my favorite and put it in my arms. "A little bird told me you might like to take this one home."

"Oh, I would, but I don't know how to arrange that."

"Luckily, I do," he said. "I've already gotten permission from your airline to carry him on the plane, bought the proper crate, and paid the extra fee for him to travel with you."

"Oh, Mr. Sentinel, I can't believe it! Thank you! I had a name already in my head for him—Pass's Shadow."

"I'm keeping Sunny's, calling him Pass's Mercy. Paradise Found doesn't seem to fit anymore." He stroked the puppy that was destined for Africa. "Just don't let that leopard eat this one!"

"Is Julia okay, now that she's had that note from Sunrose?"

"She told me since we have *two* of Dog's grandchildren, maybe her mother would come see them."

"Do you believe that?"

"No. Even if Sunny is allowed to, or chooses to, visit her folks, Julia and I may be in another country."

"What country is that?"

"I think you know," he said. "Africa."

On Sunday, I was fitting water and food bowls, pee pads and special treats into the airline crate, hoping I was leaving enough room for Shadow, when Trace called me.

"Kivuli, guess what?"

"You're coming to Africa with me?"

"This isn't quite as good as that," he said. "Father Zenwa gave my dads communion at Mass this morning!"

"Oh, wow! That is quite good. I wish I'd been there."

"And everyone welcomed them back. Tim was asked to lead a Bible study."

"Well, that might not be good."

"Why?"

"Oh, never mind. I'm sure Father Z will smooth any contradictions over. I trust him."

"What would you think if I started going to church with them?"

"Excellent for your family dynamic," I said, "But you'd better write to me about *that*. And I'll write about my next mission."

"Maybe I'll have to come to Africa and keep you out of trouble."

"Will you at least come to the airport for my flight?"

"If you don't mind seeing a boy cry."

"I thought Indians didn't cry."

"There's always a first time."

I felt the pang of leaving rise up in my chest. There had not been enough time after all. Some questions remained unanswered. Some people I loved were still lost.

"Kivuli?" Trace was trying to get my attention.

"I'm still here."

"It's not over," he said.

In the morning, I woke up aching for the Nevada I was going to leave. I got up and pulled back the curtains on the east window. The whole sky was the color champagne. I dressed quickly and started collecting my luggage and bags with my laptop and Nevada keepsakes. But I dropped all that when I heard Dancing Horse's truck coming up the drive. As I went out the front door, Hank told me he'd load my things and get Shadow from the barn.

"Remember we have to pick Trace up, so don't be too long," he said.

The Indian waved me over to the pasture fence. We leaned against it and watched Grey Sky and Lazo, the dependable ranch stock, and some finely-tuned, not-so-wild horses grazing on the summer grass.

"I have something else for you," Henry said. "To take with you to Africa."

"You have given me so much."

"I have not given you this."

A warm wind came up from the south and blew the Native American's long graying hair across his face. He closed his eyes for a moment and then moved so that our shoulders were touching. The sun rose over the ridge to the east and blessed us with its light.

"Yes. That's it," he said and opened his eyes. "I am giving you your Indian name to add to your three names."

"Henry!"

"You are Kivuli Rides-with-the-Sun."

"Oh, I love it!"

I wanted to hug him but had the feeling he didn't expect that. And it might spoil this last moment that defined our friendship. Grey Sky looked up and nickered at us, and Hank honked the horn in his truck.

"Well, Rides-with-the-Sun, hang onto that star for all your worth. Maybe it will bring you back to me," Dancing Horse said. "'Cuz who else am I gonna talk horse with that really listens to this old Indian?"

"Henry—"

"Go on now. Hank's waitin'."

As we turned under the sign *Rancho del Cielo Azul*, the first carloads of summer guests turned in. They would settle into their cabins and wander up to the barn. Some would pet the horses and perhaps admire True Passion. Others would sit on a hay bale and watch the wranglers doing their chores. And maybe one or two would notice the painting on the door of the tack room, study it, and nod their heads.

We hadn't gone far past the Crossroads when I asked my last question. I leaned forward in my seat and spoke in a cautious voice. "How did you get the painting back? The one Liana stole."

Hank gripped the wheel and glanced at me briefly, but Susan looked out the window at the pink and yellow summer cactus opening to a sudden shower.

Then, Hank said, "My dad found it at an auction and gave it to my mother on her sixtieth birthday."

"Oh, wow."

"Some things are never lost," Susan said.

"I don't know what we'll do without you," Hank said.

"I don't know what I'll do without you."

We rode in silence for a while. I held Trace's hand. Rain drummed on the roof of the truck. On the outskirts of Elko, a coyote with a pup hugging her side dashed across the highway in front of us. The animals glistened gold and umber and gray, their heads intent on their own journey before they disappeared into the wild landscape. Then, I saw the airship trembling on the runway, bound for another world.

ACKNOWLEDGEMENTS

Without these friends, the story could not be told: Lowell Prunty, who led me into the remote mountains of northeastern Nevada, through what will always be to me "heaven's door"; Buck Brannaman, who taught me the meaning of "pressure/release" with horses in the round pen and enabled me to have a better partnership with at least a dozen of my equines over the years; readers Katherine Carpenter, Marla Worden, Renee Lundberg, Jeffrie Susan, Ruth Hemming, Trace Clark, Nelda Kendall, my husband, Jerry, who cried in all the right places and let me keep the light on late into the night, and my faithful and tireless editor, Krista Hill. A very special thank you to the young artist, Andrea La Manna—andreaachasee@gmail.com—for her rendition of the bronc in the round pen with the hand through the rails offering a simple treat, or perhaps forgiveness.

Elizabeth Cain
Lincoln, Montana
August, 2023